To the Totem Shore

Ministerio de Asuntos Exteriores
Dirección General de Relaciones Culturales
Ministerio de Defensa

Instituto de Cooperación Iberoamericana
Comisión Nacional para la celebración del V Centenario
Comisario General para la Exposición Universal Sevilla 92

Banco Central of Canada

To the Totem Shore

The Spanish Presence on the Northwest Coast

World Exposition, Vancouver 1986
Pavilion of Spain

Ediciones El Viso

The plant «Fumaria cuculata» (Fumitory).
Francisco Lindo. Diario de Bodega y Quadra, 1792.
Ministerio de Asuntos Exteriores.

Contents

Symbolic representation of the Hispanic world, 1761.
Servicio Geográfico del Ejército, Madrid.

Acknowledgements

The Editor and authors of the present volume wish to express their indebtedness to
Emilio Cassinello, Comisario General de España, Vancouver 1986 and
to the following who provided information, assistance and photographs:

Paloma Acuña, Ministerio de Cultura, Madrid
Peter Barber, British Museum, London
Roberto Barreiro-Meiro, Museo Naval, Madrid
Juan Carlos Benevto, Madrid
Paz Cabello, Museo de América, Madrid
María Carmona, Archivo Histórico Nacional, Madrid
Ricardo Cerezo, Museo Naval, Madrid
Carmen Crespo, Archivo Histórico Nacional, Madrid
Juan Fernández Navarrete, Museo de América, Madrid
Concepción García Sáenz, Museo de América, Madrid
Adela González Vega, Archivo General de Simancas
Frederic V. Grunfeld, Mallorca
M.ª José Jiménez Albarran, Museo Nacional de Ciencia y Tecnología, Madrid
Carmen Liter, Biblioteca Nacional, Madrid
José María Losada Aranguren, Museo Nacional de Ciencia y Tecnología, Madrid
Josefa Lozano Rincón, Archivo Ministerio de Asuntos Exteriores, Madrid
Esperanza Manso Martín, Madrid
George Miles, Beinecke Library, Yale University, Connecticut
Toby Molenaar, Paris
Oregon Historical Society
María Ascensión Sánchez-Rubio, Madrid
Carmen Sotos, Universidad Complutense, Madrid
Elena Santiago, Biblioteca Nacional, Madrid
Manuel Sánchez Mariana, Biblioteca Nacional, Madrid
Coronel Paladini, Servicio Geográfico del Ejército, Madrid
Mercedes Palau, Museo Nacional de Ciencia y Tecnología, Madrid
Rosario Parra, Archivo General de Indias, Sevilla
Patricia Tena, Madrid
James White, Hunt Institute for Botanical Documentation, Pittsburgh

Galleons, Pirates, Pearls and Fantastic Straits: California, XVIIth Century

by Francisco Morales Padrón
Universidad de Sevilla

1.   The Manila Galleon and English Pirates

In the second half of the 16th century maritime exploration was conducted by the Spanish Crown all along the route to the Californias. The motivation for this grew out of several different concerns: the geographic interest aroused by the peninsula, centering on the question of whether it was or was not an island; the strategic significance of its coast, where a way-station for the China Galleon would prove to be of vital importance; and the interest aroused by the exploitation of the pearl beds. The Spanish Crown wished to ease the rigors of the long sea voyage that the Acapulco ship imposed on its crew and passengers, and, at the same time, eliminate any foreign presence in the area, find a passage into the North Sea (the Atlantic) and the South Sea and profit by the great riches in pearls.

The trade route New Spain-Philippines had been established since 1565 thanks to the voyage of sailors Esteban Rodríguez and Fray Andrés de Urdaneta. On their return from Manila they went up almost as far as 40° and dropped anchor off the American coast of California (27º 12'), taking advantage of the Japanese current and the northwest shore winds. This was a difficult and long route (running from July to January), but it was the only viable one, and was used by the Galleon to transport silks, tea, porcelain, gold, lacquer, spices, and passengers. It set out from Acapulco in March to arrive in May, by an almost direct route.

The months of sailing on the way back, which totalled almost half a year and greatly wore on the crew, suggested the need to find a point midway, where one could relax and regain strength, or else find a more southern route, so that one would drop anchor in Baja California (28ºN). This second route did not lighten the hardships of the voyage nor did it shorten its length very much.

The Galleon had been in operation hardly ten years when Francis Drake, with a fleet of three ships, penetrated as far as the Pacific through the Strait of Magellan and surprised Valparaiso and Callao, going on as far as the coast of California in his search for a passage to the Atlantic. He had met no resistance along the American coast; nor did he meet any on the waters of the Pacific, which, as he found no outlet, he was obliged to cross, rounding the Cape of Good Hope in 1580. This daring feat shook the Spanish Government, now aware that the great ocean was not a private lake and, therefore, not exempt from either the presence or the blows of foreigners. Many believed that Drake had gained access to the South Sea by a strait in the Northwest, or the Strait of Anian. It seemed more important than ever, then, to protect the ships from the Philippines in their arrival on the Californian coast, and desire quickened to discover a way-station. The Viceroy of New Spain, Don Pedro de Moya y Contrera, is an example of this enthusiasm. It prompted Pedro de Unamuno's expedition of 1582, which set sail from Macao in search of the islands of Rica de Oro and de Plata, believed to lie along, approximately 35º. As he never found them, he decided to head up toward the Californias (37º3'). There along the coast the came upon the San Lucas Bay where he narrowly missed clashing with the pirate Thomas Cavendish. It was Cavendish's luck to capture the galleon *Santa Ana*, which was loaded down with rich Oriental cargo. The pirate had followed the same path as Drake, crossing the Strait of Magellan and sailing along the entire pacific American coast, to sack México, Huatulco, Navidad, Acatlán, Chacala, Mazatlán... For an entire month his two spy ships were stationed on the Cape San Lucas, until their long wait was rewarded with the appearance of the coveted galleon, full of silks, brocade, spices, pearls, and passengers' fortunes. After seizing it and taking the plunder, the ship went on to the Philippines and entered the port of Plymouth in 1588. This was the year that the Spanish Crown suspended voyages of exploration.

2. False and Apocryphal Voyages

In 1558 a singular document appeared in Venice, published by one Niccolò Zeni or Zeno, who claimed that it had been found in the family archives. It was a letter from Antonio Zeno, one of Niccolò's ancestors, which told of certain voyages made by the Zeno family in 1380. First there was Niccolò Zeno, who voyaged from the coast of Flanders to an exotic land called Frisland. As in the case of Columbus, a storm was to blame for his having taken this course. The explorer was able to establish relations with the prince of those unknown lands and, later, it was said that his brother Antonio returned with thirteen ships and found a multitude of islands. The tale goes on and becomes more complicated. What is the basis for this legend (for it is a legend)? Without a doubt, the voyages of the Portuguese Corté Real brothers. It was by taking them as a model that Niccolò Zeno made up his own story, which some took seriously.

The route taken by the Zeno brothers in the North Atlantic was the one that would later be taken by the boats investigating the Northwest Passage. A passage that for many who believed in it would lead to Cathay. There is no short supply of testimony to this belief in maps and historiography. Gemma Phrysius drew the passage on his 1537 globe; Sebastian Munster traced it on his map of 1540; Gerhard Mercator put it on his globe of 1541; and Ortelius on his map of the world in 1564. Finding it was the chief ambition of many associations and seamen, who saw in it a way to circumvent the monopoly and control of the Portuguese over Africa and that of the Spanish over America.

The first man to repeat Zeno's voyage was Martin Frobisher, who carried out, unsuccessfully, three expeditions (1576-78), which are described at

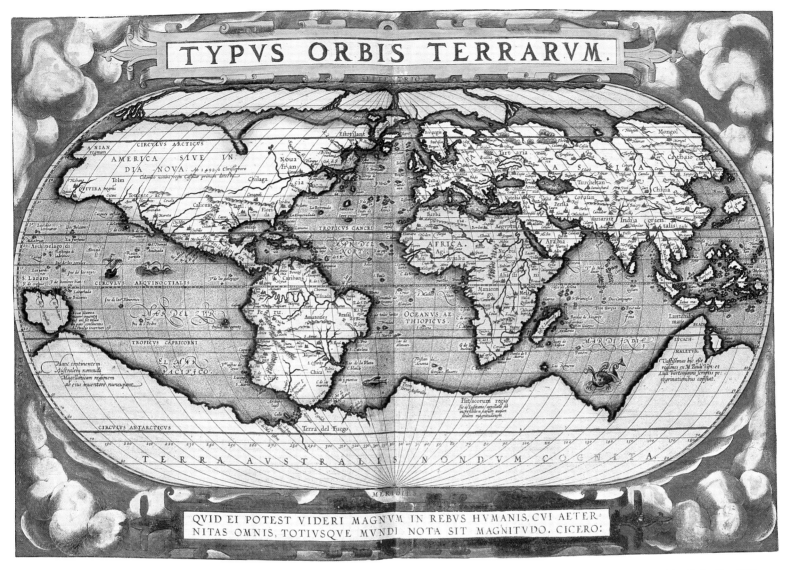

Mapa Mundi. Ortelius, 1579.
Servicio Geográfico del Ejército.

some length in Richard Hakluyt's *Voyages*. At the time, Drake was touching on the coast of the American Northwest (1577) and looking for a passage in the other direction, from the Pacific to the Atlantic, while, at the same time, sowing fear around Mexico. Frobisher's attempts were followed by those of John Davis, who was backed by the Society of Merchant Adventurers. Davis reached 72º 12'. These real explorations, which were inspired in news and reports of false voyages, were followed by the voyages of the impostor Lorenzo Ferrer Maldonado (1588) and the apocryphal Juan de Fuca (1592). Briefly, the accounts of Ferrer Maldonado's sea runs, which were made public in

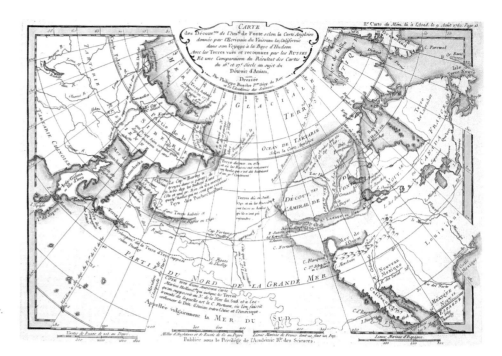

Chart of the new discoveries of Admiral Fonte.
Philippe Bauche, 1752.
Museo Naval.

the last century by the Duke of Almodóvar under the pseudonym of Eduardo Malo de Luque, tell of Captain Lorenzo Ferrer Maldonado, who in the year 1588 left Lisbon with the pilot Juan Martínez for Labrador. At the time the two Iberian Crowns were united. These two men were looking for a strait or passage not found by either Frobisher or Davis. Ferrer went beyond the strait named after the English sailor until, finally, some 1750 leagues from Spain, he entered the much sought-after passage. The navigation took from January to March, with the crew suffering from the cold, the dark, and the ice, but they never found the frozen waters. The other outlet of the strait, on the Pacific shore, lay at an altitude of 60º N. The return trip, which was calm, was made under a steady sun and warmth. In 1791 Malaspina was ordered to locate that outlet, at 60º, but he was unable to find the slightest sign of its existence.

The story of Apostolos Valerianus, alias Juan de Fuca, which was cited in Hakluyt's and Purchas' accounts as proof of the existence of the passage, proved to be equally fantastic. Valerianus, a Greek in the service of Portugal, recounted his nautical experiences to the British merchant Michael Lock in Venice (1596), who then went to Lord Cecil, Sir Walter Raleigh, and Richard Hakluyt to ask them for support in financing the Greek's voyage to England and the Northwest (Fretum Anian). Fuca had spent forty years in the New World and had been a member of the crew of the *Santa Ana*, which had been sacked by Cavendish. He had formed part of a fleet of three ships

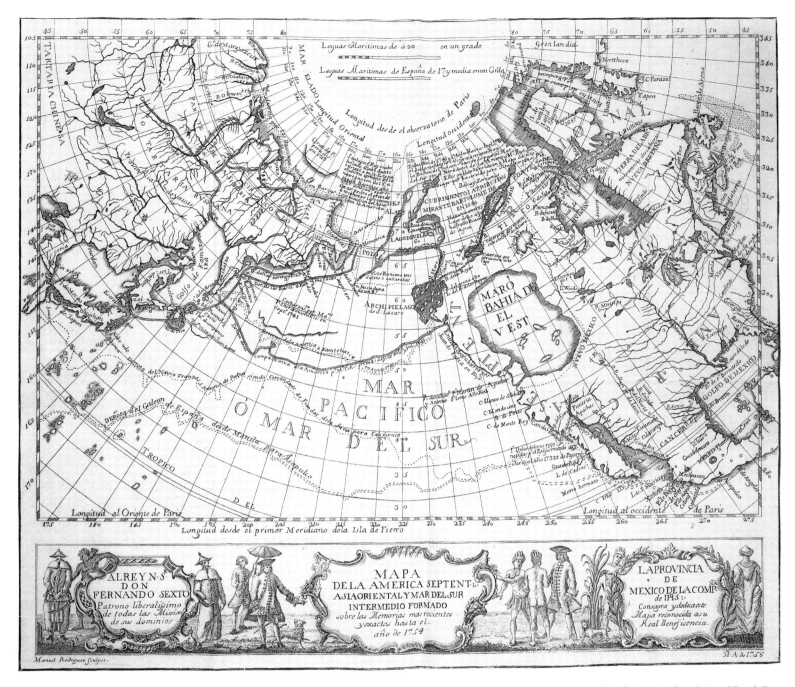

Map of North America, East Asia and South Sea, based on the most precise recollections available to 1754. In «Noticia de la California», 1757. Biblioteca Nacional.

sent by the Viceroy of New Spain to look for the Strait of Anian, an undertaking abandoned with the mutiny of the crew. But in 1592 the Viceroy sent him back to go on with the project, and Fuca —by his own account and later Lock's— found the sought-after strait at 47º and 48º. He entered it and sailed for more than twenty days until he came upon the North Sea. He was feted on return to Acapulco and, at the Viceroy's urging, he set off for Spain in search of favors. These he did not get, and he decided to go to Italy. The Spaniards' lack of interest in the project stemmed from the fact that the British had given up their efforts to discover the Northwest Passage. The money Lock was requesting to help Fuca never arrived and Fuca died. Nonetheless, his story was influential in his time, and even in the 18th century James Cook and Malaspina looked for Fuca's strait, or the Strait of Anian. When the Spanish historian Novo y Colson in 1881 dismissed the existence of this strait, considering it 'altogether impossible', he could have no idea that twenty-two years later Roald Amunsen would finally hit upon it.

3. Pearls and Voyages

Count of Monterey. Viceroy of New Spain from 1595 to 1603.
Biblioteca Nacional.

From 1533 on, it was considered that the Californian coastal waters concealed abundant oyster beds. The men on Cortés' expeditions noted the existence of this wealth, and Alarcón's and Unamuno's expeditions confirmed it. But it was only in 1585 that the Crown legalized the commercial exploitation of these beds, which, although the property of the Crown, were being illegally exploited by private citizens. Those who were favored with the first official concession failed when their boats were burned by Cavendish. In 1592 some new prospective contractors, among them Sebastián Vizcaíno, requested a twenty-year monopoly. They wished to extract pearls, fish the waters, and exploit the gold deposits in the zone extending from Navidad to California. Vizcaíno had arrived in the Indies in 1583, going on to Manila to work as a merchant. And a merchant and rich investor he was, dating from 1589, when he settled in Mexico. The company that he and other associates formed went bankrupt, and the future explorer, teaming up with other partners, presented Viceroy Velasco with a new petition that requested aid for their enterprise (ships, arms, and men of the cloth) and the right to take in *encomienda* four-fifths of whatever natives they found and subdued. The document was approved by the royal representative Don Gaspar de Zúñiga y Acevedo, the Count of Monterey and Velasco's successor. Once the new society was constituted, there were no few setbacks and disagreements among the associates, as they prepared for the expedition, which would be made up of 230 armed men and five Franciscans. They set sail from Acapulco on June 15, 1596, and ended up in Baja California where they tried, unsuccessfully, to establish a base. In October they were on their way back, with Vizcaíno attributing their failure to bad weather, although he maintained an optimistic outlook and believed that there were pearls in abundance, to judge from the shells they had seen on the beaches. It was important to keep at it and sail in the month of March to stay clear of storms.

14

November 1592 found Sebastián Vizcaíno asking for royal authorization to carry out a second expedition, for which he also requested royal backing. He wanted help to be able to convert the natives, exploit the pearl beds, the salt, and the fishing banks. Vizcaíno believed that the coast from the Cape San Lucas up toward the north was long and that in the interior there were rich cities. His idea was to explore the Gulf of California, take possession of the lands, chart them on maps, and earn from the King the title of *Adelantado* (provincial Governor), the power to appoint officials, and the reward of an hereditary tax *encomienda* in perpetuity, with 20,000 Indians. These exorbitant powers and favors were granted him, but a competitor appeared, Gabriel Maldonado, who challenged Vizcaíno's request, alleging that he had not made good on his first promises. Notwithstanding, Viceroy Zúñiga and the Council of the Indies supported Vizcaíno's request, demanding that he avoid the use of violence with the indigenous population. The *Ordenanzas de Nuevo Poblamiento* (Ordinances of New Settlement) had been in force for some time now, and they were scrupulous in all matters concerning the attraction and conversion of the natives. The death of Felipe II, author of the abovementioned ordinances, brought negotiations to a standstill (1598). The royal response came in 1599 —one year before the Dutch pirate Oliver van Nort entered the Pacific—, but until March 1602 Vizcaíno did not have the instructions which specified that, instead of stopping with the discovery of the inlet and mouth of the Californias, he should find and mark off the existing ports and inlets between the Cape San Lucas and the Cape Mendocino (22º to 42º). He was barred from going inland. It was May 1602 when Vizcaíno set sail in Acapulco and, going by way of Navidad, Cape Corrientes and Mazatlán Island, he reached California the following month. From here on, the geography that lay before them was the most interesting because it was the least known. It took them more than six months to get to Cape Mendocino; they next went beyond Magdalena Bay, Cedros and San Jerónimo Islands, the San Francisco Bay, the Cove of the Once Mil Vírgenes (Eleven Thousand Virgins), the port of San Diego... until dropping anchor in Monterey (November 16). The contemporary account affirms that, 'we find ourseves as far ahead as Cape Mendocino, which everybody has looked forward to, since it has taken so much hard work to reach it'. They were around 41º; nonetheless, aware that the new moon would bring bad weather and, with all their people lying ill, they agreed to go back to the Cape San Lucas. The results of the voyage? On the positive side: a series of sea charts, the hydrographic survey of the stretch of coast they had sailed, and the toponym Bay of Sebastián Vizcaíno given to a gulf on the western California shore. On the negative side: no colonial outpost was left behind. Frey Iñigo Abad Lasierra explains the reasons for these and other results when he states that the Spanish government was skeptical of finding the Northwest Passage, or Strait of Anian, and that it wanted, above all, to found a coastal station that

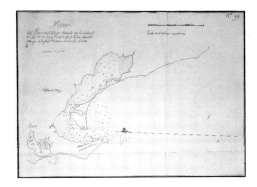

Map of the Port of San Diego, discovered by Sebastián Vizcaino in 1603. Diario de Caamaño, 1792. Ministerio de Asuntos Exteriores.

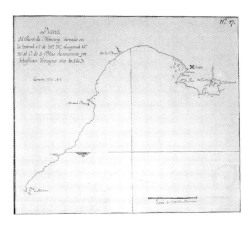

Map of the Port of Monterey, discovered by Sebastián Vizcaino in 1603.
Diario de Bodega y Quadra, 1792.
Ministerio de Asuntos Exteriores.

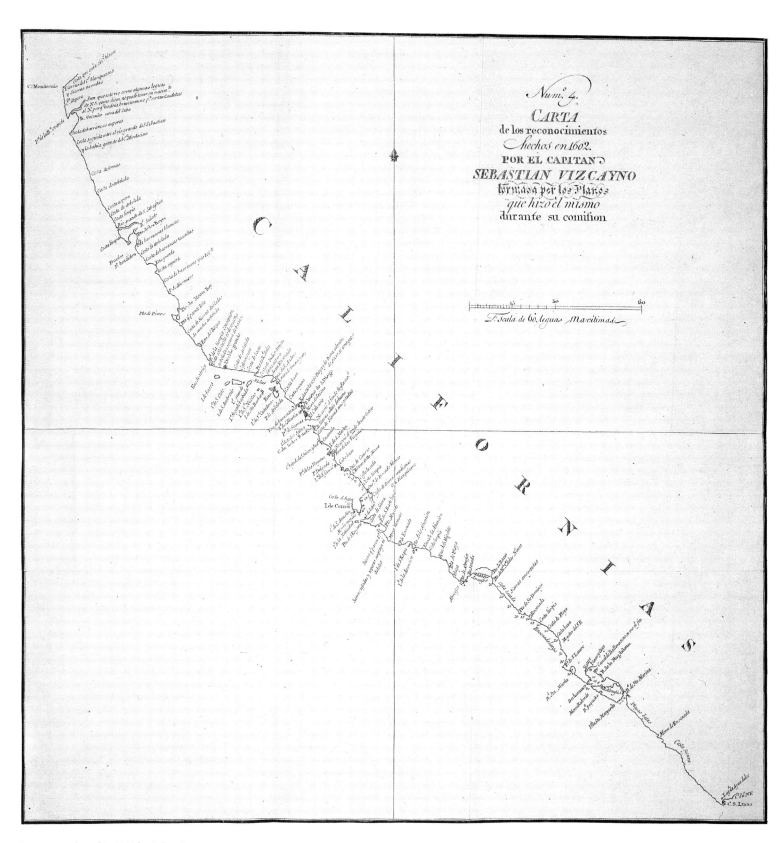

Surveys conducted in 1602 by Sebastián
Vizcaíno. Atlas de las goleras *Sutil* y *Mexicana*, 1802.
Museo Naval.

would safeguard the navigation of the Manila Galleon. This ideal, however, came to naught, on account of the presence of foreigners and because, alleging this very danger, those who might have founded such a base devoted themselves instead to barter and the fishing of pearls.

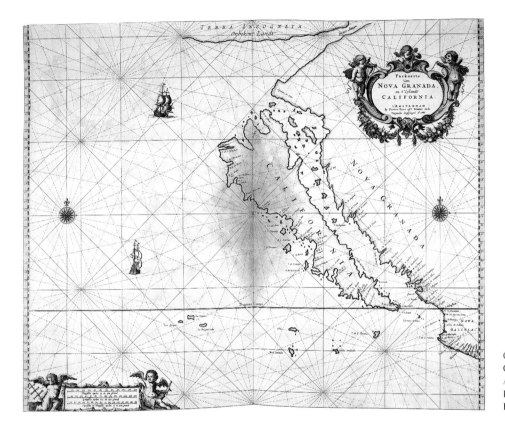

Chart of Nueva Granada and the island of California from Cape Corrientes to the Strait of Anian. In «Atlas de la mar o mundo de agua», Pieter Goos, 1669.
Biblioteca Nacional.

4.   The Obsession with Pearls

As opposed to the judgment of the Crown, which at the beginning of the 17th century felt it had sufficient strength to proceed with efforts to extend the geographic horizons of California, there appears the policy of the viceroys of New Spain, who are against taking money from the royal coffers to finance nautical enterprises. In this sense the figure of Viceroy Don Juan de Mendoza y Luna, the Marquis of Montesclaros (1603-7), stands out. He is opposed to the ideals of his predecessor, who had been in favor of exploring and settling the outermost coast of California, to erect a way-station for the Galleon. Given that Sebastián Vizcaíno owned a license, valid until 1613, to carry out this mission, it was up to him to bring this project to fruition. That is why the King in 1606 insisted that a settlement be made at Monterey and that this be entrusted to Vizcaíno. But already in Mexico, at that time, it was considered far more realistic to give up this enterprise, for by the time the Galleon arrived in Monterey it was safe. It was deemed more expedient to locate the way-station near Japan, on an island in the Pacific, such as the famous islands of Rica de Oro and de Plata. What continued to interest many private individuals about the waters and shores of California were the pearls, and nine years after the royal disposition of 1609, expeditions in search of the pearls were begun anew. The actors in these forays, and the successors to Vizcaíno, were Cardona (1615), Iturbe (1616), Ortega (1632) and Cestero (1642), for from 1615 to 1642 the navigations were repeated, without succeeding in expanding the geographic stage.

Nicolás Cardona, a Venetian based in Sevilla, left from Cádiz for New Spain in 1613. In that year, together with his uncle Tomás, he signed a contract with the Crown and formed a company of other associates for the exploration of the oyster beds in the North Sea and the discovery of the wealthy kingdom of California. One of his partners was Captain Juan de Iturbe. In May 1615 Cardona left the port of Acapulco with three ships, a boatful of land and seafaring people, and a goodly number of skilled black pearl divers. They laid claim to the land at the tip of California and then they travelled up the inner coast as far as 30°. They had been at sea nine months when winter was suddenly upon them and with it ever greater difficulties, for which reason they decided to turn back. They left the frigate *Almirante* in Sinaloa with Juan de Iturbe in charge, who went back out to California, while Cardona tried to make a report to the King about his movements and prepare to continue the venture. Just opposite Zacatula, Cardona was attacked by the Dutch pirate Joris van Spilbergen, who captured his flagship. Cardona himself, miraculously, escaped. Finding himself without boats and without money, he decided to go to Spain, while Iturbe, moving once more into the Gulf, thought he could just make out at its end a strait which, if truly there, would turn California into an island. The geographical puzzle about this land of myth continued.

The project to establish a way-station was abandoned; the fame of the pearls spread; the mistaken notion of California's insularity took hold; and the belief in a strait (of Anian) persisted. These are the results thus far of the navigations to the north. The interest in California was fading in such a fashion that in 1628 the King wrote to the Mexican that 'said discovery has always been held of little account, inasmuch as, the times it has been attempted, nothing of substance has been gotten out of it'. The King wishes the matter to be discussed and a report be made to him of the various opinions 'about how and in what way this discovery can be conducted, should it prove expedient to proceed with it'. The points of view were contradictory: the Carmelite Frey Antonio de la Ascensión, a man of experience, was in fa-

Marquis of Cerralbo, Viceroy of New Spain, XVIII c. Biblioteca Nacional.

vor of going on with the expeditions; Vizcaíno's cartographer, Enrico Martínez, was hostile to the undertaking. In 1632 the Viceroy, the Marquis of Cerralbo, announced that Francisco Ortega had just set sail to reconnoiter the
northern geography, as if Vizcaíno's voyages had never taken place and he
had not managed to obtain basic information and maps to prepare a report
for the King.

In effect, in March 1632, taking along with him as pilot Esteban Car-
bonel de Valenzuela, Ortega left San Pedro in a small frigate which, once
again, entered the Gulf of California and reached 27º. The following year Ortega repeated his attempt, unsuccessfully. It is possible that he made a third
voyage in 1636 without an official license. Two years before, in Madrid, Nicolás Cardona had offered to carry out another navigation at his own expense in exchange for exclusive navigating and pearl fishing rights. No agreement was reached regarding this proposal.

5. The Last Figure of the 17th Century: Porter de Casanate

Pedro Porter de Casanate, an Aragonese from Zaragoza, seems an unlikely
figure in this saga of conquerors and navigators. A military man, a sailor, a
gentleman, and a Knight of the Order of Santiago, Porter first came into contact with the West Indies in 1629, when he accompanied Don Fadrique de
Toledo on a mission to do away with the pirates located on the islands of
San Cristóbal and Nevis (Nieves). From 1632 on, Porter was to voyage to the
New World on several different assignments and act decisively on the European stage. He was beginning to formulate the idea of exploring California, and in 1635 he made his first offer to Viceroy Cerralbo. The following
year he repeated his offer to reconnoiter and delimit Californian lands. In
1637 he was taken prisoner by the Dutch pirate Peg Leg, who took him to
Curaçao, an island recently captured by the Dutch. Finally, in 1638 and in
later years he received the license he so much desired, but he would still
find himself obliged to serve on other, different missions. In 1640 he presented a Memorial of his plan, which is a mixture of fact and fantasy: it refers to the need to guarantee the safety of the Philippine ships, convert the
Indians, move ahead of foreign competition, establish trade with the king-
doms of Anian, Japan, China and Tartary, visit the rich and famous city with
high walls that Captain Martín de Viday had seen, find the deposits of gold,
silver, corral and amber... He asked for nothing in return; he would cover
all the expenses; the only thing he wished for was the license and the subsequent fame. It was not a very propitious moment. Spain was entering a
period of decline, beginning with the European fiascos of 1639, and in Mexico Indian uprisings held the day; but the Crown granted Porter permission
in a royal warrant dated August 8, 1640. Urged on by the Council of War

Marquis of Cadereita. Viceroy of New Spain, XVIII c.
Biblioteca Nacional.

☩

Seys Reales.

Relación Ajustada De
los Seruicios Del Almirante
Don Pedro Porter Cassanate
Cauallero De la Horden
de San Tiago. _____

Consta Por sus Papeles, Titulos sees Certificacíones
Cedulas RS. Cartas de Capitanes Generales, y otros
Ínstrumentos hauer Seruido a su Magestad de Veynte
y Ocho años a esta parte en los puestos Jornadas y ocasiónes
que se Síguen _____

Parece Por sees de Ofícios de la Armada R.l del
Mar oceano, y Guardia de las Índías hauer comencado,
A Seruír a su Mag.d con plaza ordinaria de Soldado,
y Seis Escudos particulares de Ventaja, El Año de,
1627. en la Conpañía del Capítan Gaspar de Carassa
que Yra rma de las de la Armada R.l y Esquadra de
Quatro Villas, y fue este año a la Jornada de françía, Y
Socorro de la Rochela con la Armada Real que salíó
del Puerto de la Coruña a cargo de su Capítan General
Don fadrique de Toledo Ossorío _____

El Año de 1628. fue con el Almírante Francisco De
Vallecilla a Correr las Costas De España y Reciuír
los Galeones de la plata, y en esta Ocasíón hauiéndose de=
rrotado el Nauío en que yba embarcado, peleo dos
vezes con Nauíos De Turcos sobre el Cauo de finisterra
y Sobre San Lucar _____

Los Años de 1629. y 1630. fue con el General (1) Don
fadrique de Toledo en la Jornada que hico a las
Índías con la Armada R.l A echar los enemígos

(Junta de la Guerra) Porter embarked for the Indies in the galleon commanded by General Don Francisco Díaz Pimienta, and entered Veracruz in August 1643. The Viceroy, the Count of Salvatierra, quickly offered him aid, as did the Jesuits, who were eager for the conversion of the Indians. But Porter would not realize his first expedition until 1648. What obstacles lay in the way of his plans? Misfortunes. He had chosen the banks of the Santiago River to build a dockyard, because of the woods nearby. He raised houses, shipyards, and depots, bought arms and supplies in Guadalajara, and undertook the construction of the boats. But soon a group of sailors deserted, taking with them one of the vessels, and in April 1644 a disloyal Portuguese set fire to the shipyard, which brought the enterprise temporarily to a halt. Porter, however, was not disheartened, and 1647 found him starting once more to build two vessels in the town of Sinaloa. His request that he be made captain of this town was granted, and he served in this capacity until 1651, at the same time that he managed, at last, to carry out his expeditions. The first was in 1648, when he attempted, with the cooperation of the Jesuits, to start a settlement in California. He entered the Californian gulf with two ships, and for 77 days they traced its outlines with precision, marking the location of currents and reefs, describing the islands and the customs of the natives. Having managed to go farther in than anybody else, he found, almost at the end of the line, an island which he named Salsipuedes (Get out if you can). In 1649 he undertook another voyage, but currents prevented him from getting past the Angel de la Guarda islands. He went back in 1650, neither reaching the farthest end of the lake nor seeing the mouth of the Colorado River, but he did confirm his idea that the narrowness of the gulf foretold the passage to the North Sea —as he was to write to the Viceroy, the Duke of Alba: 'what has hitherto been doubted is now assured, that there is a navigable strait to the Mar del Norte' (1651). After Porter's voyages, the shoreline between 23º and 29º latitude was much better known than before. Porter was to close the chapter of his nautical adventures in California and his experience governing Sinaloa, which he had undertaken in support of his voyages. He was quitting Mexico and heading for Peru, leaving to Isidoro de Atondo y Antillón the honor of colonization. The honor of beginning it, that is, for Atondo was also to know failure and the frustration of unfinished business. Atondo, along with the Jesuits Kino and Goñi, entered the Gulf in 1683, leaving behind a number of places they had already visited: the islet of San Juan, the Tres Marías, the Bay of la Paz, the island Grande del Carmen... He disembarked in what he called the Port of San Bruno, where they baptized thirteen natives. Nothing practical was obtained. It was not the right moment. International difficulties with Great Britain, an insurrection among the tribes of Nueva Vizcaya, and a ban in 1685 on explorations in the Northwest did away with civilian enterprise. From then on it was the Jesuits who were in charge of the annexation of the territory.

Count of Salvatierra. Viceroy of New Spain in 1642. Biblioteca Nacional.

Russian, French, British and American Incursions into "The Spanish Lake"

by Thomas Vaughan, CBE, FRGS
E. A. P. Crownhart-Vaughan, FRGS

Oregon Historical Society

In mid-August, 1775, Bruno de Hezeta y Dudagoitia stood off the mouth of a river which had hitherto eluded European explorers. Peering east through the long summer afternoon, from his 77-foot frigate *Santiago* explorer Hezeta could make out two obvious capes which he named Cape San Roque and Cape Frondoso. We know these today as Cape Disappointment and to the south, Point Adams, or more southerly, perhaps, Tillamook Head. Between the capes, which Hezeta described respectively as rocky and luxuriant, on August 25,

> *...In the afternoon of this day I discovered a large bay that I named Bahia de la Asunción [Assumption Bay] the shape of which is shown on the map...*

The hard-pressed mariner then noted,

> *...I sounded in 24* brazas. *The swirling currents were so swift that despite having a full press of sail it was difficult to get clear or separate myself from the cape to the extreme north... These currents and the seething waters had led me to believe that it may be the mouth of some great river or the passage to another sea*[1].

As some mariners later acknowledged, Hezeta had in fact discovered the Great River of the West, the Columbia River, which today separates the American states of Oregon and Washington.

Upon consulting with his subordinates, Captain pilot Don Juan Perez and pilot Don Cristobal Revilla, Hezeta determined not to anchor for more extensive investigations. His crew was so reduced and so weakened by scurvy and other debilitations that he would have had insufficient manpower to retrieve the anchor even at six fathoms; nor could he consider lowering a boat into the swirling waters, the only remaining launch available to the apprehensive crew. Caution prevailed. Hezeta continued southerly on the homeward leg of a long northern voyage undertaken by the Spanish exploring ships *Santiago* and her consort, the schooner *Sonora*. They had in fact been sailing for months in what some now regarded as Russian waters, although Spain with some vexation resisted this idea, considering the Pacific Ocean to be a «Spanish lake» quite properly awarded them by the papal decree in the Treaty of Tordesillas[2]. And while Hezeta fixed the Columbia River location and the western thrust of Cape Blanco at 43º N. Lat., his supply ship *San Carlos* had the greater good fortune to find the gateway to San Francisco Bay.

More than a century earlier Russia's tsars had despatched explorers, trappers, traders and officials across remote Siberian tracts from the Urals to the Kamchatka Peninsula and the Pacific coast. Not content with quadrupling their land mass within less than a century, the Muscovite leadership in the 18th century moved into the Pacific Ocean itself.

The essential reason Russian leaders undertook to mount their costly North Pacific expeditions is simply explained. There was uncertainty concerning the relationship of the Asian and North American continents. Were they, in the remote and foggy arctic waters, separate or joined? The question had actually been answered in 1648 when the Cossack voyager Semen Dezhnev with 90 men had sailed a singlemasted vessel equipped with reindeer hide sails from the mouth of the far north Kolyma River, along the Arctic Ocean Coast, down around the Chukotsk Peninsula (through what we now know as Bering Strait) to the mouth of the Anadyr River in the Pacific Ocean. He sent a report of his voyage to regional headquarters in Iakutsk, together with a request for back pay for himself and the surviving members of his crew. The import of his voyage was not recognized; the report was filed away and gathered dust for 86 years[3].

By 1700 the Russians had gathered a rudimentary understanding of the outline of their new conquests, the Chukotsk and Kamchatka Peninsulas, the Sea of Okhotsk and the nearest of the Kuril Islands. However they were also misled by maps showing a confusing body of apochryphal islands, bays and land masses: Gama Land, Company Land, Terra Esonis, El Dorado and the inviting Strait of Anian.

Occasional reporters excited the interest of ever curious Peter the Great. Several travelers and foreign scholars enjoined the great ruler to explore the northeast coast of Asia to resolve the geographical puzzle of the relationship between the continents.

Several factors contributed to Peter's determination to proceed: the influence of other European voyages of enlightenment; the founding of the Imperial Russian Academy of Sciences and its foreign complement of questing scholars; the desire to explore the potential of the vast waters and resources

Reindeer used as transport animals, Siberia, Kamchatka and in other parts of the far north.

of the Northwest American Coast north of Spanish claims; continuing with the extending of Russia's Colonial Empire; the youthful enthusiasm and dreams of the new Russian Navy; the possibilities of extending the seriously depleted Siberian fur harvest; the need to find food provisionment for the more northern settlements; the search for a northern sea route; competition with an obviously expanding group of foreign adventurers —the reasons become numerous. Among them certainly was the competition looming between the exploring parties of Russia and Spain[4].

Russian voyagers of the early 18th century who should be noted are Danilo Antsyferov and Ivan Kozyrevskii (1711-1713); the Bol'shoi Kamchatskii Nariad [Great Kamchatka Command] under Colonel Iakov El'chin (1716-1718); the I. M. Evreinov-F. Luzhin expedition personally despatched by Peter with the imperial command:

> You will proceed to Tobol'sk, obtain guides and go to Kamchatka and beyond [authors' italics] according to your instructions. Make a description of the places there. Are America and Asia joined? This task is to be carried out diligently, proceeding not only South and North, but also East and West, and everything is to be placed accurately on a map.

Peter certainly knew what he wanted[5].

That special knowledge was not to be his, however. Even all-powerful Peter did not know of the 1648 report mouldering in Iakutsk. In December, 1724, as he lay dying of fever, the Russian giant, between bouts of delerium, drew up orders for the first Russian naval scientific expedition, the First Kamchatka Expedition. As administrators he named General-Admiral F. M. Apraksin, the naval head, and geographer I. K. Kirilov, Over-Secretary of the Senate. It was Apraksin who chose Vitus Bering to head the expedition. Born

in Denmark, Bering had served for 20 years in the Russian Navy and was raised to the rank of senior captain. Bering chose as his seconds a Russian naval lieutenant, Aleksei I. Chirikou, and another Dane in Russian service, Martyn Spanberg.

Peter's lordly instructions were again simple: Go to Kamchatka, build two boats and

> *... sail near the land which goes to the north, which (since no one know where it ends) it seems is part of America*[6].

The expedition members were to be taken from the Baltic Fleet, and only the young and healthy were eligible. Siberia's coastline, after all, was thousands of miles away. Over 350 soldiers and laborers were picked up on the way across the continent. It took three years to transport the necessary building equipment the 6,000 miles by raft, barge, dogsled, reindeer, packhorse and manpower. Sometimes the starving men ate their dead horses, their saddle bags and other pieces of hide leather clothing and boots. The land passage was but one of many ordeals.

The First Kamchatka Expedition (1725-1731) was in essence regarded officially as a failure. Bering sailed into the middle of the elusive strait he

The Harbour of Awatcha on Kamchatka Peninsula.

26

sought, but neither he nor anyone in his command realized it. Conclusive proof was not revealed to them, although important geographical details were obtained and drawn into a map by warrant officer Peter Chaplin. This map suggested an outline of the coast from the southern tip of Kamchatka to the northeastern capes of Asia. Among others, the brilliant British voyager James Cook later paid tribute to Bering and his men:

> *...he has delineated the coast very well, and fixed the latitude and longitude of the points better than could be expected from the methods he had to go by*[7].

In the fact of scepticism, Bering returned to St. Petersburg and began drawing plans for a second expedition. In spite of opposition the plan moved forward, culminating in the second and far better known thrust, the Second Kamchatka Expedition (1733-1742). More than 600 men and one woman participated in this "Great Northern Expedition", and eight years were consumed simply crossing Siberia and building the Baltic-style packet-boats *St. Peter* and *St. Paul*. As previously, the crews suffered from scurvy and other afflictions. Terrible storms and fogs separated the vessels and Bering's *St. Peter* was eventually wrecked (on Bering Island) in the Komandorskii Islands where the expedition leader died miserably. This was but a prelude.

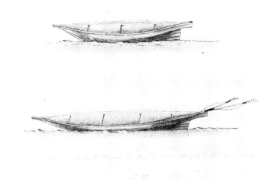

Canoes that provided transportation along the Northwest Coast.

Despite great hardship and cost in life and treasure, the expedition was a triumph. America was "rediscovered" in a Russian sense. The geographical puzzle was resolved and many important illuminating reports and observations were made in several fields, beginning with Kamchatka itself, where the young Russian scientist Stepan P. Krasheninnikov prepared an overall description which is even now accepted as the standard source[8].

What Bering, then Chirikov and Spanberg notably achieved was the establishment beyond all doubt of an emphatic Russian presence in the North Pacific, which remains powerful and permanent in our own era.

There were several important, sometimes secret Russian expeditions following through the years, along with a host if not a horde of private adventurers plundering the great fur wealth, the "soft gold" reserves unlocked by the voyages and descriptions of Bering's men. Expeditions were led by V. Ia. Chichagov, I. Sindt, F. S. Plenisner, P. K. Krenitsyn, M. D. Levashov and an elaborately planned but unfulfilled expedition of Captain G. I. Mulovskii. The names of these men, as well as those of dozens of "private" Russian fur entrepreneurs, became known for many reasons —boldness, illustriousness, cruelty, despotism, enlightenment. And all this took place before the Spanish had begun to move from the Mexican mainland on their northern push toward Baja California and San Francisco Bay.

It was in this period that European maritime powers began to discern that Russia had quickly established an ill-understood but obviously successful working monopoly in Siberia and now in the North Pacific. In the 1760's a challenge was formulated. This was rather naturally first articulated by Spain where for generations royal representatives had used the Treaty of Tordesillas to claim the west coast of both Americas, South and North. This exclusivity was claimed by right of first discovery, dating back to Columbus in 1492, not to mention Balboa and all the others.

Spanish diplomats sent to the Russian court in 1761 soon gathered information concerning the Russian encroachment. The Marques de Almodovar concluded that the Pacific's northern reaches were turbulent and inhospitable, but the royal administrator of New Spain, visitor Jose de Galvez, determined in 1769 to move his country's presence north. The establishment of presidios and missions in San Diego (1769) and Monterey (1770) came to the attention of the Russian planners, but also to a centuries-old imperial rival to Spain, the increasingly powerful English fleet and British imperial interests[9].

The English held a thin but wiry connection to the western shore of North America through the exploits of the Spanish scourge, Francis Drake, who had anchored off the coasts of Oregon and California in the 1580's —hence the name New Albion.

When Captain James Cook, the now famous sea surveyor, arrived on the Oregon coastline on his third and last great voyage of discovery (March 7, 1778), he formally noted that he was surprisingly close to Drake's landfall which had earlier been projected for Captain Anson's voyage in the early 1760's at 38º N. Lat., which would be Drake's Cape Arago anchorage.

As Cook purposefully moved north through storm, fog and long dark nights, he missed the Columbia River mouth, which had been noted by Hezeta more than two years earlier. With his captains, Charles Clerke and John Gore, Cook sailed north, dropping anchors from the *Resolution* and *Discovery* on the west coast of Vancouver Island in a roadstead Spanish voyagers had already identified as San Lorenzo, which all recognize today as Nootka.

After extensive repairs to his much worn ships, Cook moved on to the north, looking, as had all others before him, for the long-sought North West Passage, the short way home to Europe which Drake and everyone afterward had yearned for.

This brief account cannot encompass the many observations and contacts made by Cook's shipmates as they visited Kodiak, Onalaska, Unimak and other wave-swept islands. Eventually he moved through Bering Strait to the north, rounding the northern capes of Siberia, but to the east he did not find the passage for which a prize of 20,000 awaited the discoverer. It is interesting to note that the first Russian encounters were in fact arranged by a Virginian serving with Cook, Captain John Gore; and the British corporal of marines who was sent ashore was actually an effervescent Yankee from Connecticut, audacious and cocky John Ledyard.

A view of the Habitations in Nootka Sound.

A view of Snug Corner Cove in Prince William's Sound; the ship *Resolution* remained four days in this place to be examined.

Cook took time to note the rich furs, especially the sea otter pelts, but he observed:

There is no doubt but a very beneficial fur trade might be carried out with the Inhabitants of this vast coast, but unless a northern passage is found it seems rather too remote for Great Britain to receive any emolument from it[10].

Yet, as Cook's principal scholar Beaglehole records, within eight years there were five British trading vessels searching the islands and inlets for the "sea beaver" Cook had described. In the meantime Cook had sailed on to death and glory. Included in the army of merchant adventures were Captains Nathaniel Portlock, George Dizon and James Colnett. All three had at one time or another sailed in Cook's company and had then returned, driven by "the rage to possess" more of the pelts they had purchased during the first voyage for a few nails, a hatchet or a saw blade, to be sold in Canton for an amazing 50 to 70 dollars per skin. Some of these men used maps and charts based on those certain Russian fur trader had provided to Cook, which had dispelled many doubt and which "had every mark of being Authentick".

In the intervening years reports from other Spanish observers in the Russian courts, notably Viscount of de la Herreria (1764) and Count of Lacy (1773) had evalutaed the Russian Pacific conquest as being uneven and con-

Huts at Onalaska, Northwest Coast of America.

fused. It would appear that wealth through fur harvests was a larger factor than strategic land acquisition, with island advances tied essentially to the diminution and retreat of the wary furbearing animals. But we know that Catherine the Great was ever attentive to her exotic Pacific possessions despite preoccupations in the Pugachev insurrection, the Polish revolt, the Ottoman wars and her Crimean invasions. Certainly she was displeased to hear how much geographical information had been shared with Cook, and her government so stated this to her representatives in Siberia.

As far as Spanish-Russian contacts are concerned, there is little to report until the meetings of Captain Juan Martinez, and these encounters in fact yielded no great impact.

Another tragedy reminiscent of James Cook's untimely end was the fate of the important French voyage of enlightenment, that of Jean Francois de Gallup, Count of La Perouse. The French royal interest had not extended so far into the Pacific until several years after the colonial contests with Great Britain came to their first close with the signing of the Treatry of Paris in 1764. From them until the domestic upheavals of 1789 the French and their leaders were beset with economic and other domestic problems. There was no long range, logical plan for a French drive into the Pacific. When they did arrive, they were much over-extended.

In the face of these mounting crises and with surely some sense of unreality, it is interesting that a major, well planned naval expedition could be mounted at all, in spite of the examples earlier provided by Louis Antoine de Bougainville (1766-1769), Jean F. M. de Surville (1769-1770), and N. T. M. de Fresnes and Marion de F. Crozet (1771-1773). However the special interest the La Perouse voyage holds for us in long after his departure from Best on August 1, 1785 (ten years after Hezeta's explorations).

La Perouse and Captain de Langle tarried at Easter Island and the Sandwich Islands (Hawaii), and then cruised on to North America. In California they spent four months cruising the shorelines surrounding Monterey Bay, their surveys of which hold great interest for us today. Fortunately for the historical record, the French explorer with some trepidation sent his written records and his young aide, Russian-speaking Baron de Lesseps, home via the overland route from Petropavlovsk Harbour on Kamchatka. A second report was despatched from Botany Bay, before the two ships sailed on to destruction on the reefs at Vanikoro in the Santa Cruz Islands. There was no large contribution to Spanish interests by the French exploring team; one negative factor is the misinformation passed on to the Spanish by the French observers concerning Russian plans for the occupation of Nootka. If La Perouse had returned safely to Brest, he might well have been met by a Committee of Public Safety and the guillotine or other means of disposal[11].

In the midst of national turmoil and vicissitude, French publicists somehow managed to produce not only a superb journal and atlas for La Perouse, but also translations of Spanish, British and Russian explorers and atlas makers. Certainly these were all studied by Captain George Vancouver, RN as he prepared for his important voyage of confirmation, a Britisch Government intention to determine beyond all possible doubt the existence, or the myth, of a practicable North West Passage between the British Isles and the treasures of Cathay.

Vancouver ealier had sailed as a lad on Cook's second and third voyages. With the *Discovery* and *Chatham* Vancouver arrived on the Pacific shore

Russian church over looking bay in present-day town of Kodiak Island.

Ship-wreck at Port des Francais.

A typical "odinochka", a one-man fur-trading outpost, for the Russian-American Company, Alaska.

to find it more complicated than hitherto. His assignment was obviously more grinding, more taxing than laurel-laden. He does however provide us with extended views of the Russian and Spanish advances, as well as some newcomers —the profit oriented Americans, "Boston men" from New England and New York City ports[12].

Through his eyes we note advances the thrusting Russian *promyshlenniks,* fur hunters, have made along the Alaskan Coast in pursuit of sea otter pelts. Vancouver's partners have given historians some pungent descriptions of Russian domestic life as well as economic practices loftily viewed by a haughty and fastidiouus British officer class. Toward the end of April, 1794, the *Discovery,* coping with dangerous icebergs, was suddenly visited by a party of natives and "nine or ten Russians in a large whale boat made of Fir planks". As usual, communication was very awkward, due to language barriers, but the Russians through several conversations made it quite clear that "all about them was Russian land".

Vancouver had been there in 1778, and as far as he was concerned, Captain King of Cook's command had sixteen years previously formally taken possession of Cook's Inlet by displaying flags, buying coins and bottles and other recognized ceremonials associated with geographical discovery and land claim.

As Vancouver left Cook's Inlet with some sense of frustration, he recorded:

32

Sea otter, J. W. Audubon.

Thus we took our leave of Cook's inlet, where from our different interviews from the Russians settled on its shores, it might have been reasonably expected that much information would have been derived concerning the objects and advantages in contemplation, from the extension of that empire into remote regions. Ignorance of each other's language, that insurmountable obstacle to the attainment of such kind of knowledge, attended on all our inquiries, and in most cases extremely inconclusive, and often very contradictory to what we had first understood. This difficulty was not a little increased by the want of information in most of our Russian visitors, with everything that appertained to the science of geography.

Russian American Company "promyshlenniks" (fur trappers or traders), at Onalaska Island.

Referring then to the false and confusing information given him about Cook Inlet topography, fretful Vancouver stated:

...this incident will further afford sufficient proof how little dependence is to be placed or information assumed from such persons but ill-qualified to answer our questions, if understood... it will also shew, on how slight foundation the theories of mediterranean seas, and of a northwest passage may often rest[13].

As the Briton again cruised south he noted that the Russians had reached Cross Sound. Stalled there, they "encountered a more warlike race", the

Tlingit or Kolosh Indian group, who would prove harsh, implacable enemies of the Russians for the next 75 years.

Arriving in Nootka in September, 1794, the British expedition encountered a more congenial atmosphere even though Spanish and British interests were in conflict. In his "Notes and Miscellaneous Observations", written shortly after the voyage, Vancouver mentions 20 vessels trading for furs on the coast in 1792. Six were English, two from Bengal, three from Canton, six from Boston, one from New York, two from Portugal and one from France. He also excepted all Spanish ships, including those anchored at Nootka. The importance of the fur trade is so obvious, and he notes in "what important light the court of Spain beholds her interests in their valuable country". Vancouver undertook very sucessful negotiations with Spanish officers present who shared a desire to resolve the so-called "Nootka Controversy" by conversation and negotiation rather than warfare.

There is a somewhat different notion expressed by the impulsive American marine, John Ledyard. We can truly see his hand in the early arrival of Yankee shippers on the Northwest Coast, namely the merchant adventurers, captains John Kendrick and Robert Gray. Kendrick was surely responding to the Ledyard tales he had heard of "fair and comely Russians" and "fantastic profits". This was not fanciful talk, for after all, the beaver and other pelts had already been part of an important fur trade in the New England-Hudson River area for 150 years. Skippers in search of cargoes would have seen the reality in Ledyard's dreams, and we know that he visited the idling wharves of Boston.

We link him then with the important first voyages of the *Columbia Rediviva* and the *Lady Washington,* and their audacious owners and underwriters who knew with Ledyard that "there is at present little home navigation".

It was redoubtable, taciturn Robert Gray who first reached Canton with an American cargo of otter skins, Gray who first carried the American merchant flag around the world, and in 1792 Captain Gray who penetrated the river fixed as a distinct reality by the Basque sailor Hezeta, seventeen years earlier, and recorded as such in his *Diario.*

Along with the official Russian voyages of captains Adam von Kruzenstern and Iurii Lisianskii, we have the Baranov group sailing in one way or another under the authority of the newly identified Chief Administrator of the Russian American Company, headquartered in New Arkhangel (now Sitka), Alaska. It is under his aegis that the Russian sea hunters and Yankee skippers at last come together in the latest imperial combination. Many years later the French genius, de Tocqueville, would observe Russia and America as:

two great nations that seem to tend toward the same end. All other nations seem nearly to have reached their natural limits, ... but these

Tlingit family.

are still in the act of growth ... these alone are proceeding with ease and celerity along a path which no limit can be perceived.

The great social observer went on to say in a concluding thought about Russia and America:

...the starting point is different, and their courses are not the same; yet each of them seems marked out by will of Heaven to sway the destinies of half the globe.

However we view it, the Spanish, English, French and American voyages to the North Pacific in the late 18th and early 19th centuries fall far short of the total Russian voyages and expeditions to the North pacific. We know this despite the secrecy surrounding so many Russian undertakings and for which information has yet to be released from official archives. In time many Russian mariners will take a place in a history as yet unknown to us all.

Well over 250 years ago the Carmelite, Frey Antonio de la Ascension (who had been with Vizcaino) urged for political, religious and other reaons, that Spanish explorers push their king's claims from Mexico northward. He urged that these actions be taken to obstruct the designs of other European powers. Neither he nor any other person could have foreseen how all would change in the intervening years, that a vigorous new nation would wrest those territories from the grasp of all the European imperialists. No one envisioned that another great nation, Canada, also once a North American colony, would swiftly rise to take its place among world leaders . Who envisioned that the North American nations would so swiftly and confidently develop ports of international significance such as San Francisco, Portland and the Columbia River port cluster, Seattle-Tacoma, Anchorage-Whittier in the north and the magnificent installations at Vancouver-Westminster, British Columbia.

What is perceived by *all* today is that the nations facing each other across the vast reaches of the North Pacific Ocean form an arena for great world tension and very great promise. The interests of the newest world powers all meet in the North Pacific. Widsdom dictates that we learn all we can from the early, courageous leaders who brought the region to world knowledge, Hezeta and his compadres setting forth "... in search of adventures...".

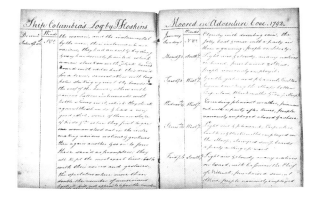

Log of the voyage of the *Columbia* around the world. John Box Hoskins. 1792.

The *Columbia* in a squall.

Notes

1. *For Honor and Country: the Diary of Bruno de Hezeta.* Translated and annotated by Herbert K. Beals. Oregon Historical Society, Portland, 1985, 3.

2. *Ibid.,* XIII.

3. See: Raymond H. Fisher, "The Early Cartography of the Bering Strait Region", *Arctic,* vol. 37, no. 4 (December 1984), 574-589.

4. E. A. P. Crownhart-Vaughan, "Eighteenth Century Russian Scientific Expeditions to the North Pacific Ocean", in press, *Papers of the Third International Congress for Soviet and East European Studies,* 1986.

5. *Pol'noe Sobranie zakonov rossiiskoi imperii,* vol. V, document no. 3266. (Hereafter: PSZ). Translated in forthcoming publication: Basil Dmytryshyn, E. A. P. Crownhart-Vaughan and Thomas Vaughan, *Russian Penetration of the North Pacific, 1700-1799: A Documentary Record.* (Vol. II of *To Siberia and Russian America: Three Centuries of Russian Eastwared Expansion, 1584-1867)* Oregon Historical Society, Portland. In press, 1986. (Hereafter: Russian penetration).

6. *PSZ,* vol. VII, document no. 4649. Translated in *Russian Penetration.*

7. James Cook and J. King, *A Voyage in the Pacific Ocean,* Vol. II. London, 1785, 473.

8. Stepan P. Krasheninnikov, *Opisanie zemli kamchatki* [Description of the land of Kamchatka]. St. Petersburg, 1755. Translated and annotated by E. A. P. Crownhart-Vaughan: *Explorations of Kamchatka 1735-1741.* Oregon Historical Society, Portland, 1972.

9. J. C. Beaglehole, *The Life of Captain James Cook.* Stanford University press, 1974. 127-133.

10. Beaglehole. 571-636.

11. *Voyages and Adventures of La Perouse:* F. Valentin Abridgement. Julius S. Gassner, Translator. University of Hawaii press, Honolulu, 1969. 133-156.

12. *The Voyage of George Vancouver, 1791-1795.* Edited by W. Kaye Lamb. The Hakluyt Society, London, 1985. Second Series, No. 163. Four volumes. IV, 1151, 1396-1397.

13. *Ibid.* IV, 1239.

The Spanish Presence on the Northwest Coast Sea-going Expeditions (1774 – 1793)

by Mercedes Palau

Museo Nacional de Ciencia y Tecnología. Madrid

Introduction

As a result of José de Gálvez's driving force, together with other reasons pertaining to science, missionary works or simply to the investigation of coasts in the face of the English and Russian presence in the Northwest a series of sea-going expeditions took place which proved to be of great scientific and political interest.

Under the auspices of the Spanish Monarchs Carlos III and Carlos IV, and supported by the ministers Arriaga and Valdés, and the Viceroys Croix, Bucareli and Revillagigedo, these expeditions were undertaken by expert pilots and seafarers trained at the Escuela de Guardiamarinas de Cádiz and the Colegio de San Telmo de Sevilla. Prominent among these were Bodega y Quadra, Esteban José Martínez, Antonio Mourelle, Bruno de Hezeta, Jacinto Caamaño and Manuel Quimper.

Three different stages could be singled out from the more than ten expeditions incorporating this period (1774 to 1793) of sea-going expansion. The first stage included the expeditions of Juan Pérez (1744), Hezeta and Bodega (1775) and Arteaga and Bodega (1779). The second, those of Martínez and Haro (1778 and 1789) and Hezeta, Fidalgo and Quimper (1790). The third and final stage, of a scientific and political nature, included the expeditions of Malaspina and Bustamante (1791), Bodega, Moziño and Maldonado (1791-1792), Caamaño and Quimper (1792), Galiano and Valdés (1792) and Seijas and Matute (1793). These voyages marked the close of one of the most outstanding chapters of Spanish involvement on the NorthWest Coast of America, in which a group of men, sailors for the most part, risked their lives individually and collectively, setting an example of vigour and courage in the service of their country. Their contribution to our knowledge of the North Pacific and its coasts, with no attempt made to seek economic benefits therefrom, and their effort and sacrifices, have been like a legacy for future generations. This work sets out to place the legacy on record.

A Port on the Pacific: San Blas de Nayarit

José Bernardo de Gálvez, appointed Visitor of New Spain upon the sudden death of Francisco Anselmo, arrived at Vera Cruz on 18 July, 1764. Renowned as an eminent, energetic, honourable and forceful jurist, he had been charged with prerogatives of some magnitude. He would have to improve the Public Treasury, institute a tabacco monopoly, introduce government reforms, inspect employee conduct and ascertain whether there was any truth in the accusations made against the Viceroy of spending two million pesos on fortifications and raising forces in 1762. Gálvez's actions led to the replacement of Cruillas with Carlos Francisco de Croix, who took over the post

San Fernando. Real Colegio de Guardiamarinas, 1850.
Museo Naval.

View of the Port of Cádiz, 1782.
Museo Naval.

on 23 August, 1766. Before his departure he had been advised by the minister Arriaga to act in compliance to Gálvez. From the outset, both Gálvez and the Viceroy "shared a peculiar contempt for the situation prevailing in the viceroyalty, the causes of which dated back more than two centuries. Faced with those who had benefitted from such a situation, and in conflict with them, they did not hesitate to inculcate the most respectable Indian administration principles. They similarly lent each other support so as to act with an authority ill-applicable to them constitutionally..." (Cárdenas, 1968: 20).

Under Croix's rule (1766-1771), two facts bearing influence on the establishment and development of the coastal department of San Blas, the point of departure and base for the NorthWest Coast expeditions, are worthy of note: the expulsion of the Compañía de Jesús replaced in the California missions by the Franciscans from the Colegio de San Fernando of Mexico, and the Sonora military expedition.

Gálvez deemed it essential to have two ships built in one of the Southcoast ports "so as to provide, promptly and inexpensively, the troops, people and other essentials needed for Sonora...".

The Port of Machatel was considered, and Alonso de Pacheco y Solís was commissioned as chief craftsman responsible for building two brigs measuring 28 feet along the keel, 10 feet abeam and with 15 oars each side.

Pacheco sited a shipyard on the river Grande or Santiago, 4 leagues to the north of Machatel, scheduling the estimated completion of the vessels for October. However, he died suddenly, and the new chief craftsman, Rivero Cordero, moved the shipyard to San Blas. By August, 1767, the *San Carlos* and the *Príncipe* were in franchise at the mouth of the port, "the masts are being fitted with all speed so that the troops and Franciscan missionaries who are to replace the Jesuits may be transported by the middle of next month..." (Cárdenas, 1968: 27).

On 1 March, Diego Peirán, in Tepic, recorded that Rivero considered the vessels *Concepción* and *Príncipe* as being commensurate with the task of shipping the troops, clergy, artillery and 25 Catalonian volunteers. The *Concepción* set sail on 13 March at ten o'clock at night, with 16 monks bound for California, amongst whom was Friar Junípero Serra.

Gálvez arrived at San Blas in May, with orders from the Viceroy to explore the North coast. During his commission as secretary, Juan Manuel Viniegra wrote: "... on 13 May we came into the Port of San Blas. In this new settlement, despite being almost uninhabitable as a consequence of its scorching climate and the host of poisonous insects littering its soil, the Inspector stayed for eleven days, presenting an external show of pleasure so as not to discredit a town he had founded at great expense and wished to sustain...".

Two days later, Gálvez said to the Viceroy: "I shall not withdraw from the present confines of California or Sonora without seeing the first-class Port of Monterey and establishing there a fortress to protect the remaining coasts of these dominions..." (AGI Guadalajara, 513; Cárdenas, 1968: 36).

It could rightly be said that during the time Gálvez was in San Blas, his legislative ability was what led to the port being built, ordering as he did the construction of all the outbuildings essential for establishing an important naval base. Materials were transferred from Machatel, and government and administrative offices, in addition to defences, were raised on his orders.

In its early days, San Blas boasted a small fleet: the *San Carlos* and the *Príncipe* in the Santiago estuary, the *San Antonio*, the schooners *Sonora* and *Sinaloa* and the ships *Concepción* and *Lauretana*, confiscated from the Jesuits (MN ms. 127, doc. 12).

That year, the navigator Juan Pérez and ten sailors from the port of Acapulco arrived. "He seems intelligent, endowed with good judgement, and will thus be of great benefit to us..." Famous visitors in the form of Abbot Chappe d'Auterouche and the seafarers Vicente Doz y Salvador Medina also arrived. They were bound for San José, California, to observe the passage of Venus across the sun. The Abbot and Doz (Medina had just died) boarded the *Concepción*, and following their arrival at San José Chappe also died, although they were able to carry out the observations with which the Paris Academy of Science had charged them. Their notes and observations were published by their mentor Cassini in *Voyage à California* (París, 1772).

Gálvez fell seriously ill during his time in the province of Sonora, and was on the point of dying, but his health improved and he returned to the viceroyalty's capital in May, 1770, where he remained until his work was completed. The ideological, political, economic and social forms he tried to

José de Gálvez, Marquis of la Sonora. 1729-1786. Biblioteca Nacional.

View of La Carraca, XVIII c. Museo Naval.

The Monterey Presidio. José Cardero.
Museo Naval.

impose were countered by powerful opponents, amongst whom the new Viceroy, Antonio María de Bucareli, was the most prominent. On arriving in México, he showed not the slightest regard for Gálvez's efforts, despite the relative calm prevailing in the internal provinces.

San Blas was thus the image of Gálvez's endeavours in Sonora. Bucareli was not taken with any of the projects implemented by the Visitor, and consequently tried from the outset, particularly once he was aware of the economic situation, to do away with the naval base.

The arrival in San Blas of Friar Junípero Serra, en route to the capital, prevented a report from the Viceroy aimed at dismantling the port from being enacted. Bucareli appointed Echeveste to draw up a new statute which he did, dividing the Department into three parts: Comisaria, Arsenal and Flota, all with a degree of independence, but all under the Viceroy's control. The statute was approved in council on 23 July, 1773, and signed by Bucareli, Valcárcel, Malo, Areche, etc. The Viceroy did not only bear in mind support to the Franciscan missions in California, but also the latest, alarming news of Russian advances and exploration on the NorthWest Coast. As early as 1761, the Minister Ricardo Wall had been informed of these expeditions by the then Spanish Ambassador, the Duke of Almodóvar, and further, of the success met by the explorers Vitus Bering and Chiricov and the establishment of a State fur-trading company. In 1773, the new ambassador, Lacy, confirmed to the Secretary of State, Grimaldi, that the Russians had been proceeding with their expeditions to Archangel, and Kamchatka and the eastern coasts. They had been bringing back an abundance of all sorts of furs and settlements were being established towards latitude 64º, The King of Spain ordered Bucareli to investigate the exact facts of the matter and inquire into the possible disadvantages for Spain arising from the Russian establishments. Bucareli had the frigate *Santiago*, captained by the only naval officer in California at that time, Juan Pérez, set sail.

Juan Pérez, 1774

Abundant and fruitful correspondence was exchanged among Lacy, the Spanish ambassador in St. Petersburgh, the minister Grimaldi and the Viceroy Bucareli. Lacy reported the Russian voyages, warning that they were near Spanish possessions, and ventured to say that they might invade California. News became increasingly intensified until Bailio Arriaga requested that Bucareli take the measures necessary to investigate the facts behind the Russian advance.

Bucareli entertained no further doubts on the appropriateness of keeping the Department of San Blas, and called upon the chief navigator, Juan Pérez (in July, 1773), to draw up a plan for an expedition to the Russian establishments. He similarly requested the presence of Luis de Córdova, marine Commander in Veracruz, but de Córdova refused to convey any views since he was not acquainted with Pacific navigation. Bucareli therefore had to accept Juan Pérez's proposals as valid. Pérez intented to stop over at Monterey, and from there head northwards "to reach latitude 45º or 50º which is where the Russian establishments are purported to be". Experience gained from voyages to Alta California assured him that they would have to sail out at sea to avoid the relentless southwest currents and, if the frigate *Santiago* was to sail, it would need: "royal yard-arms, and be fitted with 4 anchors and 4 new cables, 2 grapnels and 3 hawsers, 5 topmasts and spare yards, 3 sets of new sails, rigging and work ropes; a well-preserved spare rudder, 80 ordinary places for selected crew, a first and second warrant officer, likewise for carpenters and shipwrights, 2 good pilots, a ship's doctor with medicine box, a chaplain, 3 dozen good rifles, likewise for bastions, swords and cartridge belts, 8 cannons, food-stocks of all varieties for 12 months, 6

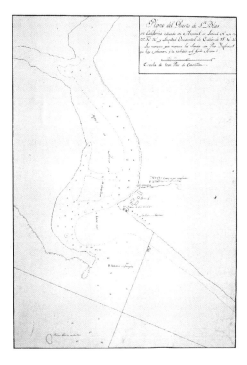

Map of the Port of San Blas. Diario de Caamaño, 1792. Ministerio de Asuntos Exteriores.

barrels of firewater, 3 of wine and 2,000 pesos" (MN ms. 331 and 575 bis).

Preparations got under way, with Francisco Hijosa being appointed to replace the sick Viergol. José Esteban Martínez was named as second pilot. The ovens to make the ship's biscuits, to accompany the expeditionaries, were built in Tepic, and new armed troops were commissioned. Pérez recommended the carpenters José Acosta and Prudencio de Altum. Pablo Mugartegui, from the Colegio de San Fernando, would be the chaplain, and José Dávila and Pedro Castan were selected as ship's doctors (Cárdenas, 1958).

In December secret orders arrived: "V. M. will keep the contents of this envelope hidden until, having left the provisions at Monterey, sail is set and the vessel is one or two leagues away from the port. Then, it shall be opened in the presence of the chaplain, the second pilot and the ship's doctor, who will testify that it has so been carried out."

The Viceroy drafted the "Instructions to be followed by midshipman Juan Pérez, chief pilot of the Department of San Blas, encharged with the discovery expedition following the Monterey coast to the North", and the "Form acting as a guide in the drawing up of deeds of possession for discoveries" (Servin, HSQ, 40, 237-48).

The following are extracts from the Instructions:

"An exact log-book shall be kept from the moment of departure of each and every item of news, bearing, sandbank, and coastline-configuration, and everything shall be demarcated with the quadrant. The depth corresponding to the coast at latitude 60º shall be taken, if possible. Landings shall be made wherever possible, where no risk is involved. Possession shall be taken on behalf of the King. No settlements shall be founded, regardless of apparent advantages. In the event of foreign settlements, investigate from afar whatever possible, taking good note of location and whether or not there are vessels to be reckoned with. Upon encountering another vessel, avoid contact. Treat Indian peoples in the most differential fashion" (Cárdenas, 1968).

Hijosa recorded in a communiqué on 23 January, 1774, that the frigate intented for the expedition was completed. The *Santiago*, alias the *Nueva Galicia*, measured 40 half-arm lenghts along its keel, 3 in fore rake, 1 and 12 inches astern, 14 half-arms and 7 inches in breadth, 10 in hold deck, 6 half-arms and 4 inches in depth and 45 half-arms in length: an exact weight of 225 registered tons...". In the same document, detailed descriptions were given of each part of the ship; outfittings, spare parts and tools, utensils, etc. (AGN, 61: 228-241).

On 22 January, Hijosa and Ruíz signed the crew-list, made up of officers, gunners, seamen, galley-boys, cooks and deck-boys, Manuel López insúa as boatswain, Pascual de Rojas and Diego Nicolás as midshipmen, Francisco Rúa as caulker, José Padilla as gunner and Carlos Ortega as coxswain. In all, 86 men plus the commanding officer. There was a further list of those families who were to go to Monterey. Hijosa recorded that Friar Junípero

Chief of Descanso Port. [José Cardero].
Museo de América.

had also decided to embark, and at sea, facing the isle of Isabela, he wrote: "'... my devout colleague and I are well and happy with our course, and with regard to the new frigate, they occasionally think better of it than they actually say...'".

Neck ring. Attributed to the Tlingit. Latter third of XVIII c.
Museo de América.

Three days after setting off, Juan Pérez recorded: "... in the three days following our departure from San Blas, we have not been able to put her (the frigate) to a greater test... however, her steering is definitely sound... the best thing experienced has been her plying, and her prompt response to the rudder when needed..." (Cárdenas, 1968: 79).

A stopover was made at San Diego, where Serra disembarked on 13 March, and on 5 April they left for Monterey, arriving on 8 May after an uneventful voyage. They remained there for 26 days and before departing once more, the monks Tomás de la Peña and Juan Crespi, responsible for spreading the Holy Word and keeping, moreover, a diary recording the customs of the natives, came on board.

On 6 June, the departure date, navigator José Cañizares's *Príncipe* arrived. They set sail on the 11th, but could not get on course until the 18th, and for several weeks afterwards the Calms prevailed. The advance seemed to last an eternity, and the boatswain Manuel López died. The fog, the rain and the severe cold began. By 13 July they had reached latitude 48º 55', by the 14th, 50º 24'. As recorded in the diary of Esteban José Martínez, the captain ordered that a survey of the waters be made: at 8 o'clock in the morning that day, my colleague Juan Pérez informed me of his wish to go ahead and discover the coast in the light of the little water we had, and the uncertainty of a port in which to take on water, and also of the strength of the winds. I deemed his judgement correct and lent him my support, at which he appointed me expeditionary notary on the occasion of a council of officers whom he informed of the fact. A certificate was signed by them and authorized by my own person..." (AGN historia, 61: 385).

On the 15th, at latitude 51º 42', a course was made towards the coast, which was discerned at a distance of 20 leagues on the 18th. On the following day, latitude 53º 43' was reached and three islands were baptized with the name Santa Margarita (presently called Queen Charlotte Islands). The strait between these islands and those of the Dixon archipelago was investigated, and the advance towards the North continued until latitude 55º (approximately) was reached. The meeting with Indians of the area was described: "... of the twenty-one canoes, two were full of women with a few suckling babies, and several older females: they were all good-looking, pale-skinned and fair-haired, and many of them had iron and copper bracelets, and some had similar small rings. They wear tight-fitting leather clothes, and the lower side of their faces are pierced through the middle, in which a rim of painted shell is placed which touches their nostrils when they talk: however, their movements were normal and it would seem that the married women wore this device, since several young girls did not. Both the women and the men had good bodies...' (AGN Historia, 61: 361).

From 23 July to 5 August they headed southwards, and at latitude 52º 2' they sighted the raised snowy peaks of a mountain range. On the 6th they found themselves facing the island which would later be known on Spanish maps as Quadra and Vancouver. On 8 August they dropped anchor "at a place which seemed ideal to claim, although not sheltered, but as the wind had dropped and our depth was 25 fathoms... the idea still seemed valid at dawn on the 9th which, in view of the weather, gave me reason to hope. I ordered the launch to sea, which was promptly executed... as I was preparing to set out for land, the West wind suddenly arose so fiercely that in an instant the sea swelled in such a way as to cause alarm. The anchorage, which extended four or five leagues out to sea, was unlevel, and the wind such as to perturb the sea. In the light of this unexpected occurence, and the fact that the frigate was dragging the kedge-anchor and heading rapidly onto the coast, I deemed it necessary to cut the cable and set sail lest we all perished..." (Cárdenas, 1968: 80).

In his "Political essay on the Kingdom of New Spain", Humboldt said that this expedition was the most significant one after that of Sebastián Vizcaíno, and that Juan Pérez and his crew were the first European seafarers to drop anchor in Nootka Sound, which would be called King George's Sound by Cook four years later (t. III: 146). The Indian canoes "... watched us throughout the night at fore and stern, and the following day they drew closer, offering us sardines, and they exchanged otter and wolf skins for Monterey shells. They are very docile people, not as lively as those previously encountered, but as fair and handsome. They are also poorer and, from what could be discerned, less inventive". Near Nootka the headlands of Santa Clara (Cape Cook) and San Esteban were identified. After leaving the anchoring berth, a high mountain was sighted and given the name of Sierra Nevada de Santa Rosalía (now Mount Olympus). Then, for 9 weeks, the *Santiago* had to battle against the sea, foul winds, fog, and downpours hampering observation of the coast given what was practically zero-visibility. Despite this, Pérez affirmed that on 22 August, at noon, he was able to chart Cape Mendocino at latitude 40° 8', and not 41° 45' as Cabrera Bueno and Sebastián Vizcaíno had done. On the 26th he made out the Farallon Islands, which they named San Francisco, in "a darkness so dense that until being right upon them they could not be discerned, being necessary for me to put the helm up so strong was the wind". Scurvy took hold of the crew, and the only wish they had was to land in a place they knew: they arrived at the Bay of Monterey on the 27th at half past four in the afternoon. On 9 October, they left Monterey and dropped anchor in San Blas at 6 o'clock in the evening on 3 November.

Apologies were made for not having carried out the instructions to the letter, especially with regard to landing and the preparation of a map of that part of the coast discovered, "made difficult by the rolling suffered off those very coasts". However, a promise was made to "send a full draft-copy, although it would not be made with the delicacy to which art teachers are accustomed".

On 14 November, Bucareli thanked Pérez for sending the ship's logs his own and that of Martínez and congratulated him, for "although everything desired and planned for in the expedition had not been achieved, the information obtained was always of value and extended knowledge to an extent which could make sailing to higher altitudes easier...". Greater euphoria was expressed in the communiqué to Arriaga: "... for having reached an altitude of 55° 49', this promising start in a nation as yet unknown, laying a basis for subsequent progress which I must, from my judgement, see enacted without delay, ensuring that those already with some knowledge of that voyage be instrumental in the selection of replacements. For this purpose I have dispatched a special communiqué to the Port of San Blas so that the frigate be refitted and prepared, without any further delay, for a second voyage..." (Cárdenas, 1968: 81-82).

Neither Cook, Barrington nor Fleurieu knew of this voyage. Humboldt was able to include it in his "Political Essay" thanks to the copy of the log-books of Juan Crespi and Tomás de la Peña forwarded to him by Guillermo Aguirre of the Mexican High Court.

Bruno de Hezeta and Bodega y Quadra, 1775

A second expedition was speedily prepared and command was given to Lieutenant Bruno de Hezeta, and the post of chief steersman and pilot to Ensign Juan Pérez.

Hezeta was one of the six officers from the Escuela de Guardiamarinas de Cádiz requested by the Viceroy for the exploration of the NorthWest Coast. Accompanying him were Miguel Manrique, Fernando Quirós, Juan de Ayala, Diego Choquet, and Juan Francisco de la Bodega y Quadra. They brought scientific instruments with them which, together with those available in the Department of San Blas which had belonged to Abbot Chappe, were taken on board the frigate and schooner earmarked for the expedition. They arrived at San Blas on 25 October.

Hezeta was given command of the the frigate *Santiago* and Ayala that of the schooner *Felicidad*, alias the *Sonora*. Bodega y Quadra, despite his rank, requested to go as second-in-command, and the chief steersman was Antonio Mourelle.

With instructions to investigate the bay of San Francisco, the packet-boat *San Carlos* was fitted out under the command of Lieutenant Miguel Manrique and steersman José de Cañizares. The three ships departed on 16 March, 1775, with water for four months and other essentials for a long voyage. The log-books of Hezeta, Bodega and Mourelle recorded that Juan de Ayala was stricken by a fit of madness shortly after the departure, so Bodega took command of the *Sonora*.

The log-books were meticulously detailed. Those of Bodega and Mourelle reciprocated each other in the main, since both had a similar temperament. Bodega, his steersman's senior by seven years, was likewise an excellent navigator, with a great eye for detail, and courageous and energetic. Capable of withstanding any trial or tribulation, Bodega and Mourelle would prove to be the driving force behind the success of the expedition (Landin, 1971: 19).

The *Sonora* measured 18 half-arm lengths along the keel, and its sole protection and accommodation was afforded by a cover and a small cabin, sparsely equipped with a bed under which a only a drawer would fit. The layout of the accommodation allowed no other posture than being sat down, and since the small size of the deck was in no way akin to permitting a stroll, they had to live in such inactivity for a period of ten months.

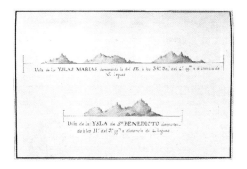

View of the Marias Islands and the Island of S. Benedicto. Montes de Oca. Diario de Bodega y Quadra, 1792. Ministerio de Asuntos Exteriores.

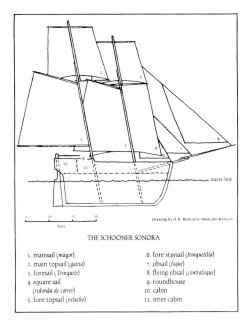

THE SCHOONER SONORA

1. mainsail (mayor)
2. main topsail (gavia)
3. foresail (Trinquete)
4. square sail
   (redonda de correr)
5. fore topsail (velacho)
6. fore staysail (trinquetilla)
7. jibsail (foque)
8. flying jibsail (contrafoque)
9. roundhouse
10. cabin
11. inter-cabin

From For Honor and Country, by Herbert K. Beals.

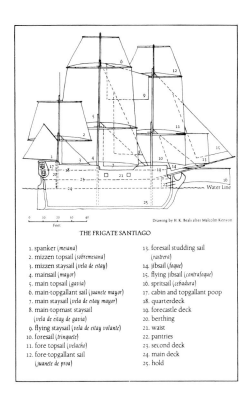

THE FRIGATE SANTIAGO

1. spanker (mesana)
2. mizzen topsail (sobremesana)
3. mizzen staysail (vela de estay)
4. mainsail (mayor)
5. main topsail (gavia)
6. main-topgallant sail (juanete mayor)
7. main staysail (vela de estay mayor)
8. main-topmast staysail
   (vela de estay de gavia)
9. flying staysail (vela de estay volante)
10. foresail (trinquete)
11. fore topsail (velacho)
12. fore-topgallant sail
   (juanete de proa)
13. foresail studding sail
   (rastrera)
14. jibsail (foque)
15. flying jibsail (contrafoque)
16. spritsail (cebadura)
17. cabin and topgallant poop
18. quarterdeck
19. forecastle deck
20. berthing
21. waist
22. pantries
23. second deck
24. main deck
25. hold

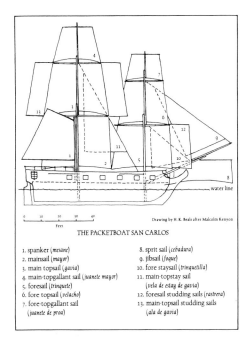

THE PACKETBOAT SAN CARLOS

1. spanker (mesane)
2. mainsail (mayor)
3. main topsail (gavia)
4. main-topgallant sail (juanete mayor)
5. foresail (trinquete)
6. fore topsail (velacho)
7. fore-topgallant sail
   (juanete de proa)
8. sprit sail (cebadura)
9. jibsail (foque)
10. fore staysail (trinquetilla)
11. main-topstay sail
   (vela de estay de gavia)
12. foresail studding sail (rastrera)
13. main-topsail studding sails
   (ala de gavia)

The crew was made up of 14 men, the captain and the steersman, and only four of them had sailed before. The rest were ranch-hands, recently departed from estates. The captain and the steersman worked the same as the sailors, and when the latter were struck by the sea, it was they who would operate the pump to bale the water out: "fortunately such fatigue, not in keeping with their position, was overcome, and that the two young men were able through their drive and ambition for fame to resist...". Bodega y Quadra constantly spurred his men on, frightened as they were by the sizeable heel of the boat, "reminding them many a time of the glory awaiting those on their return who, having stuck with it, were fortunate enough to see the expedition's goal attained. They were also told not to fear the press of sail, since we valued our lives as much as they did theirs, and that care would be taken in avoiding unnecessary risks..." (MN ms. 331: 81).

On the 24th, five of the Marías Islands were spotted and species such as frigate-birds and penguins were recorded. There the packetboat San Carlos broke off to verify the first discrepancies of the Belling map which had already been pointed out by Bougainville. Towards 10 April, the island of Socorro was sighted, being the same, according to Mourelle, as that which Grijalba discovered and named Santo Tomé in 1533. High winds and overcast skies accompanied them until mid-May. After 60 days of nothing but sea and sky, an officers' meeting was held to express opinions —to continue northwards or to head directly for Monterey. Bodega and Mourelle favoured push-

Pocket longitudinal clock. John Arnold, no. 71,
XVIII C.
Museo Naval.

49

ing on, and so declared this by passing a communiqué to the frigate in a barrel attached to a rope, prevented from handing it over in person by the bad weather.

Towards June they began to sight seaweed and algae, and on the 7th the coast was spotted. They anchored at latitude 41º 0,6' at a port called La Santísima Trinidad —between Cape Mendocino and Cape Blanco— and took possession of it in the habitual fashion. Bodega ordered the schooner to be repaired and explored the port until the 18th.

Bodega said of the schooner *Sonora*: "there is no hiding her small size, bad steering, frailty, slowness and the fact that I am forced to give more sail than should be necessary. All these reasons, together with the following, should have been brought to his Excellency's notice by those responsible, informing him of the danger her attributes constitute. However, what is done is done, and no fear will stand in our way. Mourelle, my steersman, and the few men I have, are willingly sacrificing themselves alongside me, accepting their fate with measured realism. Up to now, not the slightest water has been discovered, even in the light of the seas covered, and if the sails be too many and also frail, the continuous watchfulness of my steersman and I will yet see us through. Recently God has lent force to great undertakings, and if our fate results so adverse that it may not be overcome, what greater glory than to die at one's post in the service of the King" (Landin, 1971: 21).

Mourelle observed and described the Indians. He said they were friendly and sociable, and inhabited very low, wooden, square huts, with a circular entrance with room for only one person. Inside, on a clean and levelled floor, a deep, square hole was used to keep a fire going, to help the inhabitants fend off the cold. The men wore leather skins, although when the cold was biting —not an unusual occurence— they would throw sea-lion and other animal skins on their backs, and would wear a garland of fragrant herbs on their heads. They would wear their hair long, and have a bone-type adornment through their ear-lobes and a thread or thong around their waist and ankles. They painted their faces and bodies black and liked to tattoo their arms "in the same way that uncouth Spaniards would have ships or anchors tattooed on them".

"The women cover their heads with a woven crown of pita thread and other fibres, and arrange their hair in two plaits decorated with fragrant herbs. They use the same adornments in their ears as the men, and around their necks were a string of shells, bones and fruit. They protect themselves from the cold with furs similar to the men's, and below the waist they wear a mesh, saffron-coloured skirt or underskirt, skilfully woven with skins, from which tassel-like threads hang. On their lower lips, two cuts are made dividing it into three lobules which hang down as far as their jaws..." (MN ms. 622).

They lived under a chief who decided how goods were shared out. They were skilful in the use of the bow, and well disposed to iron, be it in the form of knives or tools, and waged war with neighbouring villages. They grew tabacco in small plantations and smoked it in wooden pipes "similar to small trumpets". They hunted and ate deer, bison, seals and otters, and their fishing incorporated sardines, smelt and mussels. There were fresh-water streams, and fragrant green meadows where roses, irises, oregano, celery, plantain, camomille and other well-known herbs grew. They also saw strawberries, blackberries, mulberries, sweet onions, truffles and magnificent, upright pine trees. Hezeta, Bodega and Mourelle drew up a map of the port of Trinidad and noted down facts they considered of interest (Landin, 1971: 24).

At the end of May they had reached latitude 48º at the site of a natural bay they called Bucareli —now known as Grenville Bay. They claimed it the following day but, upon disembarking to collect water and firewood, six men died at the hands of the Indians, which is why this place was also called Martyrs' Cove.

At that time, it was debated whether the *Sonora* should head back to Monterey in view of her frailty. Bodega was firmly against it and believed, moreover, that "a direct northward course must be adhered to, and no more time must be wasted taking coastal routes". The crew began to protest, and on 19 July the ship's doctor reported 28 seamen as unfit for duty. Consequently, the expedition appeared to be on the point of being called off, and on 30 July both vessels took different routes.

In early August, when they were near what is now Vancouver, Hezeta, at the request of the ships' doctors, started the return voyage. On the 29th they arrived at Monterey and set about exploring the North coast as far as San Francisco until the *Sonora's* arrival. They discovered the river mouth to which they gave the name Bay of Asuncion, or Entrance of Hezeta, the very same as was found in 1792 by Captain Gray in his vessel *Columbia Rediviva*, the river's present name.

On the 17th the *Sonora* headed towards a port on the island of Kruzof, near that of Barenov and Chicagov of the Alexander archipelago, calling it Guadalupe. On the 18th they came across a further port at latitude 57º 20' which "... although smaller than the previous one, it nevertheless has a magnificent beach, a river 4 or 5 yards wide with a depth of eight fathoms, sheltered on three sides and defended on the foruth by protruding islands, all joined together at a depth of 6 fathoms "a rifle-shot distance away from the coast... the Indian dwellings are no more than a single house, not badly built, with a parapet for their defence...". It would be claimed and given the name of Nuestra Señora de los Remedios. On the 21st they headed on and on the 22nd, because of the wind, the cold, the soaking rain, the lack of adequate clothing and the spread of scurvy, they were forced to turn back. At latitude 57º 17' they found "a vast, endless arm of the sea, extremely calm, sheltered

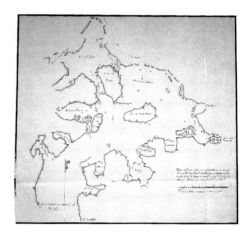

Map of the Port of Bucareli, discovered in 1775 by Juan Francisco de la Bodega y Quadra. Diario de Caamaño, 1792. Ministerio de Asuntos Exteriores.

and tranquil, and with splendid waters". They took possession of it on 24 August and named it Port of Bucareli, charting it accordingly.

On the 26th, they investigated the Island of San Carlos, spotting the Cape of San Agustin on the 27th. Having almost reached the 59th parallel, they decided to head back along the coast. Towards 3 October, they entered what they took to be the Bay of San Francisco. Their error did not prevent the place being charted years later as Bay of Bodega. On the 8th, they reached Monterey (AGI Estado, 20, doc. 22; Cárdenas, 1968: 86).

During the course of the crossing from Monterey to San Blas, the steersman Juan Pérez, "grey-haired and with ruddy countenance... passed peacefully away... perhaps he knew little of nautical calculations and books, but he knew all too well of the heroic virtues needed to live at sea upon the frail wood of a ship, and of the sacrifices involved..." (Majó Framis: 1113).

Bodega and Mourelle arrived with their weakened schooner as far as the 58th parallel, and their minutely-detailed description of the coast extended geographical knowledge enormously. Mourelle's log-book was published by Barrington and used by Cook on his third voyage, and drew on the instructions given to Count of La Perouse. The expedition's charts were printed in Mexico in 1778 and included details of the area between latitudes 17º and 58º (Humboldt, III: 147).

Arteaga and Bodega, 1779

Fired with enthusiasm at the voyage's success, the Viceroy set about preparing a new expedition, even though the previous one had yet to return. In August he called upon Lieutenant Ignacio Arteaga, in conjunction with Francisco Hijosa, Shipping Master in the Department of San Blas, to prepare a list of arsenal requirements with a view to "arming and fitting out the King's vessels for war, and to proceed to claim those places discovered". However, the international background was marked by a state of political disarray. The 13 American colonies had declared their independence and embarked upon the struggle to obtain it. Even though this news was well received in Spain, since in the event of war Spain would have France as an ally against England, the Madrid authorities ordered the expedition to be postponed. During this period, the very same coasts were visited by Cook.

While the *Princesa* was being built in San Blas, Bucareli sent Bodega to Perú to buy the frigate *Favorita*, both vessels being well-suited to long sea-voyages.

Mourelle, promoted to Ensign as a result of his distinguished conduct on the previous expedition, went to help out at the San Diego fortress and ascertained the accuracy of the description of the Californian coasts en route.

Towards the end of 1778, preparations were well under way: the frigates were already prepared and stocked with victuals, supplies, crew and spare parts for the new campaign which, it was hoped, would go further than ever before. The officers, Bodega and Mourelle, studied the route meticulously using Spanish, Russian and French maps which would later have to be thoroughly re-plotted.

Lieutenant Ignacio de Arteaga was commissioned as Commander of the frigate *Princesa*, and Lieutenant Fernández Quirós as second-in-command. Bodega y Quadra was given command over the *Favorita*, and his friend and colleague Mourelle took second-in-command.

The *Princesa*, measuring 40 half-arm lengths along the keel and 13 in breadth, carried 98 men, and the *Favorita*, 100. Besides the commander and second-in-command, the remaining posts were: chief steersman José Camacho; steersman's mate; Juan Pantoja; ship's doctor; Juan García; chaplains; Juan Riobó and Friar Matías Nogueira. On the *Favorita*, the chief steersman was José Cañizares, thes ship's doctor Mariano Núñez Esquivel and chaplain Cristóbal Díaz. Provisions consisted of bread, ship's biscuits, sliced beef, beans, salted fish, lentils, cheese, chick-peas, rice, peppers, garlic, onions, lard, oil, bacon, salt and syrup.

On 11 Febraury they set sail with supplies for 15 months and 195 men on board. By 1 May they could already see the snowy mountain peaks, and at dawn on the 3rd, the *Favorita* dropped anchor off the Entrance of Bucareli; the *Princesa* did likewise that afternoon. Two days later they changed anchorage ground to a nearby port sheltered from the wind.

At Santa Cruz port they stocked up with water, firewood and ballast, and everyone rested. To avoid being caught unawares by the natives, ever mindful of the tragic fate of those members of the *Sonora*, they organized groups of infantrymen and gunners for their defence.

Arteaga and Bodega ordered a thorough exploration of the nearest shores (Prince of Wales archipelago). Mourelle commanded the launches to be used for plotting charts and pinpointing locations, accompanied by the steersmen José Camacho, Juan Bautista Aguirre, Juan Pantoja and the ship's doctor Juan García. Their captains gave them "the brightest amongst the seamen, 5 soldiers, a gunner, 8 stone-cutters, 6 emeries, 20 rifles and provisions for 18 days".

They set off on 18 May and observed, with the greatest detail, and named the following locations: the ports of San Antonio, La Asunción, and Mayoral, the Islands of San Ignacio and Santa Rita, Port of La Real Marina, Isle of San Fernando, Point of La Amargura, Channel of Portillo, Bay of Esquivel, Mouths of Juan Arriaga, Channel of San Cristóbal, Inlet of San Alberto, Mouth of Almirante, Caño de la Cruz, Point of Cuervo, Isle of San Juan, Port of Bagial, Caños del Trocadero, Isle of La Madre de Dios, Ports of La Caldera, La Estrella, El Refugio and Los Dolores, and Point of La Arboleda. Some of these names have been preserved on present charts, and on the latest maps there can be found a group called the Mourelle Islands.

Mourelle returned with the launches on 13 June. In his log-book he described the Indians as "olive-skinned, some a normal white, and well-built. The women seemed decent, and agreeable to look at: some were very beautiful and we thought that if dressed otherwise, they would compare favourably with the finest-looking women of the Kingdom. They used one device which made them look abominable: this was a wooden oval which was inserted in a hole pierced especially in the lower lip; only the married women bore this incision, as the younger girls wore a copper clip which, with time, would give way to the oval. They wore fur tunics, fastened around the waist, falling down to their feet, with sleeves extending to their wrists. When waging war, they would don a breast and backplate plaited out of wood and bark which left their arms free for combat, in addition to gorgets and fur helmets. Finally, a cord tunic was used to protect them from arrows. Weapons used were arrows, iron-tipped lances, long knives and stone axes made from extremely hard green stone."

The bird «Gracula». José Cardero.
Museo Naval.

Their language was difficult to transcribe for the Spaniards as they formed their consonants with a guttural sound made moving the tongue against the palate. Influencing such language must, according to Mourelle, have been the difficulty for the women of pronouncing labial sounds, owing to the aforementioned device scarcely letting their lips touch. Fruit of their labour were everyday objects such as woven fur mats, woolen blankets and girdles, wooden troughs, canoes with unusual drawings of heads, wooden boxes in the form of frogs, and other bigger boxes displaying several animals, human figures, birds and other creatures made of wood and similarly-made helmets, imitating heads of fierce animals. There were also fishing nets and whistles which they played like a transverse flute".

They ate a large variety of fish and sea-food, such as hake, sole, sardines and salmon, which they would cook or dry. They relished venison and other meats. They appeared to have no religion, although they did show an inclination for the sun. They would place their dead with their furs on boxes mounted on four small supports (Landín, 1971).

Shortly before setting off, Mourelle recorded in his log-book: "... there are lofty mountains nearby whose slopes plummet sharply to the sea". Huge forests of tall, upright, solid pine trees grew there, often being flattened by the storms. Among the plants to be found were camomille, nettles, wild celery, aniseed, plantain, celandine, elder, wormwood and sorrel. There was a wide variety of birds; ducks, seagulls, grebes, crows, kites, geese, cranes, goldfinches and others they were unable to identify. They found what was apparently copper-bearing rock, which made it logical to presume that that used by the Indians in their jewellery had been extracted. Nevertheless, the Spaniards believed that the iron came from dealings with other people (the

English or the Russians, perhaps), traces of whose presence could not be found.

The last stage of the expedition started at latitude 55º. On the 9th, after sailing northwards through dense cloud, they came across land which was completely covered in snow. 7 days later they sighted a very high mountain "whose peak could equal that of Orizaba in height". This mountain was San Elías, the second highest (5,489 m) in U.S.A., where the Pacific coast curves towards the East, forming the Alaskan Gulf. Mourelle recorded a latitude of 59º 2' —the furthest North attained by the Spaniards at that point.

On 17 July, 3 leagues from San Elias Cape, Mourelle plotted the location as 59º 53' and continued to head West, hugging the coast so as to re-chart ranges and locations and maximize accuracy.

On the 20th two manned canoes appeared, each with a single pilot. They confidently approached the frigates offering them arrows, as if it were the most natural thing in the world. Mourelle described the eskimo kayaks we are so familiar with today. He said they wore hats similar to those worn at the Entrance of Bucareli, and leather tunics. Their language bore no resemblance to that of the Bucareli Indians.

The bird «Tetrao Lagopus Var. Amer.». José Cardero. Museo Naval.

On 22 July they dropped anchor at the Island known today as Hinchinbroke referred to on Spanish charts at that time as Magdalena. The next day they sailed by, and claimed, an inlet, naming it Port of Santiago. They reached latitude 60º 13', which would be the most northerly point of their voyage, and received a visit from natives, coming to greet them in 6 canoes "some 26 half-arm lengths long and 4 wide, lined with white leather, and whose sterns were similar to those of our own boats. They brought their women with them, who could be distinguished from the menfolk by the string of beads hanging from the corners of their mouths...".

The documented the presence of copper, furs and fishing grounds, three elements which, together with gold, have always constituted the basis of the Alaskan economy.

Arteaga called a meeting on board the *Princesa* and the ships' doctors confirmed the spread of scurvy. It was decided that, weather conditions permitting, they should leave the port as soon as possible, sailing westwards in an attempt to reach a greater latitude (MN ms. 331: 109).

They sailed along the coast of Montagu Island and claimed the Islands of Quirós and Regla (one of the many which stretch along the Southeast shore of the Kenai Peninsula from the Chugach to the Outer, Rabbit and Ragged Isles. Near the Volcano Ipiamna, one of the Spaniards, Miranda or Quirós, discovered more lofty peaks which were no doubt Redout, Douglas and Denison.

On the Isle of Regla they found signs of Indian presence in the form of huts and seal carcases. Eventually a canoe appeared, but they did no more than shout incomprehensibly and then disappear rowing at top speed, frightened, perhaps, by the size of the "floating houses". Sickness got a hold of the crew and, with bad weather additionally, they decided to return (MN ms. 331, f. 113).

They surveyed Cape Mendocino and entered the port of San Francisco where they received orders to bring the expedition to a halt and return to San Blas.

Martínez and Haro, 1788

The Spanish government was concerned by the news of Russian settlements, the existence of which did not come to their knowledge before the publication of Cook's third voyage. They viewed unfavourably the fact that the fur-trade attracted English, French and American vessels to the Northwest Coast. Following the voyages of Cook, Dixon, Portlock, Meares and Duncan, the Europeans began to consider the port of Nootka as the chief fur-market on the Northwest Coast, making it necessary for the Madrid authorities to do what they should have done 15 years previously (Humboldt, t. III: 150).

Having seen a chart obtained by La Perouse of the Russian settlements in Nootka, Trinidad Island, Onalaska Island and Prince William Island, the Viceroy set about preparing a new expedition. However, in full preparation, made difficult by the lack of seamen and staff, Bernardo de Gálvez died and was replaced by the Viceroy Manuel Antonio Florez. From 1787 onwards he took charge of preparations. He issued the same Instructions as those given for previous expeditions to Lieutenant José Camacho, commander of the *Concepción* alias *San Matías*. With Hijosa's assistance, Camacho prepared the victuals, stores, foodstuffs, medicine, clothing, barrels, beams, boxes, etc., and the Public Treasury allocated 30,000 pesos for expenses. He asembled the navigation diaries, reports, maps, plans and charts from previous voyages, but then, two days before departure, Camacho lost all will to undertake the voyage and backed down. The Viceroy, in the absence of Mourelle who was in the Philippines at that time, appointed Esteban José Martínez as commander of the frigate *Princesa* and López de Haro as commander of the packetboat *San Carlos*. The steersmen Antonio Fernández and Esteban Mandolia, the steersman's assistant Antonio Palacios, the chaplains Inés López and José Díaz and the ship's doctor Diego Muñoz completed the crew of 89 men boarding the frigate. The *San Carlos*. with a crew of 83 men, had José María Narváez and Juan Zayas as steersmen, José Verdiaz as steersman's assistant, and Nicolás López as chaplain (Cárdenas, 1968: 133-4).

Florez reported to Valdés that they set sail on 9 march, and by 15 May they had already reached a latitude of 58º 32'. It seems that it was Martínez's decision to head straight for this latitude following his talks with La Pe-

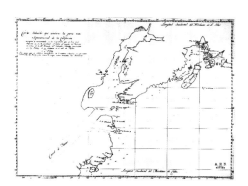

Reduced chart of the northernmost area of California. Salvador Fidalgo, 1790. Houses indicate Russian settlements.
Archivo Histórico Nacional.

rouse. Three days later they were off the coast of Prince William Island and reached two islands which they called Hijosa. On the 25th they sighted the Island of Montagu and a volcano which was named Palacios in honour of the steersman's assistant who spotted it. At dawn on the 28th they dropped anchor in an inlet which was henceforth known as Port of Florez. In the logbook, Martínez showed himself to be an expert, keen-eyed seaman and cosmographer with a great capacity for description, revealing a cultured, sensitive man with extraordinary scientific curiosity (Vila, 1966: 69-89). On 15 June they left Port of Florez, and dropped anchor on the 18th at latitude 59º 53' where several Indian boats came with the news that nearby was a single-masted vessel which had killed one of them from a cannon-shot. Martínez would not believe the story, whereas Haro did, and from that moment friction between the two reared its head.

Martínez headed towards Trinidad Island, one of the many in the Kodiak group, whereas López de Haro went off to Cape Dos Puntas. Martínez came across an Indian "dressed in a blue blanket-shirt, boots made of leather which looked like guts, shoes like the slippers worn by the Indo-Chinese, with cordovan and a sole, more gut on his tunic and hood, and with a sickly, olive-skinned appearance... he speaks Russian, but answers questions in an abrupt and furtive manner..." (Cárdenas, 1968: 135).

On 3 July the *San Carlos* arrived with the news that they had made contact with the Russians. In his report, Haro said that the Russians they had come across in Dos Puntas "... are all well-built, well-dressed, white and courteous... they have two vessels grounded on the beach under the command of a captain called Haro". They obtained information on the trading of otter-skins and showed on a chart where the establishments were located: at Cape Dos Puntas: 60 Russians with 2 schooners; at Onalaska: 120 Russians and one schooner; at latitude 55º 15': 40 Russians; at Cape Elisabeth: 40 Russians; at Cape Rada at the start of Cook shore: 37; and on Prince William Island: 40 Russians, a house and a sloop which ran along the coast as far as Nootka, collecting the furs (Vila, 1966: 135-6).

In the light of this information, Martínez decided to head for the largest establishment, that at Onalaska. From the 19th to the 28th he remained in the port, procuring much information from the Russians by whom he was cordially received. He was lodged at the house of chief Cumic, who stated his wishes to establish himself at Nootka so as to prevent the English from fur-trading. This concerned Martínez, who decided to return immediately and inform the Viceroy, and subsequently beat the Russians and the English in the race to take possession of Nootka and establish a settlement. He ordered Haro to set sail for Monterey so as to gain time, but the latter disobeyed and headed directly for San Blas, believing that the Commander was not following the instructions received. The frigate *Princesa* reached Monterey on 17 September and waited there in vain for the *San Carlos* to arrive.

Whilst the crew was recovering, Martínez completed the charts of those places visited and arrivel at San Blas on 5 December (MN ms. 331, fol. 137).

Martínez, Eliza, Fidalgo and Quimper, 1789-1790

On 6 December, Martínez reached San Blas, and on the 7th he received an order from the new Viceroy to depart alongside Lieutenants Francisco Eliza and Salvador Fidalgo, and sub-lieutenant Manuel Quimper, at the command of the frigate *Princesa* and the packetboat *San Carlos* and the *Aranzazu* in order to occupy the port of Nootka before the Russians or the English did.

The orders stated that the ships were to be armed and suitably equiped and staffed by officers and seamen, troops and arms. They would leave at the end of January. The frigate *Aranzazu*, carrying the same number of people as the *San Carlos*, and under the command of Cañizares, would take provisions to the New California fortresses and then continue on to Nootka. From there it would return to San Blas with news of the venture. Friendship would be sought with the Indians through gifts and trading, and the four members of the clergy would try and spread the Holy Word to the natives, but without forcing them. Any Russian or English vessels arriving at the port would be received and made to see the rightfulness of our possessing Nootka, and if they attempted to use force they would be driven back once all friendly and peaceful channels of diplomacy had been exhausted.

The packetboat *San Carlos* would have to investigate the coast, recording all ports, islands and inlets missed by Cook, from latitude 50º to 55º, which had likewise been missed by previous expeditions. The steersman López de Haro would take official possession of the country, and describe in full detail in his log-book the place and its inhabitants. He would then head for the port of Bucareli, rectifying and correcting previously-made discoveries as far as Prince William Sound.

The frigates *Concepción* and *Aranzazu* would be continuously involved in shipping those reinforcements and stores needed in Nootka, simultaneously surveying, with the greatest accuracy, the coast from San Francisco to Nootka (MN ms. 332: 126).

The frigate *Princesa*, with 106 people on board, and the *San Carlos*, with 89, departed on 17 February, 1789. Martínez kept a meticulously-detailed log-book, and complained, towards 21 April, about the lack of spare sails, the ship's dirty state, its poor fittings and the general lack of care taken by the Department. The crew was assailed by sickness: colds, coughs, venereal diseases, etc.

On 5 May they arrived at Nootka, and the launch of a ship which had come from Macao came out to greet them, their captain offering himself as

The bird «Larua melano cephalos». José Cardero.
Museo Naval.

pilot. Martínez accepted, and at 11 o'clock in the morning they dropped anchor in the port. Verses of welcome were sung, and 15 cannon-salutes were
fired in accompaniment to three utterings of "God Save the King!". The Macao packetboat replied with 13 cannon-salutes, and their captain Francisco
José Viana and purser, William Douglas, from Lisbon and Scotland, respectively, came on board. Captain Kendrik of Boston, whose vessel was anchored in-shore, also came aboard and informed them that the Indians were peaceful. The Franciscans incorporated in the expedition went to visit the chief
of the port, Macuina, who, together with Chief Keleken, held a feast in their
honour, with music and dancing. Macuina showed Martínez the shells from

59

Monterey he had been given as a present in 1774 (Humboldt). Kendrik's steersman, Ingraham, acted as interpreter as he knew the langugage of the Nootkans.

Martínez immediately set about undertaking the work needed for establishing a settlement. On a nearby hill a small stronghold was built, in which ten cannons were placed. It was given the name of Bastion of San Miguel.

On 15 June the sloop *Princesa Real,* from the London Free Trading Company, arrived under the command of Thomas Hudson, and on the 17th the sloop *Lady Washington,* commanded by Captain Robert Grey, arrived after a 116-day voyage from Macao. He requested leave for rest and was granted it by Martínez.

In the meantime work continued on the Spanish settlement, and a captured schooner was re-fitted and baptized with the name *Santa Gertrudis.* The steersman José M.[a] Narváez was appointed captain and given the mission of exploring the strait of Fuca, sighted by Martínez in 1774 and whose existence was denied by the English voyagers.

Martínez, accompanied by all his men and by the captains and crews of the foreign vessels, took formal possession of the port of Santa Cruz, located at the entrance of Nootka. Cries of "God Save the King" in honour of Carlos III, and the customary speeches were made. The official deed of possession was placed in a tightly-sealed bottle, and then a meal was offered by the Commander for all those present.

On 2 July the ship the *Argonaut* arrived, under the command of James Colnet, bearing orders from the King of England to take possession of the port, found a settlement, and build a frigate and a schooner.

On the 29th the frigate *Aranzazu* arrived with orders for Martínez to leave the port and return to San Blas. Accompanied by Captain Kendrik's son, who acted as interpreter, he visited Macuina and told him to look after the port and the Spanish settlement. He also left goats, kids and pigs under his care.

Before leaving, Martínez gave a meticulously-detailed description of the place in his log-book (Martínez, 1964: 117), including words "... taken from the report delivered to me by the chief steersman of the Boston frigate *"Columbia",* José Ingraham, translated into Spanish by our Englishman, Gabriel del Castillo, with the remaining terms we ourselves have been able to acquire, since the report made by Cook is defective with regard to pronunciation..." (MN ms. 732, Martínez, 1964: 117).

On 7 December, 1789, the new Viceroy, the Count of Revillagigedo, ordered the commander-in-chief of the Department of San Blas to have the frigate *Concepción,* the packetboat *Argonaut* and the sloop *Princesa Real* leave in January to relieve the frigate *Princesa* in the port of Nootka and not to leave the settlement.

The crew of the frigate *Concepción* consisted of Lieutenant Francisco

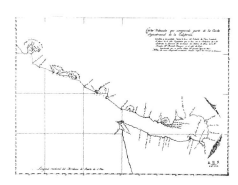

Reduced chart including a section of the northern California coast to the Mouth of the Fuca Strait. Manuel Quimper, 1790. Archivo Histórico Nacional.

Eliza, ship's commander, captain pedro Alberni from the Catalunyan Volunteer Company, lieutenant Mariano Jaulia, chaplain Alejandro Jordán, sub-lieutenant Esteban José Martínez, chief steersman Gonzalo López de Haro and assistant José Verdía, and the ship's doctor Friar Juan Ferrón. There were, moreover, 16 sea-officers, a gunner, 50 Catalunyan volunteers and 92 ordinary seamen. It was well stocked with anchors, cables, sails, water and rations for 10 months, and fitted with 22 cannons (4 and 3), 6 stone-cutters, 20 rifles, 40 pistols, knives for all the crew, 80, 25lb-bags of gunpowder, and all other necessary items for handling artillery. There were also trinkets and 192 cooper plates for trading otter furs with the Indians.

The packetboat *San Carlos,* alias the *Filipino,* was under the command of Lieutenant Salvador Fidalgo, and its crew was made up of a chaplain, two steersmen, a ship's doctor, 14 officers, 23 troops and 58 ordinary seamen. Like the frigate, it had anchors, cables, sails, rigging and water plus victuals for 10 months. It was also fitted with 14 cannons (3) and other utensils for weapon-handling, in addition to swords and knives.

The sloop *Princesa Real,* commanded by sub-lieutenant Manuel Quimper, had two steersmen, 7 naval officers, 4 soldiers and 18 ordinary crew-members. It was well-endowed with anchors, cables, sails, rigging and victuals for 10 months. The artillery consisted of small cannons, rifles, pistols, etc.

They set sail on 3 February and reached Nootka on 5 April. There they tried to strengthen their position by forming a new battery where they raised the national flag. Once the formalities were over, Eliza gave Lieutenant Salvador Fidalgo the orders and instructions from the Viceroy to explore the coast from latitude 60º.

Fidalgo departed on 4 May from Nootka towards the North coast in the packetboat *San Carlos.* They dropped anchor at Prince William, took possession of it and charted it. They named the inlet after Revillagigedo, the island at the mouth after the Count, the volcano after Fidalgo, and the last inlet after Valdés. A further port to the South was named after Mazarredo. Fidalgo gave an exact description of the country, its natural products, the nature and customs of its inhabitants, and the settlements set up there by the Russians, by whom he was told that they had been established in 1787. On 21 June they departed to explore the Southwest coast. On the 4th they dropped anchor within sight of a Russian settlement on the River Cook, whose chief gave him the help he required. On the following day they entered a more sheltered port which they named Revillagigedo, and from there a launch explored as far as Cape Elisabeth —perhaps the same one that Arteaga named as Regla in 1779. There they received news of a Russian war-frigate which had left Ochoskoy in May with astronomers on board to ascertain the real location of the islands and immediate coastline as far as Mount San Elías. Aware that there was a Spanish ship in the area, they set

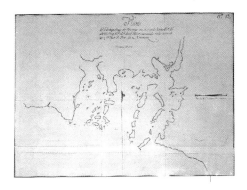

Map of the Carrasco Archipielago, surveyed in 1789 and 1791 by José de Narváez. Diario de Bodega y Quadra, 1792. Ministerio de Asuntos Exteriores.

sail to visit her, but a storm had obliged them to head for Prince William Sound (Malaspina, 1985: 430).

They then dropped anchor near Cape Dos Cabezas where they landed to go and visit the Russian settlements, procuring news of their industry, trade, fishing, relationship with the natives, etc.

On the 17th they set off to continue their exploration of the coast, but foul winds and a shortage of supplies discouraged them and they headed for Monterey. From there they returned to San Blas, arriving on 14 November.

Manuel Quimper, in command of the sloop *Princesa Real,* received orders from Commander Eliza to carry on the exploration of the strait of Fuca first undertaken by the steersman Narváez. He left the port of Nootka on 31 May, explored the Port of Claucaud, cut into the Fuca Channel, and visited several ports and part of the coast. He charted his findings and headed back at the beginning of August.

In 1790 he received a new order from Viceroy Revillagigedo to continue exploration of the strait. Once more he left Nootka in charge of the packetboat *San Carlos* and the schooner *Santa Saturnina* alias the *Orcasita,* accompanied by Captain José Villaverde, the ship's doctor Friar Juan Ferrón, the second steersman Juan Pantoja and the steersman's assistant José Verdiaz (MN ms., 332; 63). His intention was to reach latitude 60°, and come back down exploring the coast. However, adverse weather conditions prevented this, so he decided to begin explorations from latitude 40° and sail up the Fuca Channel, where he arrived on 27 May. Two long months later he returned, with most of his crew suffering from scurvy. He charted several ports and explored the coast as far as the Great Channel of Nuestra Señora del Rosario.

Quimper joined up with Fidalgo in Monterey, and they both returned to San Blas, arriving on 14 November, 1790 (Malaspina, 1885: 433).

Malaspina and Bustamante, 1791

Alejandro Malaspina, head of the expedition of the corvettes *Descubierta* and *Atrevida* (1789-1794), was an Italian sailor from a noble family which, like many, was at the service of the Spanish Crown. This was not unusual, all the less so if the numerous 18th-century emigrations to Spain of experts from all fields are taken into account. He had been born a subject of the Duke of Parma, who was also a Prince of Spain.

He planned the voyage and was helped in its preparations by the Spanish seaman José de Bustamente y Guerra, who was to accompany him as second-in-command and Commander of the *Atrevida.* The expedition got un-

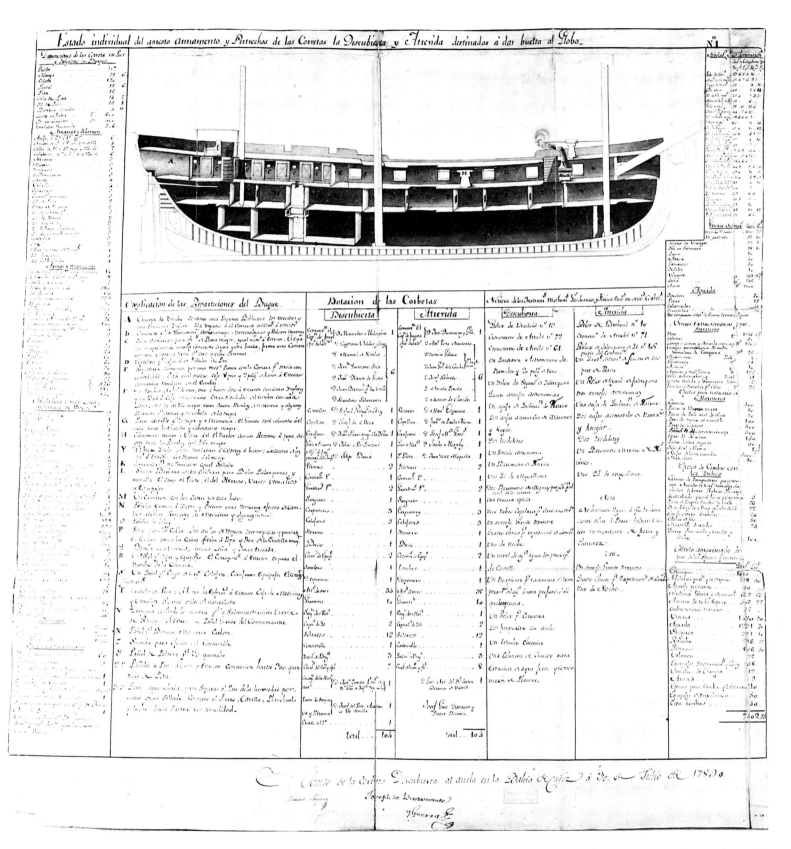

Account of equipment, arms and supplies of the corvettes *Descubierta* and *Atrevida*.
Malaspina and Bustamante, Cádiz, July 30, 1789. Museo de América.

derway in 1789, a key year in European history in the light of the French Revolution, and no less decisive a year for Spanish history: a change of Kingdom was enacted upon the death of Carlos III and the accession to the throne of Carlos IV, during the course of which it cannot be rightly said that the vigour of noble spirit nor its institutions flagged. In accompaniment to the important changes about to take place in Europe, and indeed, as a consequence of such events, new information and knowledge pertaining to America was to be sought by the expedition. This would be undertaken on the basis of all sorts of research, and in-depth exploration and analysis of the American continent and Pacific islands geared to furnishing instruments for its better organization, administration and defence. It was also intended to enrich the Real Gabinete de Historia Natural (Royal Natural History Collection) with contributions such as the 10,000 botanical species catalogued by Nee and Haenke, Pineda's minerals and animals, and further highly-valuable objects pertaining to the fields of anthropology and ethnography which, together with the rich collection of Bauza drawings, are preserved in the Museo de América in Madrid (Palau, 1890: 16).

The Spanish naval Minister Antonio Valdés began with the thought of remodeling the mortar ship *Santa Rosa* for the daring expedition, but Malaspina wanted two new ships, and he eventually undertook the construction of the 306-ton corvettes *Descubierta* (Discovery) and *Atrevida* (Daring) —109 feet in length with a 14-foot draft loaded— best identified as sloops. He followed the early example of James Cook in this and other important details, mindful of the fact that a consort, large or small, could be of vital importance in unknown waters and treacherous circumstances. One interesting detail is that Malaspina sheathed the hulls inside as well as out for further protection against rocks and shoals. He also sought professional advice from new scientists and physicians concerning chronometers, other measuring instruments, related technical equipment as well as dietary suggestions.

The Spanish fleet physician José Salvaresa was very helpful with new findings in food and diet, a distinct improvement on the previous generation, when ceews three times the size necessary for ship handling were routinely signed on to ensure enough living hands to work the ship home. Malaspina checked on venting for air circulation and proper food storage and preparation. Certainly he was ahead of his time in experiments to distill water, prepare antiscorbutics, preserve meat and serve fresh fruits and vegetables. He ruled out almost all hard liquor and salted codfish and went into detail on proper clothing for the varying climates the ships would experience. In writing his specific instructions to officers of the expedition Malaspina referred to his own sailing experiences as well as the feats of Cook and the French explorers.

He kept close watch on the yard officers and the arsenal, always se-

Brigadier Malaspina.
Museo Naval.

64

lecting and maintaining the best of them. The ships carried six anchors between them and an adequate amount of cannon and shot, balancing this armament with a harpsichord. To José Bustamante, his second in command and captain of the *Atrevida,* he gave some very sound advice: "In ordinary ships of the fleet discipline is imperative", but on this long voyage of discovery he wished to win obedience and discipline through example, "not what the orders are, but rather what can be done and with what intent. On this commission, the scientific aspect rather than the military is what will contribute to public usefulness". And so this enlightened leader strove in his best judgment toward the attainment of harmonious solutions for his men, "the essential basis of service". But to be realistic, these were much more than hydrographic surveys and collectors' dream voyages.

Astronomy and natural history were all very well, but the expedition was also instructed to assess the political and military situation in restive Spanish territories scattered across the globe. In particular an assessment was wanted in light of the important dispatches sent from St. Petersburg by the Duke of Almodóvar, the Viscount of La Herrería and the Count Lacy, Minister of King Carlos III to the Court of Russia, during a number of years to the Secretary of State, Marquis of Grimaldi and Count Floridablanca in Madrid. These cipher dispatches concerned Russian plans and encroachments along the Northwest Coast of America, a source of interest to the Spanish for a long time. And now there were the grasping English, not to mention French designs, to be contended with.

Malaspina was formally promoted to Captain on September 21, 1789, after he had held sea trials off the harbour of Cádiz and the expedition had sailed on its diagonal course across the Atlantic on July 30. The corvettes passed the Canary Islands and the Cape Verdes, noted distant Trinidad in the log, and anchored off Montevideo, then an Argentine colony. They undertook a survey of the Rio de la Plata and the Patagonian coast as far as Port Deseado, Argentina. They then separated to rendez-vous at the Malvinas (Falkland Islands), explored the forbidding east coast of Tierra del Fuego, and rounded the Horn far south at 62°.

Subsequently they stopped over at San Carlos de Chile, sailed north to Valparaíso, tacked outward to the islands of Juan Fernández, the supposed site of Robinson Crusoe's shipwreck, and returned shoreward to visit Concepción. Coquimbo, Chile, was followed by Callao, with a formal visit to Lima, capital of the viceroyalty of Perú. "Following the coast", they explored Guayaquil on the Guayas River in Ecuador and moved up around the shoulder of Tierra Firme and Costa Rica towards Panamá. Noting the volcanoes of Guatemala on February 19, 1790, the *Descubierta* pushed on through foul weather and headwinds towards New Spain. Bustamante, re-assigned to Panamá, had gone directly to Acapulco, arriving on February 1. There he sent messages to the newly arrived Viceroy, the talented Count Revillagigedo in

José Bustamante y Guerra, 1759-1825.
Museo Naval.

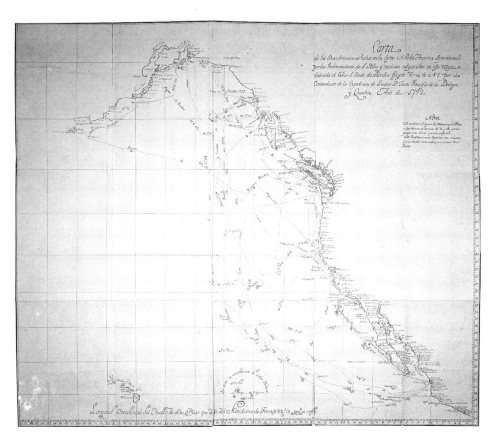

Survey chart of the Northwestern American
coast. Diario de Caamaño, 1792.
Ministerio de Asuntos Exteriores.

México City, reporting the Expedition's progress and his intention to move
on to San Blas ship repair yards after drawing up a plan of Acapulco Port.
On March 26 he sailed north, and the following day Malaspina arrived in the
same roadstead after "an exhausting journey".

Early afternoon on March 29, Bustamante in the *Atrevida* "described
the coast of San Blas and especially the mountain of San Juan over the prow;
its elevation and configuration at the summit served as a very distinctive
landmark to find the port". There he was met by the famous Pacific navigator of 1775, Francisco de la Bodega y Quadra who had returned from Madrid with the newly appointed viceroy. As Commandante and Chief of the
Departament de San Blas, Bodega y Quadra offered every assistance to Bustamante's worn ship. The vitalized but ill-located depot of San Blas had been
established in 1767 to give support and supplies to the Northern fortresses
of Monterey, San Diego and Loreto, and to oppose Russian plans.

While Bustamante was supervising the repairs, a royal messenger arrived with jarring news. This was, of course, a time of great tension with the
continuing reverberations from the Nootka imbroglio. Rather than continue
on to the Sandwich Islands, the ownership of which was contested by Spain

on the basis of a centuries old discovery claim on the Hawaian archipelago, Madrid ordered Malaspina North. He was to determine the truth of the Maldonado memoir which had just been discovered in the Archives of the Duke of Infantado. The memoir stated that in 1588 Lorenzo Ferrer Maldonado had sailed from the New England coast across to the Pacific near the 50th parallel. Of course, this impossible claim aside, the Spanish government was deeply interested in the new claims and contentions of the British through Cook (and no doubt knowledge of Vancouver's proposed voyage), the findings of La Perouse and the ever expanding claims of the Russian hunters (or *promyshlenniki)* hunting sea otters from the Northwest south towards the Columbia River. A new plan was therefore drawn up for Malaspina's perusal to move far out from the coast to catch the northerly wind, sail up to the 60th parallel, head in towards the unknown coast and sail south towards the 18,008 foot peak, Mount San Elías. The passage described in the memoir would be located near that political marker; if it were not found, the flotilla should continue south, tracing that part of the embayed coastline as yet unpenetrated by the Spanish or other foreigners. After a stop at Nootka the commanders would sail toward the Oregon coast, to Monterey and on to Acapulco. On April 11 Bustamante received news of Malaspina's arrival in Acapulco, and on the 13th, sailed to join his chief for the Northern Passage (Vaughan, Crownhart, Palau, 1976: 2-5).

With regard to the staff acompanying Malaspina and Bustamante —astrónomers, mapmakers, botanists, naturalists, etc.— we have given a brief biography of those particularly prominent in the exploration of the North-West coast, and omitted those who remained in New Spain such as Pineda, Neé, Guio, etc., or the painters Brambila and Ravenet, since they did not participate until the return of the Northwest Coast expedition.

José Bustamante y Guerra was born in Santander in 1757. he entered the navy at 11 years of age and was promoted to frigate commander in 1784. In 1788 he assisted Malaspina in planning the Expedition. he successfully commanded the *Atrevida* until the final return to Spain. In 1795 he was made Governor of Uruguay and Naval Chief of the Viceroyalty of La Plata. In 1809 he became President of the Audiencia de Charcas y del Cuzco, of Perú. He then served as Captain General of Guatemala, and died in Madrid in 1825.

Cayetano Valdés, subaltern to Malaspina, was brother of Naval Minister Antonio Valdés. He sailed with Malaspina from Cádiz to México and to the Northwest Coast. Upon returning to México, Malaspina and the Mexican Viceroy Revillagigedo ordered him to prepare a second expedition to the Northwest Coast with the Dionisio Alcalá-Galiano, to explore the Strait of Juan de Fuca. Valdés returned to Spain via México and took part in the historic battles off El Ferrol, La Coruña and Trafalgar (1805), commanding the ships *Pelayo* and *Neptune,* respectively. Although he served as Governor of strategic Cádiz he was twice exiled. In 1823 he was provisionally made Prince

Cayetano Valdés y Flores Bazán, 1767-1834. Museo Naval.

Regent and was then promoted to the historic title of Captain General of the Armada, of Commander of the Spanish Fleet.

Two subalterns from the *Descubierta,* Juan Vernacci and Secundino Salamanca, returned north with Valdés and Alcalá-Galiano in the schooners *Sutil* and *Mexicana.* They engaged in successful exploration of Nootka and beyond the Strait of Juan de Fuca through what is now called the Inside Passage. Rafael Rodríguez Arias was bookkeeper and José de Mesa served as chaplain. The surgeon and assistant to the botanist was Francisco Flores; Fabio Aliponzoni served as midshipman.

Of greater interest to us is Felipe Bauza y Cañas, in charge of charting. He oversaw the preparation of all charts and maps on the Expedition. A native of Mallorca and a pilot's mate in the Spanish Fleet, Bauza had served a hard apprenticeship under Vicente Tofiño preparing the *Atlas Marítimo* of Spain. In 1787 he was made Professor of Fortifications and Military Drawing in the Naval School of Cádiz, where two years later he was promoted to lieutenant, obiously on merit. Malaspina had chosen him for the Expedition, and he worked intensely drawing up mostly coastal profiles from the Río de la Plata as far as Alaska and among the islands of Oceania. When Bauza returned to the Americas in July, 1793, he disembarked at Callao with Espinosa y Tello and sailed to Valparaíso in the frigate *El Aguila.* They travelled overland to Santiago, crossed the mountain range and the Pampas to Buenos Aires and sailed thence to Spain.

When the Dirección de Hidrografía was created in 1797 Bauza was named deputy chief, and there he initiated the publication of materials from the Expedition. This would have had special ramifications, with the leader then in disgrace. In 1807 Bauza became a member of the Real Academia de la Historia, delivering a paper on South American geography. When the Napoleonic armies invaded Spain Bauza placed the hydrographic archives in "twelve well loaded carts" and left Madrid for Cádiz. In 1815 he was named Director of the Dirección Hidrografía succeeding Espinosa y Tello. Bauza then worked on the *Atlas of North America* (1828) and the *Atlas of South America* (1830).

With the advent of the absolutist government of Ferdnando VII, the liberal cartographer went to London until his death in 1834, continuing studies in geography and cartography which brought him worldwide fame. He was honoured by the monarchs of England and Russia, the Royal Geographic Society, and the scientific and maritime societies of Turin and Lisbon. Valdés y Navarrete and von Humboldt wrote to him concerning the extensive archive being assembled for final deposit in Spain. After his death Bauza's widow eventually sold the collection to the Venezuelan Michele y Rojas, who subsequently sold the Bauza Collection to the British Museum. However, the Malaspina Expedition drawings went to Spain in 1846. Carlos Sanz López acquired them in 1953 and donated them to the Museo de América in Madrid in 1961. Today we pay tribute to all those who preserved this priceless archive.

Antonio Tova y Arredondo was second in command to Bustamante on the *Atrevida*. He was born in 1760 and was made midshipman in 1773. He had one year of service in the American Station and was subsequently proposed for the Expedition by Bustamante. He kept a diary of ethnographic and visual interest which was eventually discovered in the municipal library of Santander and published in its incomplete form by San Feliu Ortiz.

Dionisio Alcalá Galiano was the subaltern assigned to astronomy. As a midshipman he sailed along the coasts of Brazil and Argentina in 1775, campaigning against the Portugese. In Spain he worked under Tofino on the *Atlas Marítimo* and in 1785 he sailed in the Antonio de Córdoba Expedition to the Straits of Magellan. At 29 he undertook all the astronomical work along the Pacific Coast as far as Acapulco. Acalá Galiano was the first man to establish latitude by means of a polar elevation observed at a certain distance from the meridian (Mendoza y Ríos published this finding in 1809). As earlier stated, he was sent north after the return of Malaspina's first Northwest Coast voyage to explore the Strait of Juan de Fuca for a Northwest passage in company with Cayetano Valdés. During their exploration of the Strait and the first circumnavigation of Vancouver Island, they spent some time in nearby waters while Commander Bodega y Quadra and Captain George Vancouver, R. N. were conducting protracted negotiations at the island subsequently named after both of them: Island Quadra y Vancouver.

Martín Fernández de Navarrete. 1765-1844. Biblioteca Nacional.

This voyage description was published by the Dirección Hidrográfica in 1802 with a lot of interesting ethnographic material by José Moziño, as well as an illustrated atlas of maps and drawings, of which several originals are now in the Bauza Collection. Malaspina is referred to in the account simply as Commander.

Alcalá Galiano returned to Spain intending to undertake some naval commissions of a scientific nature. But instead he took command of the *Bahama* in the Spanish wing of the fleet under command of the French Admiral Villeneuve. Sortying from La Coruña with the combined fleet, he was killed at Trafalgar. His son Antonio Alcala Galiano achieved fame as a political leader and orator.

Juan Gutiérrez de la Concha was officer in the department of astronomy. Born in 1760, he served the entire duration of the Expedition but was assigned to Montevideo in November 1794 to make a detailed reconnaissance of the Argentine coast.

In 1806 he was decorated by the Spanish government, and one year later assigned to the province of Córdoba de Tucumán as Intendant Governor. During the British incursions in Argentina he fought their invasion along the Río de la Plata. In 1810 he was killed at Cabeza de Tigre when his group of insurgents endeavored to depose the Spanish Governor.

Tadeo Haenke, a botanist and naturalist, joined the *Atrevida* at Valparaíso. The famous botanist Jacquin had recommended this Central European protégé. Subsequently accepted, Haenke missed the Cádiz departure. Following along by merchant ship, misfortune assaulted him when the ship was wrecked off Montevideo. Although he managed to save himself by swimming, all his baggage and instruments went down. Viceroy Vertiz sent him across the pampas and the rugged Cordillera trail. By the time he reached Santiago and Malaspina the enterprising botanist had collected 2,500 specimens.

He sailed north with the Expedition to Callao and explored the interior of Moxos and Chiquitos, he described the Lagoon of Chiquito (Lake Titicaca) in detail with botanist Tafalla and the artist Pulgar. Throughout the voyage his investigations were impressive: Ecuador, Panamá, Nicaragua, México, Alaska, and the islands of Oceanía (especially Guam, the Philippines and Vavao).

Upon his return to Callao he went off to examine the Altiplano Andino where for obscure reasons he decided to settle, in Cochabamba, Bolivia, and lived there until his death in 1817. His work during this 23-year period was frankly monumental, including 40 cases of botanical and zoological speciments he sent to Spain for preservation in his home institutions.

In Perú Malaspina reassigned José Cardero, who was serving as an orderly or perhaps a cabin boy on the *Descubierta*. He was informally taken on as a painter-cartographer for the Expedition when José del Pozo was reassigned to Callao. His first rough drawings on record are from Guayaquil, Nicaragua and Panamá. From México north to Alaska the gifted young Spaniard concentrated on natural history interspersed with some individual native and village drawings. Malaspina first recorded that these drawings of "Pepe" Cardero were "those of a simple amateur, not devoid of taste or artistic feeling". Very soon howver the simple and accurate drawings of the "amateur" received the recognition and value with which ethnographers credit them today.

His unstylized drawings from the first and second northern voyages tell us many things glossed over in the more stylized and finished drawings of his professional superior. Many scenes sketched from the *Sutil* and *Mexicana* were taken back to México City and enhanced at the Academia de San Carlos. They were then taken to Spain for engraving by Fernando Selma serving as the illustrated record for an account of the voyage. After Cardero's return to Spain on the frigate *Minerva*, captained by Cayetano Valdés, he was made a ship's accountant —essentially onshore duty. Eventually he was promoted to lieutenant in naval supply assigned to the Cádiz depot where his name last appears in the Naval Register of 1810.

José de Espinosa y Tello came to the *Descubierta* in 1791 at the Acapulco anchorage. Born into a well-known Seville family, Espinosa had worked under the tutelage of Vicente Tofiño. He began to officially gather information for the Expedition in 1788, but illness prevented his departure when the ships left Cádiz. On November 25, 1790, he sailed on the *Santa Rosalía* with a companion, Lieutenant Ciriaco Cevallos. He took Malaspina the latest naval almanac and other recent publications of interest, no doubt including official news of the latter's promotion to Captain. Mazarredo had also entrusted him with two superb Arnold chronometers, and a longitudinal clock, together with a constant pendulum for simple gravitational experiments.

Scenes in the Mulgrave Sound.
Malaspina Expedition.
Museo de América.

Landing in Cuba, Espinosa moved on to the mainland at Vera Cruz, up to México City and down the long Pacific slope to Acapulco, where he rejoined the Expedition. He sailed with Malaspina to Alaska, Nootka and the Spanish settlements in Oceania. Upon his return to South America he left the Expedition at Valparaíso with Bauza and crossed overland to Buenos Aires. In 1794 he returned to Spain and was made Chief of the Dirección de Hidrografía. Among other duties, he oversaw the publication of *Relación de Viaje de las Goletas Sutil y Mexicana* as well as accounts of his own voyages and observations in Chile and Argentina.

Ciriaco Cevallos, who journeyed from Cádiz with Espinosa, was ship's captain. he had achieved distinction in drawing a very precise "Hydrographic chart of the Yucatán peninsula from Campeche Sound and its bays and of the entire length of coast from Vera Cruz to Campeche". He also wrote a conclusive article demonstrating the non-existence of the fictitious passage which Ferrer Maldonado had persuasively described betwwen the Pacific and Atlantic oceans in 1609.

Tomás de Suria signed on in México. He had left his native city of Madrid and travelled to México City with his painting master Jerónimo Gil. There they founded a school of engraving at the Mint. Viceroy Revillagigedo recommended the young medal maker and engraver to Malaspina and he reached Acapulco on February 16, 1791. By March he was aboard the *Descubierta* working for Pineda, the naturalist. Fortunately, Suria kept a diary filled with observations about the countryside and the natives. Henry Wagner published this incomplete record in 1936, as did his biographer Justino Fernández in 1939.

Suria did many portraits of the natives of Mulgrave Sound (Yakutat Bay) and Nootka, including detailed scenes of their rites and customs. Upon his return to México he was obliged to remain there to produce better delineations of the numerous field Sketches. His loss was compensated for by Fernando Brambila and Juan Ravenet, two painters sent expressly to Acapulco from Italy by Malaspina's family friend, the Count of Greppi.

Suria lived in México until his death, achieving fame in 1805 for his engraving of a medal commemorating Fernando VII (Palau, 1980: 15).

On May 1, 1791, then, the corvettes left Acapulco each carrying fourteen six-pound cannons two four-pounders, and eight additional six-pounders in their holds. On June 23 they were north of San Bartolomé which Bodega y Quadra had explored in 1775, James Cook in 1778, and Captain George Dixon, had verified in 1786. On the 25th they sighted Cape of Buen Tiempo (Cape Edgecumbe ?) and in Bering Bay Malaspina decided to move northeast through the long daylight to explore Mulgrave Sound (Yakutat).

Near the entrance to Yakutat an opening in the mountain range was observed. Could this actually be the Maldonado passage? In a mood of aprehensive excitement they entered Mulgrave (Yakutat) surrounded by dramatically decorated natives singing chants of peace and welcome, or so it seemed at the time. Troubles with these awesome Tlingits would come later, especially for the Russian fur traders. Anchoring in a beautiful location, the crews noted the snow covered mountain ranges, hills clothed with conifers, and the curious Indians offering fresh water, furs and exotic objects from their culture. The observatory tent was set up at a stable point on land where accurate positions were fixed, and the chronometers reset. Not only was latitude determined, but Mount St. Elías and other peaks were measured for height. "A great mountain range which is constantly covered with snow on its slopes forms the entire coast from the Monte de la Cruz to the extreme east of Cook Inlet. It is hard to believe that even in the months of June and July these mountains are covered with snow and... are destined to be forever inhabited only by bears."

Two cutters were prepared for a fortnight's exploration of the inlet, but very shortly the party met floating ice and then a frozen ice barrier denoting a giant glacier. While Port Mulgrave, named after a British Lord of the Admiralty, was eventually discarded as a name, the giant ice mass was later named Malaspina Glacier. Although disappointed by the inlet, known as Bahía del Desengaño (Bay of Disappointment) the intellectually curious leader spent many days in the Yakutat Bay recording, measuring, exploring, und drawing; describing every aspect of the unknown land in the very best Encyclopedist tradition. With time the Indians became older and more acquisitve and problems developed because of petty thieving and over-intimate contact These tense confrontations allowed the artist and scientists ever more opportunity to describe the complicated culture of the powerful northern villages and tribes. After sailing north to Hinchinbroke Island (near the present town of Córdova), the Expedition ceased collecting among the savage Chugach and headed south on July 27. On August 12 they approached Nootka at sunset. A launch from the Spanish corvette *Concepción* came out to meet them and in the morning they entered Friendly Cove (Cala de los Amigos in Spanish) to the salutes of cannons in the already famous Fort San Miguel, the recently constructed fortification of Nootka.

Esteban Martínez, a regular northern traveller had been instructed to fortify the site to frustrate Russian and English intentions. He had arrived on May 5, 1789, with orders to treat the Indians with the utmost consideration and to build barracks and entrenchments. Of course the site chosen had been an Indian summer campground from time immemorial. Impetuous Martínez had since departed and in his diary Malaspina noted down that Francisco Elisa was in command, while Ramón Saavedra commanded the *Concepción* and Pedro Alberni headed a crack company of Catalonian infantry, formerly stationed in the Southwest, and probably used against the Apaches.

Malaspina noted: "in the depth of the port various dwellings built of planks could be seen. Alberni watched over them vigilantly and kept all in order with the troops billeted on land; fresh bread was baked [daily]". He commented on "the cultivation of the gardens on which Nature had already lavished her gifts; the care of the provisions and defense equipment".

The natives such as could be seen "were not unlike other Americans [natives] who live on this continent, except that those in Nootka have a pyramid shaped head, which is no doubt due to the fact that when they are born, before they are placed in little oblong cradles, their heads are shaped with strong ligatures which reach down almost to their eyes". Malaspina went on to say: "They have a custom that when the child is an infant they pierce three or four openings in the lower part of the ears and one or two in the cartilage of the nose." He suggested the existence of cannibalism a widely accepted historial fact today.

Juan José Pérez, a pilot on an official voyage of exploration, had first come along the coast in 1774. The former Manila galleon pilot had with him as his second, another pilot of less experience, Esteban José Martínez. They had sailed north in the *Santiago* in January of 1775. On their southern return from approximately 50° north latitude. Pérez sighted Vancouver Island, and August 8, 1792, he was in the roadstead (Surgidero de San Lorenzo) of Nootka. Thus he was the first European recorded at the famous anchorage, but it would seem Captain Cook was first to sail inside the sound, and to the cove which he named Friendly Harbour before the displaced Indians began to show their deeper feelings. Of course we know that Captain Cook had named the large sound after King George and eventually he called the inlet Nooka and finally Nootka, which is not a recognizable Indian word. And now 16 years after the first visit Friendly Cove (Santa Cruz de Nuca) was an important and highly controversial settlement known to every European embassy.

The Malaspina party immediately moved their observatories ashore and notes were made about the much enlarged outpost. The natives were invited to parley with Malaspina as well as the local commanders, Pedro Alberni and Ramón Saavedra. As usual the negotiations were complex. The villages were involved in their own struggles for power among the tribes and individual chiefs —not to mention the surely confusing European rivalries, with occasional contributions by American merchant traders such as Robert Gray and William Kendrick. But scientific inquiry was assisted by the fact that in Nootka there were people to interpret the questions as well as the answers.

On an exploratory voyage by cutter, Espinosa and Cevallos concluded that the inhabitants in the island complex numbered no more than 4,000 —that is, those under the sovereignity of the aged chief Macuina. They also made a rough chart of the Bay of Buena Esperanza. "The land which comprises the archipelago is altogether singular. There are as many as five channels or arms not generally wider than a third of a mile, penetrating in different directions, ending in several small coves or bays chosen by the natives for their settlements." They returned to Malaspina on August 25, 1791, Macuina then agreed to come aboard the *Descubierta* for tea, of which he had several cups. "On his head he wore a kind of band of scarlet cloth in which were fastened some little glass stars... the scarcity of food had made him very weak and thin... whereas earlier many had remarked on his strength and dexterity, to the point where he would singlehandedly harpoon a whale."

On the 28th the two ships moved slowly out of the tricky harbor carrying with them twenty children who had been variously purchased in order to save them from being eaten by their Indian captors or owners. Malaspina was bound for the Entrance of Hezeta, reported by the *Santiago* in 1775 and not seen since. Malaspina's intention in all these sightings, profile drawings and landings, was to confirm locations and to establish the fact that they were unoccupied lands properly claimed by the King of Spain. However a summer fog obscured the coast where the (Columbia) river mouth was

Termination of the Salamanca Channel.
[Fernando Brambila].
Museo de América.

thought to be and Malaspina proceeded south towards Monterey. Captain Robert Gray of Boston was to take possession of the elusive River of the West (Entrance of Hezeta) the following spring, further frustrating Spanish colonial designs.

Fog prevailed in Monterey as well. Cannon fire was used to guide the Expedition to a safe anchorage ground at the fortresses on September 11, 1791. The tents were landed, and many collections gathered and described in close detail. The artist' drawings reveal that, while more familiar and pleasant, life was less dramatic than with the primitive tribesmen of the north.

On September 26 the captains moved away from the beautiful harbor to their prearranged revictualing in Acapulco. The *Atrevida* completed a previous survey of the waters between Cape Corriente and Acapulco, then Bustamante rejoined Malaspina in port. After working out arrangements for the now obviously necessary second Northwest Coast expedition of the two small draft schooners *Sutil* and *Mexicana* built in San Blas, Malaspina sailed west for the Marianas (visited earlier by Spanish explorers Marquina, Ayeusa and Sánchez). Although Malaspina had to go on his Hawaian Islands trip, he did

75

correct the position of the Cape of San Bartolomé, discovered in the days of cruder navigational aids by Alonso de Salazar. Explorations of Guam and the Carolines were followed by visits to the Philippine Ports of Palapa, Sorsogon and Manila. The Islands of Luzon, Mindoro, Mindanao and Negros were charted. The *Atrevida* cruised in the China Sea as far as Formosa and Portuguese Macao below Canton. Gathering surveys and specimens they moved south to Espíritu Santo and the area of Dusky Sound in New Zealand, so well described in Cook's earlier travel accounts. The course was then to Sydney, Australia, up to the Friendly (Tonga) Islands, then south to the 50th parallel. Sailing to 80º longitude west of the meridian of San Fernando, Chile, they moved in almost a circular route north to Callao. After further observations on the Peruvian coastline Malaspina turned south again, rounding the Horn far away from the Straits of Magellan. Passing the Falkland Islands and the Aurora Islands they reached the South Atlantic and Montevideo, the last rendezvous for scattered Expedition members.

Homeward bound at last, the Expedition crossed the Atlantic approximately following the 20th west meridian reading up to the Azores and then northeast to Cádiz. When they arrived on September 21, 1793 a five-year voyage of immense scientific benefit, as well as a superb feat of seamanship was at last completed. The officers and crew had lived up to their commander's best expectations, but so too had the scientists and learned men who had so generously given of themselves during the five-year "pursuit of knowledge". Although Malaspina had received his captaincy belatedly he was immediateley promoted to Brigadier (Rear Admiral), (Vaughan, Crownhart, Palau, 1976: 10-14).

The results of the voyage to the Northwest Coast were well-expressed in the letter sent from San Blas by Malaspina to his friend Count of Greppi, on 11 October, 1791. A copy of this letter is preserved in Academia de la Historia and has been reproduced in the recently-published *Diario de Alejandro Malaspina* (Alejandro Malaspina's Log-Book, Madrid, 1985: 563-4).

San Blas, 11 October, 1691

María, Tetaku's wife. [José Cardero]. Museo Naval.

Dear Greppi:

After six months' fairly hard sailing, and having travelled in such a short time from the icy cold of Mount St. Elías to a temperature like the present one, where the open-air themometer constantly reads 90º, believe me, dear friend, that a forgiveable abandon is due from even one's most intimate friends. Add to this that not a single letter was waiting for us and the fact that having to send news to México allows me but little leeway, and you will, I trust, better appreciate this letter, albeit frugal and badly written.

The voyage we undertook last May from Acapulco was designed, as I believe I told you, to investigate whether, at the 60th parallel, there existed a mouth through which a former seafarer, Ferrer Maldonado, claimed to have passed to the Atlantic... Such a possibility, although recently defended by Mr. de Buache in the Paris Academy, seemed higly remote, but in Europe, the explorations carried out by ourselves and the English from Cook's voyage up to the present time, had not been made known.

At first the voyage went perfectly; on about 26 June we were off the bay of Bering, where we discarded any further doubts concerning the English captain, and the following day we dropped anchor at the Mulgrave Sound, at latitude 59,5°, intending to get water and firewood supplies, carry out simple, constant pendulum experiments to determine the face of the earth, and explore a mouth, I approached it with the corvettes but it did not seem a good port given the excessive depth on both sides of the coast. I personally undertook the exploration of this mouth with the launches. We cut into the mouth and after a few leagues we came across floating banks of ice surrounding a small island. As it was early July, we knew that beneath its structure it would be permanently linked to the contiguous coast. Despite all Mr. Haenke's cultivated botanical specimens, positive results were achieved on the plains of the neighbouring port, and its inhabitants let us land and discover a thousand and one entirely new things about their customs, nature and religion, which would be worthy of interest in Spain. Our dealings with the natives were friendly, although matters almost got out of hand on a couple of occasions; once, when the advantage was on our side, and another when not, involving a serious risk for Bustamente who, with rifle unloaded, came across an armed and fierce native supported by many more who were prepared to attack Bustamente.

After leaving the port in early July, we spent the rest of the month seeking the answer to the above-mentioned issue. We limited ourselves to exploring scrupulously the coast as far as Prince William entrance, adding new islands to Captain Cook's charts, and we discovered that his Kaye Island was really a peninsula, linked by land under the continent.

Having fulfilled our first objective, we explored the coast with great accuracy as far as latitude 35°, and we were about to sail through the Dupon channel when a series of fierce storms disrupted our plans, preventing our entry to Nootka until 13 August. A further incursion by the launches into this port determined the direction and term of all those channels that Captain Cook had been unable to explore, with one of them linked through another port to the sea, hence converting the land that Cook believed to be part of the continent into a large island. Great knowledge of the internal geography, religion and social and penal laws of these people were obtained, proving to be quite distinct from those living further North or South. We then continued exploring the coast from Cape Mendocino as far as Monte-

Tetaku's second wife. [José Cardero].
Museo de América.

Map of the Floridablanca Port, discovered by Jacinto Caamaño. Diario de Caamaño, 1792. Ministerio de Asuntos Exteriores.

Map of the Port of Los Dolores, surveyed by Jacinto Caamaño in July of 1792. Diario de Caamaño, 1792. Ministerio de Asuntos Exteriores.

rey, where we ran the serious risk of getting lost for 8 to 10 days. Finally, following the California coast, we touched land at Cape San Lucas, so complementing, by means of the marine watches, the excellent observations made by Abbot Chappe and Mr. Roy with our own. We dropped anchor the day before yesterday in this bay. We have already dispatched Bustamante to Acapulco, where I plan to join him within a few days once we have received the trinkets we requested and, in particular, our orders from the Court, I shall write at greater length and with more time to you from there, replying to any of your much-welcomed letters awaiting me. I would be grateful if you would send your correspondence to me to Canton this year, to the English or Swedish Works. Please forward my news to my brother, and accept the warmest regards from your friend.

(Signed) Malaspina

Caamaño, 1792

Viceroy Revillagigedo wanted to send another expedition to confirm Admiral Fonte's findings. The inner part of Port of Bucareli and the coastline stretching from there as far as Nootka port would have to be explored. The frigate *Aranzazu* was designated, under the command of Lieutenant Jacinto Caamaño. They sailed from San Blas on 20 March, 1792, and arrived at Nootka on 14 May. They continued their voyage on the 23rd of the same month, arriving at Bucareli on 12 June. On 28 June, having made a thorough exploration of the mouth, capes, shallows, islets and anchoring berths, two well-armed steersmen were sent out in the launch and in the ship's boat with 20 days of supplies to explore the inland channels. They returned on 8 July having discovered that in the Northwest there were a lot of islets, thus indicating shallows, and an exit to the sea in the Southwest. Having completed this survey, amended various points on the port chart, and made several tidal observations, Caamaño set sail on the 11th. However; bad weather forced his return on the 16th. When the adverse weather conditions had cleared, he continued along a short coastal course as far as the Port of Baílio Bazán, where the launch was sent out to explore. On 20 May they anchored in the port of Floridablanca, a league's distance from the Island of Lángara, having sighted the passage between this island and Cape Muñoz, the entrance of which they named Juan Pérez and where they traded with the natives.

That very night an English schooner from Macao passed by. On the 20th Caamaño saw two canoes coming from the island of Lángara. The first to arrive was that of the main chief of the port, Taglas-Cania, accompanied by other Indians singing noisy songs. Some wore traditional costume, and others trousers, jackets and overcoats. It was a big canoe; 53 feet long, 6 wide and 4,5 deep. Cania came on board, greeted the commander, and presented him with his daughter as a servant. In the meantime the other canoe, carrying the chief Eltasen, boarded. They said that the port was good, and the former offered to act as pilot. Caamaño went off to the anchorage ground, keeping a short distance ahead of the two chiefs and their retinue. Next day, the 21st, he commissioned the steersmen to explore the port and chart it. A large number of natives bearing good-quality furs gathered wishing to exchange them for mother-of-pearl shells or clothing.

Cania returned in the evening with other Indians, and before leaving they paid tribute to Caamaño with songs and dances, and they seemed visibly moved when Caamaño announced their departure.

The Port of Floridablanca was well-sheltered, but small. There was another anchoring-ground on the Eastern side of the Island of Navarro. On the 23rd Caamaño sighted a large inlet at the entrance of Córdoba Port, and he set about exploring one of the inlets with a launch. There he found a good port, naming it Nuestra Señora de los Dolores. He charted its location and described it in great detail. He came across a Boston brig anchored there. The exploration continued, and that same day he sighted the vast opening at Port of Chacón (naming it Nuestra Señora del Carmen), forming Evia headland to the West and Cape Caamaño to the East. It was so wide that its full extension could not be ascertained. On the morning of the 25th he sighted Point Invisible, saw the ports of La Estrada and Mazarredo, and came into contact with the natives, who urged him to drop anchor, promising fruitful fur-trading. On the 28th the Once Mil Vírgenes Archipelago came under his scrutiny, and he went on to explore the coast thoroughly. On the evening of the 29th he sighted the Príncipe Channel, formed by Calamidad Island and the coast. From that point onwards, Caamaño took his life in his own hands many times whilst charting the location, where, according to Captain Colnet's news, the entrance to the Fonte Strait (constituting the main reason underlying the voyage) should have been (Relación, 1802; CXXVI-VII).

He continued his course along the channel and dropped anchor at the location known as San Roque, having sought fruitlessly with a launch a port marked on Colnet's chart.

Foul weather prevented their sailing until the 23rd, and, 3 times in all, Caamaño had to drop anchor anew. Each return was heralded by the Indians, dancing and brandishing pine branches. During this time they would often visit the frigate, chanting cheerfully and returning gifts from our people with feasts and dances held in their homesteads. Caamaño finally left the straits on the 20th. He sailed into the Laredo Channel, and then into that formed by the Isle of Aristizábal and the coast. He charted several headlands and islands, and explored the rest of the coast at great risk. On 1 September he explored the Isle of San Joaquín, whose whereabouts were much mistaken with respect to the maps and charts in his possession. On the 2nd he

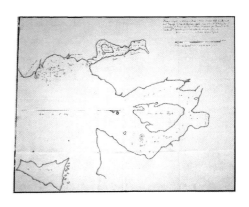

Map of the Port of Gastón, discovered by Jacinto Caamaño. Diario de Bodega y Quadra, 1792. Ministerio de Asuntos Exteriores.

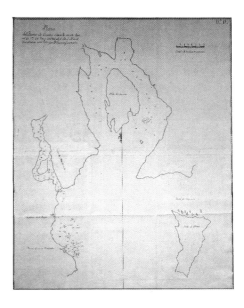

Map of the anchorage of San Roque and the Port of Gaston, discovered by Jacinto Caamaño in August of 1792. Diario de Caamaño, 1792. Ministerio de Asuntos Exteriores.

sighted the entrance to Port Grook, and the point of Cape Frondoso, and on the afternoon of the 7th he dropped anchor in the Port of Nootka.

He made charts from latitude 55º, the Bay of Bucareli, to latitude 49º, San Lorenzo de Nootka, making use of 39 place-names. He plotted out the most important Ports —Bucareli, Bazán, and Dolores— and disproved the existence of the imaginary Fonte Strait (MAE, ms. 143).

On arriving at Nootka he took over command until relieved by Salvador Fidalgo, who had been in the Fuca Strait. On 1 October, 1792, he handed over command to Fidalgo and left for Monterey. He dropped anchor on the 22nd and met up with Bodega y Quadra with the brig *Activo*, the frigate *Gertrudis* and the schooners *Sutil*, *Mexicana* and *Saturnina*. His stay saw the arrival of the frigates *Discovery* and the brig *Chathan*, under the command of Vancouver, head of the English Commission.

The English Commander asked his Spanish counterpart to take the *Chathan's* captain with him, so that he could go from México to London to give a report of the situation. Vancouver made a gift of the Carmelo and the Soledad to the missionaries.

On 14 January Caamaño left for San Blas, sailing in convoy with the brig *Activo* and the sloop *Orcasitas*. They dropped anchor on 6 February, 1773.

Alcalá Galiano and Cayetano Valdés, 1792

It was previously stated, with reference to the 1790 expeditions, that the exploration of the Fuca strait by Manuel Quimper was cut short owing to the sickness of most of the crew. On his return he wrote to the Viceroy: "... the passage to the Atlantic, so fervently sought by other nations on this coast, can be, if it does exist, in no other part than this vast channel...".

In the light of this report, and the interest in the strait, a new expedition was prepared under the command of Antonio Mourelle at the same time that the expedition of the corvettes *Descubierta* and *Atrevida* was returning to Acapulco from the Northwest Coast, where they had been unable to explore the mouth of the Fuca Strait due to foul winds. The same had been the case for that part of the coast between Sonsonate and Acapulco, and nor had they been able to locate the Santa Bárbara channel, merely a few of the islands forming it.

Malaspina therefore put it to the Viceroy that the officers taking part in his expedition —Dionisio Alcalá Galiano and Cayetano Valdés— should take responsibility for the above-mentioned explorations, assisted by marine watches and precision-instruments.

The schooners *Sutil* and *Mexicana* were chosen, as their light draught would be ideal for sailing through shallow channels. The Port of Acapulco was chosen in preference to San Blas for preparing the schooners.

Dionisio Alcalá Galiano, 1762-1805.
Museo Naval.

Everything was approved by the Viceroy who designated the command of the expedition to the aforementioned frigate captains, accompanied by Lieutenants Juan Vernacci and Secundino Salamanca. "... Malaspina and Bustamante left the port for the Philippines on 20 December, 8 days before the schooners arrived, leaving us all that was required for fitting out these vessels..." (Relación, 1802: 2-4).

Once the schooners arrived at Acapulco, their faulty structure was noted: "their limited breadth which, besides detracting from their resilience, diminished hold-space and the possibility of taking sufficient water and victuals for a long voyage...". Several changes were made to improve them, using some of the few white carpenters in the country and some Philippines from the crew of the *San Andrés*.

As specially selected provisions, geared to preventing illness, had to be taken, great care was taken with the stores. Once covered with pitch they

The schooners *Sutil* and *Mexicana* José Cardero. Museo Naval.

were given a layer of canvas, pitched once more and then sheathed with tin plate "ending up like two biscuit-barrels, each capable of holding sixty quintals of bread instead of the previous thirty-seven".

José Manuel de Alava, regiment colonel of Puebla and a Castilian from Acapulco, provided them with the fittings for the schooners; arms, lancets, books, medicine, money, scurvy-treating drugs, and objects with which to trade with the Indians.

Astronomical and physics instruments were taken on board; a quarter-circle, a pendulum, two chromatic telescopes, an equator device, a reflecting circle, a chronometer, a longitude watch, two barometers, four thermometers and a glass gas-tube (Relación, 1802: 10).

Throughout the morning of 8 March they awaited the breeze which would enable them to leave the port. At 1 o'clock they were able to set sail, but until the 18th they could not follow course "... on the fourth quadrant, trying by all means to set the ships at their greatest speed and pressing sail to the point of having the gunwales almost always to the water...". After a slow voyage, they managed to anchor in Nootka. Chief Macuina came out to greet them accompanied by his relatives and friends, and immediately recognized the officers Valdés, Vernacci and Salamanca, who had been there the previous year with Malaspina.

In the port were the frigate *Concepción,* under the command of Francisco de Eliza, and the war-frigate *Santa Gertrudis,* under Alonso de Torres, carrying Commander Bodega y Quadra, commissioned with enforcing the agreement signed between England and Spain. Also accompanying Bodega were the naturalists and botanists Moziño and Maldonado, and the artist Echevarría, all forming part of the New Spain botanical expedition and whose works are dealt with by Grunfeld and Sota in this book.

While preparations were being made to go to the Fuca strait, the frigate *Aranzazu* arrived to explore the North coast. The French vessel *La Flavia,* under the command of Captain Magon and bearing the new national flag, also arrived, as did the American frigate *Columbia,* captained by Gray.

A few days later they set sail for the Fuca Strait at the mouth of which Salvador Fidalgo was establishing the settlement of Núñez Gaona. The Indians spoke a language different from that in Nootka, but their customs were the same. They were "taller and stronger, and the women fairer. They thought little of the shells from Monterey". The officers charted the port, took note of the latitude using sextants and of the longitude using marine watches.

While they were at the mouth of the strait, they were visited by the chiefs Taisoun and Tetaku. The latter was one of the most important chiefs in this area and, it was said, was one of those most favouring the Spaniards. He went on board to see the ships, accompanied by his wife who, to the surprise of the officers, was called María.

Work in this port was restricted to charting and observing latitude and longitude, by which it was deduced that an error of 57' in estimating the difference between the Entrance of Juan de Fuca and Nootka had been recorded with respect to its real location. This signified a considerably different coastal course.

On the morning of the 8th they were ready to set sail and continue their voyage, "having received a working saw, tallow and medicine from Fidalgo, they were only waiting for the wind to leave...".

Tetaku came out to the *Mexicana* at 8 o'clock, leaving his wife María in the canoe, and came on board to greet the officers, who offered him a small cup of drinking-chocolate. After a brief visit, he asked permission to withdraw, since he had to leave for his homestead that morning. Valdés offered to take him in the schooners and Tetaku accepted. "Then he took a little dried fish from the canoe, hung it from the rigging of the schooner, and ordered his wife to continue on her journey. Only a short time had gone by before a canoe drew up carrying one of his older wives, not at all like María. Whereas María had let her husband have his way, the second wife showed her greater affection by the fear she felt at his delivering himself to us so confidently... she let it be known to Valdés that he should leave us and accompany her. Valdés made her understand that if we came across María in the channel, or any of those that knew him and had been persuaded that Tectaku was in the *Mexicana,* they might suspect that we had done him harm. In such an event we would be exposed to entering into war with nations with whom we had taken every care in maintaining peaceful relations... Thus we explained it to Tetaku, who tried to persuade his wife using the same reasons... he made signs to Valdés and Vernacci to embrace him and take him to the cabin and not let him go. The quarrels continued for some time, and the woman, in despair at the failure of her plan, withdrew weeping loudly after having been given some glass beads. There was much to admire in the conduct of the chief, who was owner of much property and assets, and ruler of an extensive territory. Alone unarmed, in a ship whose safety and functioning were unknown to him, he had given himself over to strangers he had seen for the first time the previous day in a manner free from concern, suspicion and regret. Indeed, he showed nothing but the greatest satisfaction at being with us. He would observe and ask questions with great curiosity, letting it be known that it had been his desire to be admitted and transported on the vessel so that he might see our inner facets and the workings of our vessels. He would attentively watch manoeuvres, seek out the run of the ropes, inquire into their names and generally let nothing escape his notice, yet without bothering anyone unduly. His questions would be kindly asked and he would inform of his country's practices, giving the names of certain things he thought could be of interest to us.

In the evening we were on shore, visiting Tetaku's homesteads where

Juan Vernacci (d. 1810). Museo Naval.

View of a natural gallery in the Port of Descanso,
Juan de Fuca Strait. Engraving, Maura, xix c.
Museo Naval.

there were 50 Indians. They gave us blankets to sit on, and all surrounded us, offering us a portion of the octopus they had. Tetaku showed the greatest friendliness to his hosts... at that point we were unaware of the great respect and obedience he commanded among his people. We later learned that he was one of the most feared rulers amongst those inhabiting the coast, and that his respect and authority was the result of his courage and skill" (Relación, 1802: 402).

The schooners left for the Port of Cordova, which Tetaku called Chachimutupusa, saying that they had to leave him there and that there were two large ships in the strait. The Indians gave them a woolen, feathered blanket and a tanned deer-skin.

They sent a ship's boat towards the Mouth of Floridablanca for sounding. "Having found closed one of the mouths charted the previous year as linked to the Floridablanca Channel, our imagination was fired with the idea we had conceived of the expedition made at that time and hopeful about the pass before our eyes... we hurried to seek the entrance to the North of Punta Langara (Relación, 1802: 50).

As Tetaku had said, there were two English vessels in the strait under the command of Vancouver and Broughton. Both had set off from England;

Vancouver in April, 1791, on a voyage of discovery visiting the coasts of New Holland, New Zealand, Tahiti and Sandwich. Then, having followed the Northwest Coast to latitude 45º, he had entered the strait on 5 May. Valdés and Galiano informed him that Bodega y Quadra was waiting for him at Nootka to finalize the Madrid treaty.

The schooners arrived nearby the Port of Descanso, where they came across several Indians in canoes: "... we noticed no great physical difference between them and other natives, but, strangely, a lot of them only had one eye. They had goatee beards and fairly thick eyebrows. Their clothes would usually consist simply of thick, well-woven woolen shawls, held on with two shoulder clasps and and only knee-length. A few were wearing deer-skins, being of note that worn by the Tais, who also wore a woolen shawl over it, a hat in the form of a broken-off cone, five brass bracelets on his left wrist, and a copper hoop on his neck similar to those we had seen on an Indian the year before at latitude 60º. Some wore hats, and many were painted with red ochre. They came out smiling and seemed docile. if not stupid, they appeared rather slow. The language is totally different from that at Nootka, and involves greater effort and guttural aspirations, hence our difficulty in learning it..." (Relación, 1802: 57).

They headed out from Descanso Cove to the strait at Point Langara, where they met the English boats and decided to go together. They explored Floridablanca Channel and anchored off the Island of Quema. They were visited by Indians, most of them naked, in canoes similar to those at the mouth of the strait. They had proportionate features and were lively and intelligent. With them they had numerous and solid iron-tipped weapons, pouches with metal and stone barbs, bows and clubs, etc.

From 26 June onwards they sailed in convoy with the English ships. Valdés in the launch and with provisions for 8 days, explored the Tabla and Arco Channels and the Muedres Mouths.

They anchored at a spot which came to be called Separación, which is where they left the English. The schooners continued to two bays they named Malaspina and Bustamante. On the 6th Vernacci and Quintano cut into an arm of the sea which they named Quirós, and reached the Angosturas (Narrows) de los Comandantes. They came across several settlements whose inhabitants practised sardine-fishing in a most ingenious way. They used "a round stick three yards long, with a third part of it covered with sharp points. They would put the stick in the water, and having given it a few shakes, would pull it and the impaled sardines out the water. There were about 140 Indians and they seemed the happiest along the strait because they lived in a fertile area with beautiful countryside full of trees and bushes and abundant foliage".

On the 12th the English boats returned with the news that they had found an exit to the sea around latitude 51º, at which they had agreed to

The plant «Rubus notkanus» (Bramble). Nootka. Hunt Institute for Botanical Documentation, Pittsburgh.

Otter kidneys. José Cardero. Museo Naval.

split up since the schooners could penetrate areas with less depth than the English vessels.

They sailed steadfastly, noting down the anchoring-ground of Marías, Cevallos, Robredo Murphy and Concha, and reached a cove they named Refugio after great difficulty because of the force of the water. The Indians told them not to go with the launches into the channel as they would be swallowed by the whirlpools and stand no chance of survival. They also said they would tell them when the time was right. So, at three in the afternoon the force of the current began to subside and the schooners were able to pass without danger. Near Refugio Cove, they studied the inlet they named Aliponzoni and dropped anchor at the location known as Salamanca. They passed through Engaño Channel and explored the coast between the continent and the island, later dropping anchor in Viana. On 27 July they passed along the Nuevos Remolinos Channel and by the Novales anchorage-ground. Valdés studied the arms of Canonigo and they headed for the Bauza anchorage-ground (Relación, 1802:92).

That evening several natives who could understand the Nootka language came out in canoes, and it was clear that they had already dealt with Europeans. One of the chiefs, or Tais, wore a hat which was very similar to that used by the Mulgrave Sound chief, and he put great stock by it as it had been won from his enemies in battle. They managed to buy it.

On the 31st Juan Vernacci went out in the launch to explore the arm heading towards the North and potentially the exit to the sea. Vernacci related that on this journey he saw beautiful lands covered with trees and meadows and many beaches with good anchorage-points. In the channel he named after himself he came across an enormous waterfall falling from high up. He also encountered many settlements near rivers where salmon would go to spawn, and he observed that the Indians preferred to live inland for the abundance of fish and the ease of trading amongst one another. Vernacci regretted not having brought more objects for trading and he was surprised to see such small boats in such remote places, which led to their mistrust of him. Vernacci related how he underwent moments of great danger, but that he tried to please everybody he met, even in the absence of presents with which to do it.

After the exploration he wanted to return along a new route, believing that he would find a shorter one by cutting across the archipelago. However, there were so many islands and channels that it was difficult to move through them at any speed. An Indian deceived him promising to show him the exit, for once he had led him to the most impenetrable place, he vanished. He therefore decided to leave along the same route. he came out onto Torres Channel where he saw a gulf bordered on the West by a multitude of islands and believed that the channels formed therein would lead to the sea.

On Vernacci's return, Valdés and Galiano considered it more useful to spend their remaining time exploring the Mouth of the Hezeta and locating points along the coast from Fuca to the sea, mainly the Santa Bárbara Channel.

They remained in the Port of Güemes, and explored the Salida Channel, and the Mier and Villavicencio anchorage-grounds before heading out to sea. They anchored off Sutil Point and Cape Scot. They went to Port Valdés as a result of the bad weather, and headed for Nootka from there. On 30 August the port was in sight, four months after their departure. The exploration of the Fuca Entrance had only been of use from a geographical and mapmaking point of view, and for studying the region's inhabitants: the famous passage to the Atlantic had not been found. The editor of the log-book declared: "only philosophers could find subject-matter of interest in these places in view of the land layout and the practically primitive inhabitants" (Relación, 1802: 112).

The way the natives of the Fuca entrance and channels lived, the inner

View of Vernacci Channel. [Fernando Brambila]. Museo de América.

View of the big Majoa settlement. José Cardero.
Museo de América.

appearance of their houses, and the tools and clothes they used were very similar to those of Nootka.

After a brief stay in Nootka, they returned to Acapulco stopping off at Monterey. Galiano and Valdés returned to Spain via Veracruz. The account of this voyage was published in Madrid in 1802, with the title *Relación del viaje de las goletas sutil y mexicana* to the Fuca Strait in 1792", written by Galiano and preceded by a learned introduction by the eminent and wise old seafarer Martín Fernández de Navarrete. Included therein are Spanish voyages in search of the Northwest Passage or Strait of Anian described by Lorenzo Ferrer Maldonado; that of Admiral Fonte and Juan de Fuca which appeared on Delisle's maps and in whose existence Purchas, Seijas y Lobera, Dalrymple, Meares and Buache believed. Malaspina and his officers, Galiano and Valdés, proved by their explorations, as did Cook and La Perouse, the inexistence of a passage between the Pacific and the Atlantic, a passage which only existed in the imagination of a handful of writers and geographers.

Seijas and Matute, 1793

The steersman Seijas, on the schooner *Mexicana* and under the orders of Francisco Eliza, commander of the frigate *Activa,* departed on 26 May from the Strait of Fuca to explore the coast thoroughly as far as San Francisco. The account of this little-known voyage can be found in the Museo Naval (ms. 575 bis, fol. 97). In short, the steersman made note of the following places; Point Futosi, Islotes Deseados, Isle of Los Dolores and port Greek. He drew up his chart and compared its location with that appearing on Vancouver's map, finding it to be exact. He demarcated the Cape of San Roque, to the North of the river-mouth of the Hezeta (Columbia), and dropped anchor under the lee of the Cape of San Roque. He cut in to study the river Columbia and was followed by numerous canoes. He explored the South side of the river entrance and came across well-built, wooden-roofed houses. He continued southwards, noting down a series of places, some of which had been described by Vancouver; Cape Perpetua, Sigmar port, Cape Gregori, Cape Toledo, Cape Diligencia, Trinidad Port, Cape Mendaña, Cape Vizcaíno, Bodega Port and San Francisco Port, from where he headed to the fortress. He arrived on 17 October, and on 4 November he came into San Blas with the schooner *Sutil* from San Diego.

The Por of Bodega was explored that same year by frigate Lieutenant Juan Bautista Matute in the schooner *Sutil* (MN ms. 575 bis: 104).

The bird «Anonigmos». José Cardero. Museo Naval.

Spanish Cartografic Surveys of the Northwest Coast in the xviiith Century; The Corps of Naval Steersmen

by M.ª Luisa Martín-Merás and M.ª Dolores Higueras

Heads of Investigation of the Museo Naval, Madrid

I. Training of Steersmen in the XVIIIth Century

Background

Although there have in fact been steersmen from the earliest beginnings of sailing, the first more or less systematic regulations governing the art were to spring from the *Universidad para Mareantes*, founded in Cádiz by Fernando III.

However, the first institution to have its own decrees and jurisdiction was the *Colegio de Pilotos Vizcaínos de Cádiz*, which was promoted by the Catholic Kings Fernando and Isabel in 1500.

The first great stimulus for the scientific training of steersmen arose as a consequence of the requierements imposed by transmarine navigation. The discovery of the New World and the proliferation of transoceanic voyages underlined the precariousness of the "traditional" ideas applied to medieval coastal navigation, and brought about a need for new knowledge of mathematics and astronomy for sailing on the high seas.

The XVIth Century

The *Casa y Tribunal de Contratación*, instituted in 1503 and divided into departments of cosmography, navigation, instrument and map making, artillery and ship-building, attempted to provide this training for those who would journey abroad. Nonetheless, the Casa de Contratación cosmographers continued to complain about the "ignorance of the steersmen", and attributed a large part of the losses suffered in the voyages to the Indies to this shortcoming.

From 1552 onwards the Casa de Contratación upheld three independent posts:

Chair of Cosmography.

Post of Chief Steersman.

Cosmographer responsible for map and instrument making.

The *studies for steersmen*[1], under the guidance of the Chief Steersman, included the following areas: studies of the globe; tracking of the height of the sun; determination of the altitude of the pole; use and construction of compasses, quadrant astrolabes and staff astrolabes, variation of the compass needle and determination of the hour. These studies prepared the student for oceanic navigation "without reference to the coastline", as well as for calculation of latitude. On the other hand, and due to the lack of chronometers, they did not prepare the mariner for calculation of longitude, an old navigational problem that was not solved until the middle of the XVIIIth century.

The XVIIIth Century

However, the abuses that arose in the examinations for steersmen,

Detail of theodolite measurement. Section of the «plano geométrico de la isla Trinidad levantado por Churruca con el bergantín *Descubridor* en 1792». Museo Naval.

which were already rarely held by the beginning of the XVIIth century, meant that the studies at the Casa de Contratación fell into decadence, a situation that gave rise to a reform of the training and eventually, in 1681, to the creation of the Colegio de San Telmo in Sevilla.

The constant criticism effectively gave birth to the idea of founding a special establishment for nautical training that might serve at the same time as an orphanage for the children of poor sailors.

In 1607 the Duke of Medinasidonia made an initial attempt at founding this new establishment, but failed owing to a lack of finance. Therefore, the same situation continued to exist in spite of the fact that the Casa de Contratación had established a set of regulations for the examination of steersmen and requiered that the corresponding diploma be held by all who wished to set course for the Indies.

In 1633 Porter y Casanate made the steersmen's examination public, in spite fo which the training would appear to have continued being insufficient and certainly continued to invite criticism.

Colegio de San Telmo. Sevilla 1681

Following a further attempt by the Universidad de Mareantes[2] to establish a Nautical College in 1629, an enterprise that failed in spite of the crown's authorization having been obtained, Carlos II finally created the Colegio de San Telmo in 1681, both the Universidad de Mareantes and the Casa de Contratación joining in requesting this of the training of steersmen capable of navigating to the Indies.

The college was founded in Sevilla, in the suburb of Triana, and had a capacity for 150 nautical students. Work on the new college buildings on the San Telmo site started in 1686. However, in 1682, only one year after the college's foundation, "Students well prepared for the art of navigation had begun to leave to start their career in the Americas"[3].

92

In 1786 a second college for 150 nautical students was founded in the city of Málaga under the same decree as the Sevilla school.

The students of the Colegio de San Telmo studied Mathematics, Navigation and Pilotage, Manoeuvres, Artillery, Cosmography, Political economics, Commerce, Geography, French, English and Drawing. The examinations were public and the examiners could ask questions at the students as long as these coincided with the printed programme that was distributed among those attending.

On finishing their studies, the students of the Colegio de San Telmo had to make at least two round trips to the Indies or two training voyages in order to be able to take the examinations necessary to become a naval or private steersman's assistant.

During the initial stage of the college's existence the nautical training was given by the Chief Steersman and the Cosmographer of the Casa de Contratación; the studies were of an eminently technical nature, and centred on the art of navigation and on the design and building of ships. When it is remmembered that in 1681 (before the foundation of the college) 100 students embarked on a training voyage, it is logical to suppose that the knowledge acquiered by the steersmen at the college during this initial stage was practically non-existent, and that they would learn far more on these trips organized by the Universidad de Mareantes, which in this manner obtained a cheap labour force for its constant voyages to America.

In any case, the Colegio de San Telmo in Sevilla went a long way to alleviating the constant contracting of foreign steersmen that had come about as a result of the decadent situation of the training given at the Casa de Contratación, and nourished a tradition of expert steersmen, even though these were more often than not self-taught through experience than as a result of the knowledge acquired in the classroom.

Responsibilities of steersmen in the XVIIIth Century

Throughout the XVIIth century the responsibilities of the steersmen were confined to the fields of navigation and keeping on course. No organized body had yet existed (and was not to exist until the middle of the XVIIIth century[4]) and only graduate steersmen empowered to navigate to the Indies in ships of the navy or private vessels were available.

During the XVIIth century the art of pilotage was limited both in Spain and abroad to a few of the elemental principles of Trigonometry and to the observation of the height of the sun and the pole star for determination of latitude.

As regards longitude, and to quote Guillén[5], "by means of a map and a compass, and with the speed *judged* by sight and *time* measured with a sandglass, whose accuracy depended on the boy in charge of turning it (...), it was possible to obtain what we now call a reckoning, always wrong at the speed of a sailing ship, a reading then so completely inaccurate as to merit the name 'fantasy'".

Throughout the century controversy grew between the steersmen of the theoretical school and those whose knowledge was based on experience of the sea. The ex-student of the Colegio de San Telmo Cedillo[6] in his "Trigonometría aplicada a la navegación", published in Sevilla in 1718, underlined the controversy then raging between those officers of the navy that he called scientific officers and those of the "hunting and punting" brigade. The former defended the need for Mathematics and other basic studies, whilst the latter championed the cause of experience at sea.

In short, the transition from the "art" of sailing to the "science" of navigation was a gradual one, and the day was not entirely won until well into the XVIIIth century, and not before giving rise to lengthy and bitter controversy between the officers and men of the navy.

However, between 1730 and 1748, the year of publication of the Naval Regulations that created the Corps of Steersmen and prescribed its organization and responsibilities, several treatises on navigation and pilotage[7] had been published in Madrid and Sevilla which emphasized the growing need for a scientific training for steersmen incorporating knowledge of the new instruments developed abroad and of the latest geographical theories.

The XVIIIth Century

Neverthless, the definitive impetus for recuperation of the Spanish navy was to come at the beginning of the XVIIIth century with the creation in 1717 in Cádiz, and later in Ferrol and Cartagena, of the *Compañía de Guardiamarinas*.

Each of these companies had a Director and eight science teachers, a course of higher studies and an astronomical observatory for the necessary practical lessons. The new generation of officers, trained in the systematic study of Astronomy and its application to navigation, and later equipped with the new chronometers developed by Harrison in England, would be in a position to undertake in the second half of the century the great Spanish maritime-scientific enterprise corresponding to the belated age of enlightenment that these mariners, scientists and pro-Europeans helped to put under way in Spain.

On the other hand, the old conflict of the status of the steersman, then considered a civilian and consequently without authority on board ships of the navy, continued to produce endless complaints among those affected, whose standing was often reduced in spite of the importance of their work.

The Regulations of 1748 partially solved this conflict. According to the regulations the steersman was to have the rank of *officer of the line,* which gave him a clearer status on board ships of the navy; nevertheless, the seagoing steersmen had to fight a continuous institutional battle throughout the

Navy officers carrying out
hydrographic work. Back cover of
"Tratado instructivo y práctico de
maniobras navales...". Agustín
Zuloaga. Cádiz, 1766.
Museo Naval.

XVIIIth century in order to have the ships' officers recognize their quelification regarding the technical handling of the vessels; in this respect their new rank established an heirarchical subordinacy that was favourable to the officers in comparison with the previous situation, in which the steersmen had had no military status.

In 1795 Antonio de Ulloa[8] described the responsibilities of the steersman on warships of his time: "the steersman is directly in charge of the helm and log and responsible for the course". However, during the different explorations carried out along the Northwest Coast the role played by the steersmen was in fact of much greater importance and, as is explained in the second half of this work, almost all of the important works of Cartography carried out in the second half of the century were directly attributable to them.

The Regulations of 1748 distinguished between two classes of steersmen: sea-going and coastal. Within the first of these classes, which is the one which interests us here, the different grades of leading steersman, second steersman and assistant were established. Initially[9], the leading steersmen were ranked as Ensigns and the second steersmen as non-commissioned officers, later the graduation was changed to Lieutenant or Junior-lieutenant for the leading steersmen and to Sub-lieutenant or Ensign for the second steersmen, according to antiquity.

Cover of «Ordenanzas de Su Majestad para el gobierno militar, político y económico de Su Armada Naval». Madrid, 1748.
Museo Naval.

Training of Steersmen in the XVIIIth Century

The Regulations of 1748 also transferred the functions of the previous cosmographers of the Casa de Contratación to the new Chief Helmsman (Commander of the new Corps of steersmen) and to the different directors of departments. These functions included the following:

Examination of the steersmen.

Centralization of logs, both naval and private.

Compilation of news relative to journies to the Indies.

Drawing up of charts and maps.

In this way the Navy was to take complete control[10] of pilotage, as even private steersmen would have to be controlled and examined by the Corp's Chief Helmsman and the departmental directors, who would also control the course to be taken by any ship, either private or belonging to the Navy, which set sail from their different ports.

The steersmen of the new Corps would be trained in the Nautical Colleges created within each department, and the level of education to be achieved was also established in the 1748 Regulations[11]. This training would include: navigation, use of instruments, the necessary precepts of Geometry and Astronomy and Drawing, "in order that they might learn to draw maps of harbours, make charts and represent coasts and hills".

As the XVIIIth century advanced the figure of the *steersman*, considered traditionally to be fundamental on board ship, was replaced by that of the new Naval Officer trained at the *Academia de Guardiamarinas* (Academy of Midshipmen) in Cádiz.

The "Compendio de Navegación" (Compendium of Navigation) (Cádiz, 1757) published by Jorge Juan represented a real change of course in nautical training in Spain, and changed the traditional practical approach for the new concept of the mathematical treatment of problems deduced from theoretical principles. However, it should be pointed out that this text, which was decisive in establishing the teaching of the new nautical science, was aimed at the new officers trained in the *Academia de Guardiamarinas* and not at the steersmen.

For its own part the *Colegio de San Telmo* in Sevilla continued its course, although the education given could not now be considered as comparable to that offered by the *Academia de Guardiamarinas* nor even by the Naval College in Cádiz.

The establishment of the course of "Higher Studies" for midshipmen in 1783 and the starting of this course in the *Observatorio Astronómico* in Cádiz[12] was to enable the training of a group of exceptionally well prepared officers who were later to play a leading role in the great scientific revival of the Spanish Navy and carry out an extremely important series of hydrographic campaigns through which the coastlines of Spain, the Americas and the Phillipines were entirely re-mapped, using the most up-to-date and accurate techniques. These maps, published by the Depósito Hidrográfico in the last years of the XVIIIth century and the first of the XIXth, were to be widely used at the time.

This was the case in the increasing Spanish presence along the northest coast, which will be dealt with below. This expansion generated a wide and reliable set of maps, the most significant of which were also engraved at the Depósito Hidrográfico.

II.   The Increasing Spanish presence on the NorthWest Coast of Northern America During the XVIIIth Century

The expeditions to the Northwest Coast of America or northern coast of California were carried out by the Spanish Navy from the Naval Station of San Blas, which was created not only to provide a back-up for these explorations but also for the garrisons set up under the influence of friar Junípero Serra.

It should be noted that in the 18-year period between the first expedition, undertaken by Juan Pérez in 1774, at a time when nothing certain was known of the coast further up than Monterey, and 1792, when the *Sutil* and *Mexicana* expedition was completed, the entire coastline up to a latitude of 61º N was explored and mapped.

Most of these expeditions were based on political motives: the first three —1774, 1775 and 1779— sought to determine the presence of the Russians, and the rest the presence of the English; however, the expeditions were also undertaken with a view to verifying the ideas received from the Academy of Sciences of Paris with respect to the search for the famous Northwest Passage.

These expeditions, although fundamentally political in nature, generated a great deal of scientific, ethnographic, zoological, botanical and medical information, which was only to be expected in this century of enlightenment; also, as is always the case with new possessions and settlements in unknown territories, the expeditions created a basic need for greater geographical knowledge. Therefore, map-making, with all the accompanying calculations of longitude and latitude and astronomical measurement, was a means and an end.

Creation of the San Blas Naval Station

During the reign of Carlos III, D. José de Gálvez, then Visitor General of the New Spain, found himself faced with the need for a well supplied port close to the San Diego and Monterey garrisons which would also serve as a back-up to the expeditions aimed at pacifying Sonora, Sinaloa and New Mexico, and founded in 1768 the San Blas Naval Station on the west coast of New Spain at latitude 21º, 30' N. These original objectives were accompanied by others to be achieved in the longer term, such as the exploration and taking of the coasts of northern California.

The San Blas Naval Station or department maintained always its identity as a stronghold and base for the Royal Navy. It depended directly on the

Juan Francisco de la Bodega y Quadra,
1743-1794.
Museo Naval.

viceroy, who delegated his authority to a commandant acting as supreme chief, both of the naval units appointed to him and of the rest of the advanced positions ón the Northwest Coast.

In spite of its strategic importance, the San Blas Naval Station was initially provided with very meagre human and material resources, only six ships.

The first expedition to leave San Blas set sail as a result of news from the Count of Lacy, then Spanish ambassador in St. Petersburg, who warned of the descent of the Russians through the Bering Straits in order to establish factories dealing in furs along the Northwest Coast of the continent. The viceroy, D. Antonio de Bucareli, received orders to send an expedition to verify this news and, to this effect, commissioned the chief of the department, the Sub-Lieutenant graded steersman Juan Pérez, who set sail on the 24th of January 1774 in the only ship available, the frigate *Santiago.* Pérez, whose orders were to sail up the coast as far as latitude 60º N to find the Russians, carried with him as second in command Estéban José Martínez, later famous in his own right. Without the help of maps nor any reference to the coast, he set course for the northwest, later swinging to the north at about 50º. At approximately 54º he sighted land, but decided not to disembark because of the mists and the adverse weather conditions which were also to make it impossible to continue to 60º. The journey home was algo eventful because of the constantly bad weather and the impossibility of manoeuvring among the innumerable islands and channels. The only thing worthy of mention as regards this voyage is that Pérez sailed along the coast of the island that was later to be called Vancouver, that he believed to be part of the mainland, and that he anchored in a berth that he named San Lorenzo (Nootka) without disembarking. Pérez arrived back at San Blas on the 3rd of November of the same year with a sick crew and results that were far from encouraging. As he had been unable to explore he had not produced any maps, and his observations were either incorrect or at best vague; on the other hand he was able to demonstrate that up to 55º N the coast did not deviate either to the east or to the west. At 55º he discovered a point that he named Santa Margarita, this being the northern end of the island of Lángara at the extreme northestern tip of the Queen Charlotte archipelago.

Development of the San Blas Naval Station

Given the interest that was awoken in Spain in relation to the Northwest Coast, a new contingent of officers was sent to reinforce the deparment of San Blas, thus allowing a more systematic approach to be adopted in the expeditions without leaving the garrisons unattended. With these new resources a second expedition was organized the following year (1775) under the command of D. Bruno Hezeta, who sailed on the frigate *Santiago* with Juan Pérez as second in command, D. Juan Manuel de Ayala on the schooner *So-*

ELEXMO. SR. BAILIO FREY D. ANTONIO MARIA D. BUCARELI, y Vrsua & Virrey Governador, y Cap. Gen. de esta nueva España. & Nació en Sevilla á 24 de Enero de 1717. Murio en Mexico á 9 de Abril de 1779.

Antonio María Bucareli y Ursua, Viceroy of New Spain, 1717-1779.
Biblioteca Nacional.

nora with D. Juan Francisco de la Bodega y Quadra as second officer, and D. Miguel Manrique, who commanded the packetboat *San Carlos* which was going along to bring aid to the garrisons. They set sail from San Blas on the 16th of March 1775 and not long afterwards it became clear that Manrique was suffering from mental derangement, for which reason Ayala took over command of the *San Carlos* and Bodega y Quadra of the schooner *Sonora*, alias *Felicidad*.

The viceroy's instructions were to reach 65º and not allow any foreigners to settle on the coast. The expedition explored an island that they named Socorro and reached 48º. At 41º they discovered a harbour that they named Trinidad, and Hezeta, Bodega and Bodega's steersman, Mourelle drew up a map of it. Because of the bad weather and the damage suffered by the ship, the frigate *Santiago* had to return to Monterey while Bodega continued as far as 58º. Before reaching this point they discovered the "punta de los Mártires", now known as Greenville Point. Bodega, following Bellin's Chart sailed north-west as Pérez had done before, and later swung to the north in order to gain height as rapidly as possible. At 57º they sighted the coast again and rode at anchor in what is now Mount Edgecumbe, which they called San Jacinto, the "Susto" Creek, and the harbours of Guadalupe and Los Remedios. At 55º 17' they rounded a cape called San Bartolomé and entered a very sheltered stretch of water whose far side could not be seen. The ship anchored in this stretch, which they named the Bucareli Inlet, and Mourelle drew a map[13].

Given the adverse winds, Bodega was not able to go any further than 58º 30', and returned to San Blas with the schooner and her crew in very poor shape. During the return voyage the ship sailed engulfed without coming very close to the dangerous island-infested coast, although between 45º and 42º they searched for the famous river that Martín de Aguilar, Sebastián Vizcaíno's companion, claimed to have seen. At 38º the ship made land in a bay that the men believed to be the bay of San Francisco, as yet unexplored from the sea. Upon realizing their error, they named it Bodega Bay, now known as Tomales Bay.

For his part, Hezeta, on his return journey, sailed through the Straits of Fuca without realizing and discovered a bay that he chirstened with his own name. Hezeta was not able to sail into this bay, which was in fact the mouth of the Columbia River, because of the strength of the current. He named the capes on either side of the Mouth San Roque and Frondoso, and believed that he was looking at the entrance to the Straits of Fuca, in spite of the fact that the latitude did not coincide. Hezeta waited for Bodega in Monterey, where he and Mourelle finally arrived seriously ill and where Juan Pérez died as a result of the hardships suffered during two consecutive years of expeditions at those latitudes.

From that second expedition we still conserve an abundancy of maps which reflect the doubts and uncertainties caused by a still scarcely explored coast full of legends.

These maps were drawn by Bodega and Mourelle; the latter kept a diary illustrated with maps of the coast that Cook, as he himself confessed, copied and used on his third journey.

Towards 70º

The third expedition was undertaken in the year '79 and was ordered by Gálvez, who wished to neutralize the journey that Cook had made in '77. As from that moment onwards, the Spanish expeditions tried mainly to neutralize the advance of the English, as they had been doing previously with regard to the Russians. The success enjoyed by the previous expedition nurtured the interest of the Government in such matters. In any case, Bucareli was not able to confront the next expedition as soon as he would have liked owing to a lack of ships; consequently, Bodega meanwhile sailed to Perú in order to take command of the frigate *Favorita*, which had been constructed in that port.

Meanwhile, the officers of the Department drew up a map on which they reflected all the information they had at the time regarding the Spanish and Russian discoveries, attempting to put all this information in order and reflect the different versions of certain parts of the coast so that it might serve as a point of reference for the expedition that was being prepared. To this end they used the maps of Bellin, Bodega, Stahlin and Anson, as well as Mourelle's recent observations.

The new expedition finally set forth on the 2nd of February 1779, returning on the 25th of November of the same year. The head of the expedition was Ignacio Arteaga, who was in command of the frigate *Princesa*, with Fernando Quirós as second in command and Juan Pantoja y Arriaga and José Camacho as mates. Bodega was in command of the frigate *Nuestra Señora del Rosario*, alias la *Favorita*, with Mourelle as second in command and José Cañizares and Juan Bautista Aguirre as mates. The objective was to reach 70º in order to determine in which direction the coast continued, a detail that was not shown in any of the previous charts. They anchored once more in Bucareli Bay, carrying out soundings and checking measurements of latitudes, and later continued northward until they sighted Mount San Elias on the coast of the Gulf of Alaska, and an island that they called "La Isla del Carmen" (Kayak) and the Santiago Inlet, now prince William Sound. They also went to the "puerto de Santiago", now Port Etches, on the Island of Santa Magdalena, and the Island of Hinchinbroke, which can be said to be the frontier of the area explored by the Spaniards, an area that never extended beyond the latitude of 61º. They then sailed south-west and arrived at a harbour situated on the Kenai Peninsula on the Island of Afognak, christening it "Nuestra Señora de la Regla". They found

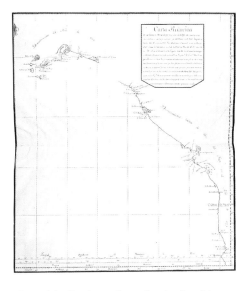

Chart of the Northwest Coast showing Spanish discoveries of 1775 and 1779. Mourelle de la Rua. Museo Naval.

no signs of the English, and came to the conclusion that the Russians had not descended further than the Aleutians. Because of the scurvy they had to return to San Blas without reaching 70º and without finding the North-west Passage that figured on the Russian maps. After eight years of inactivity due to the war with the English, the new provided by the Count of La Pèrouse with respect to the Russian settlements at Nootka, prince William Sound, Trinidad and Onalaska gave rise to another expedition that set sail on the 6th of March 1788, returning on the 5th of December of the same year. This expedition was headed by Estéban Martínez aboard the frigate *Princesa* and by the steersman Gonzalo López de Haro, who commanded the packetboat San Carlos, alias *El Filipino*. The bad weather and mists did not allow them to anchor in Prince William Sound, but they did find a small bay, on the Island of Montagu, that they named Florez Harbour in honour of the then viceroy. At Cook Inlet they discovered a Russian settlement where they were well received and given all kinds of information.

Sailing down towards the south-west, they touched the islands of Kodiak and Shumagin, as well as Unimak and Onalaska on the southern tip of the Alaska Peninsula. In both places they obtained new information on the Russian and English factories, returning to San Blas with definite news for the viceroy, D. Manuel Florez.

No sooner had he returned, Martínez was given orders to set sail once more in order to take Nootka before the English. He set forth from San Blas on the 9th of March 1789 and took solemn possession of the objective.

As regards this eminently political and diplomatic expedition, the only thing of interest from the cartographic point of view was that Martínez sent the steersman José María Narváez to explore a very wide mouth that he had seen at 48º 20' during the journey that he had made with Juan Pérez. The exploration confirmed that this mouth could be a passage to the Atlantic, a fact that he communicated to the Court. This news gave rise to a new expedition.

In 1790, Bodega y Quadra, who had been the commander of the Department of San Blas since the previous year, sent Manuel Quimper, skipper of the sloop *Princesa Real,* to explore from Nootka to the south, Salvador Fidalgo, on the packetboat *San Carlos,* alias *El Filipino,* to explore from Nootka to the north and Francisco Eliza to establish a settlement on the island.

Quimper visited the above-mentioned Straits of Juan de Fuca and drew up some maps, finally having to retire because of the adverse winds. On the basis of the information received, Eliza sent a report to Revillagigedo, saying that if there were a passage it would be found in these straits. This gave rise to another expedition.

At the end of 1790, during a voyage around the world, the corvettes *Descubierta* and *Atrevida* received orders from the Spanish Court to cruise towards the north-west with a view to checking the news given that same year to the Academy of Sciences of Paris by the geographer Buache, who claimed that the accounts of a journey made by Ferrer Maldonado in 1588 were true, and that there really was a passage joining the two oceans at latitude 60º N. The corvettes received this order in Acapulco, and captain Malaspina immediately ran northwards. The two ships sailed up to Bering Bay, Mount San Elias and Kaye Island as far as Cape Hinchinbroke at prince William Sound, which had been explored by Fidalgo the previous year. At 57º

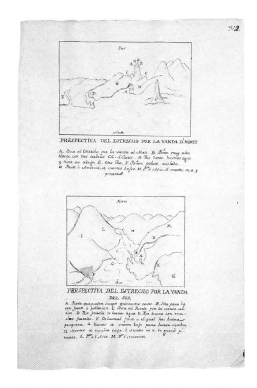

View of the Anian Strait. Ferrer Maldonado, 1588 (copy of Juan Bautista Muñoz, 1781). Malaspina Expedition.
Museo Naval.

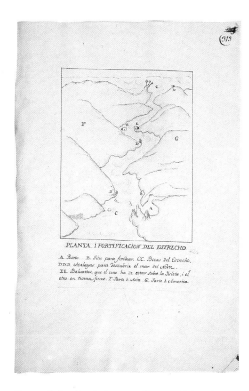

Fort at Anian Strait. Lorenzo Ferrer Maldonado, 1588 (copy of Juan Bautista Muñoz, 1781). Malaspina Expedition.
Museo Naval.

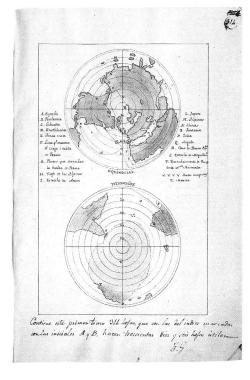

Planisphere of a representation of the world. Ferrer Maldonado, 1588 (copy of Juan Bautista Muñoz, 1781). Malaspina Expedition.
Museo Naval.

they found no sign of any passage, and at approximately 60º to the east of Mount San Elias they found an inlet. They explored this inlet, but found it to be simply a channel. They determined the latitude of Nootka by means of the precision instruments that they were carrying, and explored its channels, sailing out by way of the Bay of Esperanza and thus definitively demonstrating that it was an island. It was not possible during this campaign

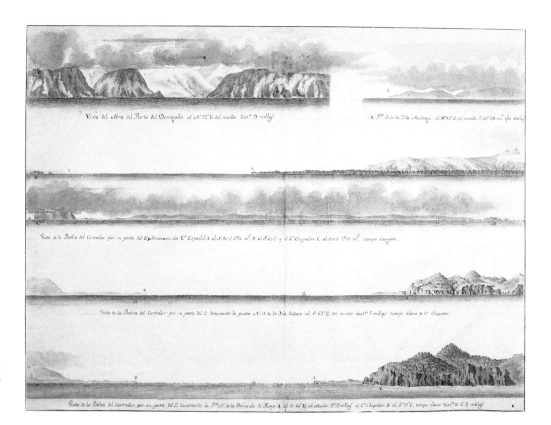

Views of the Northwest Coast from the Port of
Desengaño to the Kaye Península, prepared for
engraving. Felipe Bauzá.
Museo Naval.

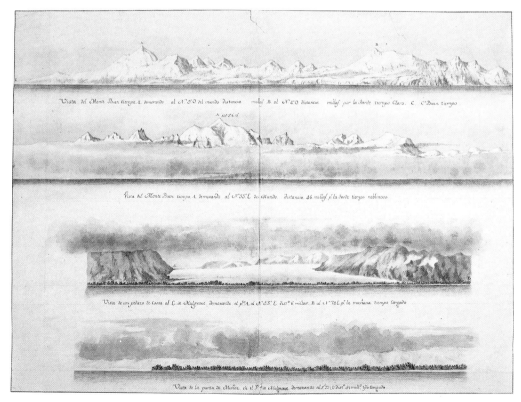

Views of the Northwest Coast, from Mount Buen
Tiempo to Mulgrave Sound, prepared for
engraving. Felipe Bauzá.
Museo Naval.

of the north to explore the Juan de Fuca Straits, and the doubts as to whether its inland channels communicated with the Atlantic remained.

The cartographic results of the expedition were many and reliable, due to the fact that the measurements had been made by means of the latest and most modern precision instruments. These maps and measurements were published soon after by the Depósito Hidrográfico of Madrid, and the astronomical results in the records of the Dirección de Hidrografía by Espinosa y Tello.

Malaspina then proposed to Revillagigedo that the following summer he send the schooners *Sutil* and *Mexicana,* which had just been built in San Blas, to finish the campaign that he had not been able to complete the year before. To this end he proposed to send two of his officers, Alcalá Galiano and Cayetano Valdés, with Juan Vernacci and Secundino Salamanca as second officers in command. The proposal having been accepted, they set sail from Acapulco in March 1792. After taking fresh supplies on board in Nootka, they sailed up to the northern part of the Strait of Juan de Fuca, to the Harbour of Núñez Gaona; here they met Fidalgo, who was establishing a settlement. They thoroughly explored all the channels and islands, and met Vancouver, who was engaged in the same task. After verifying that there was no passage to the north-west, they sailed out from the northern end and discovered a harbour which they baptised with the expressive name of "Puerto Desengaño" (The harbour of Disappointment). The records of this voyage were published in 1802, to steal a march on the edition of Vancouver's journey, and included a great many maps apart from those already published

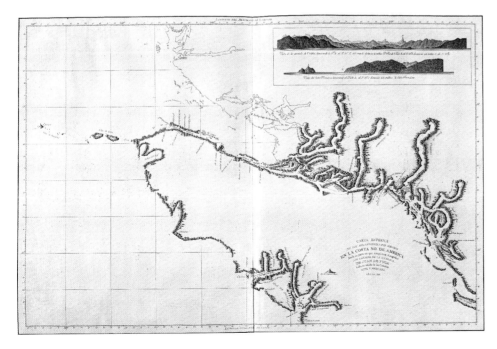

Spherical map of the channels at the entrance of Juan de Fuca Strait by the schooners *Sutil* and *Mexicana,* 1795.
Museo Naval.

in the Hydrographic Suvey's atlases. The last Spanish expedition to the coasts of Canada was the one carried out by Jacinto Caamaño and Salvador Fidalgo on the frigate *Princesa,* and was motivated by a map that the Englishman James Colnett had handed over to Eliza in Nootka, and which showed a sound at 55º that would be the Fonte Strait. This alerted the Spaniards, who had not explored the coast to the north of Nootka as far as 55º.

And so Caamaño was sent in the frigate *Aránzazu,* which was not particularly suited to sailing on the high seas and had insufficient manoeuverability for exploration of the channels. Caamaño arrived at the Bay of Bucareli and discovered a harbour which he named after the Knight of the Order of San Juan, Bazán; this harbour still carries Bazán's name. A second harbour he christened Valdés, and another Núñez Gaona. He sailed in through the Dixon Gate, christening the channel with the name of "Nuestra Señora del Carmen", the present Clarence Strait, and reached the two harbours "Estrada" and "Mazarredo", now known as Masset Harbor and Virago Sound. He also discovered the "Príncipe" channel between the Islands of "Calamidad" (Banks) and "Enríquez" (Mac Cauley and Pitt) where, according to Colnett, the entry to the Fonte Straits was to be found, only to discover that there was no Passage to the Northwest. Some of the names given by Caamaño have survived to this day because Vancouver maintained them on a map of this expedition that he managed to obtain.

Once the mysteries of the straits of Fuca, Fonte and Ferrer Maldonado had been clared up, the expeditions from Nootka to San Francisco continued with a view to completing the exploration of the coast in order to draw up a hydrographical chart of Northern America that would be included in the atlas of Spanish possessions in America.

The coast from Nootka to San Francisco, especially the area of the River Columbia, called "río de Martín Aguilar" on the Spanish maps, and of the Hezeta Sound, was explored by Martínez Zayas on the schooner *Mexicana* without the aid of his companion Eliza, who was driven off course by contrary winds and had to return to San Blas after exploring the harbours of Trinidad and Bodega and a third now known as Tomales Bay. Abundant maps are conserved of this expedition.

III. Cartographic problems Encountered in the Surveys

Cartography and surveying was generally entrusted to the steersmen of the ships, members of a special corps who only in cases of special merit or antiquity could rise to the lower ranks of te general corps, or "graduate" as it was then known, that is become Lieutenants.

On the expeditions to the Northwest Coast of America the steersmen played the most important role in the production of maps, although in most cases they did not sign the results of their work and authorship can only be established through study of the ships' log-books. Among these steersmen some are worthy of special mention, for example, Gonzalo López de Haro, author of several maps, not only of the Northwest Coast but also of the inner provinces of New Spain. This work includes a reproduction of a map showing the Russian settlements discovered during the 1788 expedition on which Estéban Martínez, also a steersman, was the commander.

Another steersman to whom many cartographical documents are owed was Juan Pantoja y Arriaga, who participated in Arteaga's expedition and later in the expedition led by Jacinto Caamaño in 1792; the abundant charts drawn up on this expedition are the work of Pantoja and of Martínez de Zayas, the author of the maps of the River Columbia that mark the end of the Spanish expeditions to the northern coasts of America.

However, the cartographic basis of all the activities in these latitudes was the work of Mourelle and Bodega y Quadra.

After the expedition by Juan Pérez, a steersman who did not produce any maps, the two following expeditions of 1775 and 1779, on which Bodega y Quadra was the commanding officer and Francisco Antonio Mourelle the steersman, generated an ample cartographic documentation that served as the basis for later voyages. Later on, upon being named commandant of the Department of San Blas, Bodega had occasion, and undoubtedly the necessary aptitude, to centralize all the maps that were being produced. In this

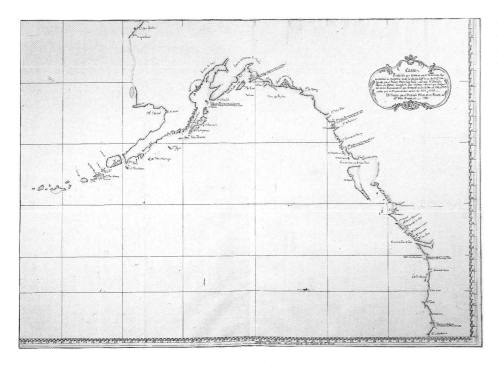

Chart of surveys conducted on the Northwest Coast by Gonzalo López de Haro, with Russian settlements, 1790.
Museo Naval.

respect it is interesting to note on how many occasions he was consulted by the different viceroys when they were organizing expeditions and deciding on the routes to be taken. Mourelle for his part continued his map-making activities, now during the journey that the *Princesa* embarked upon from the Phillipines in 1781, discovering and mapping the Vavao Islands in the Tonga Archipelago.

Following the war with the English, Mourelle was stationed in Mexico, in the secretariat of viceroy Revillagigedo, the second of this name, and given the task of organizing and systematizing all the ships' logs corresponding to the expeditions to the Northwest; here he was able to complete his cartographic collection.

The Spanish crown's interest in producing reliable maps of this part of America, previously based on a desire to locate the Russian settlements and take possession of them before the English, now began to take a scientific slant as a result of the accounts of Ferrer Maldonado, Fonte and Fuca, and represented also an attempt at mapping all of the Spanish possessions in America in the wake of the success of the 1789 Atlas marítimo de España.

During the 1779 expedition, whose aim was to sail up as far as latitude 70º N, problems were encountered as of 58º, a point which the previous expeditions had not passed; thus Bodega y Quadra states in his diary: "... from 58º onwards we had no idea whom we might believe, as the accounts of the different surveyors varied to such a degree that while some claimed that the coast swung to the southwest at 62º, others had it going west and others to the northwest, and when the different bases for these conclusions are studied it is seen that most of them are founded on the same reasoning" (sic). Faced by this problem Bodega y Quadra opts for an eclectic solution: "And so I decided to draw a map including everything discovered up to 58º, considering this part of the coast to be beyond doubt as I myself had discovered and explored it, and from this point onwards show on my map all of Mr. Bellin's Chart, in red so that it might be easily distinguished, and also show the chart included in the history of California (by Father Venegas Consag) by means of a black dotted-line and, finally, the chart of the Imperial Academy of St. Petersburg in yellow, by means of which variety on one same map it might be easy to take into account all the different suppositions so that at first glance not the slightest reflection should remain hidden" (sic)[14].

Bodega ends this entry by saying that drawing of the map was possible thanks to the steersman Mourelle being the second in command and to the ship's steersman being José Cañizares, whose invaluable help meant that several copies could be made for the purpose of navigation.

Bodega, along with his steersman Mourelle, was also entrusted with the production of a map including all the discoveries made up to that time for use by the Malaspina Expedition; an original of this map is exhibited here. From his post in Nootka Bodega also undertook to collect and prepare all

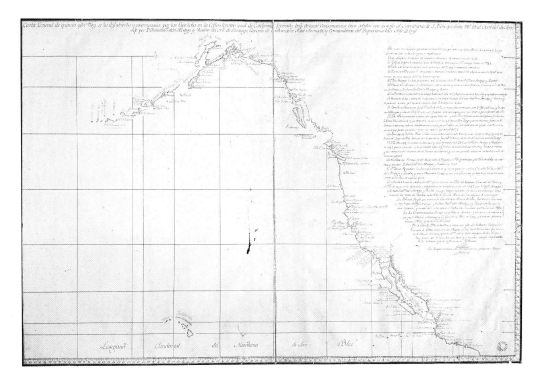

General chart of Spanish discoveries on the northern California coast. Bodega y Quadra, 1791. Museo Naval.

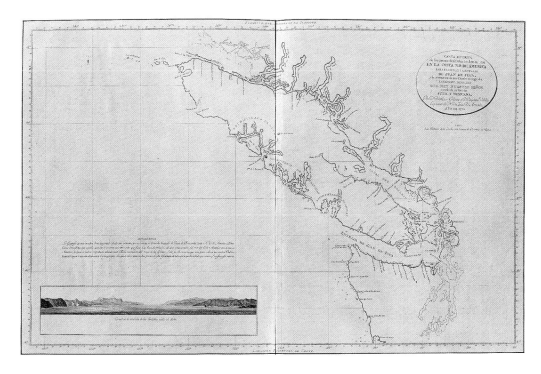

Spherical map of the surveys conducted in 1792 of the entrance of Juan de Fuca and its navigable channels. Dionisio Alcalá Galiano and Cayetano Valdés, 1795. Museo Naval.

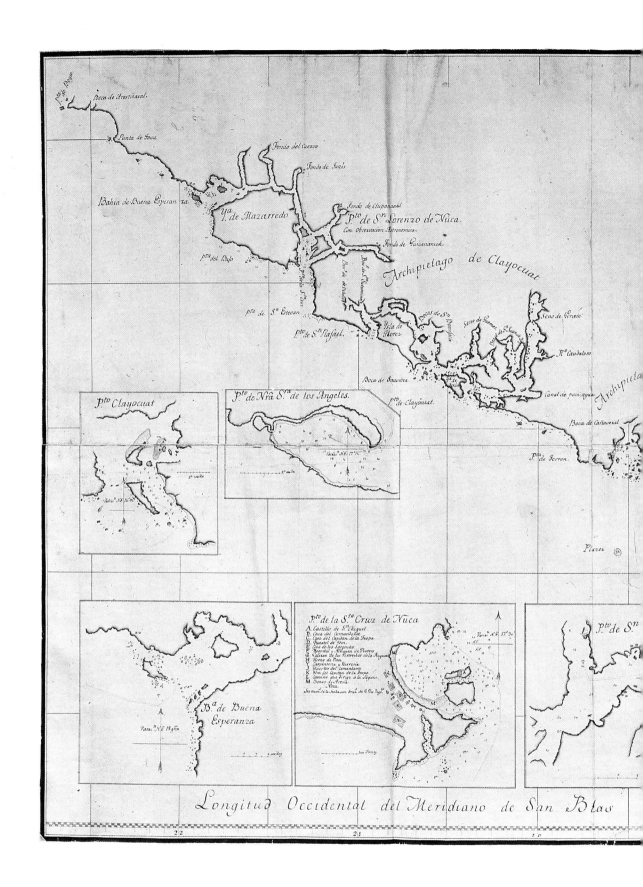

Boca de Arrestizaval.

Punta de Gova.

Fondo del Cuervo.

Fondo de Iuzis.

Bahia de Buena Esperanza.

Fondo de Clupananul.

Ya. T. de Mazarredo.

Pto. de Sn. Lorenzo de Nuca.

Con Observacion Astronomica.

Fondo de Guicananich.

pta. del Baso.

Archipielago de Clayocuat.

pta. de Sn. Estevan.

Bocas de Sn. Bonifacio.

Seno de Guemes.

Seno de Peroote.

pto. de Sn. Rafael.

Ysla de Florez.

Rio. Caudaloso.

Boca de Saavedra.

Canal de poca agua.

Archipiela

Boca de Cañaveral.

Pto. Clayocuat.

Pto. de Nra. Sra. de los Angeles.

pto. de Clayocuat.

Pta. de Ferron.

Plazes.

Ba. de Buena Esperanza.

Pto. de la Sta. Cruz de Nuca

Pto. de Sn.

A. Castillo de Sn. Miguel
B. Casa del Comandante
C. Casa del Capitan de la Tropa
D. Quartel de Tropa
E. Casa de los Sargentos
F. Hospital y Botiquin de Viveres
G. Galeran He. de los Ferreros dela Fragata
H. Horno de Pan.
Y. Carpinteria, y Herreria
J. Huertas del Comandante
K. Hm. del Capitan de la Tropa
L. Camino que dirige a la Laguna.
M. Banco de Arena.
Nota.

Longitud Occidental del Meridiano de San Blas

22   24   26

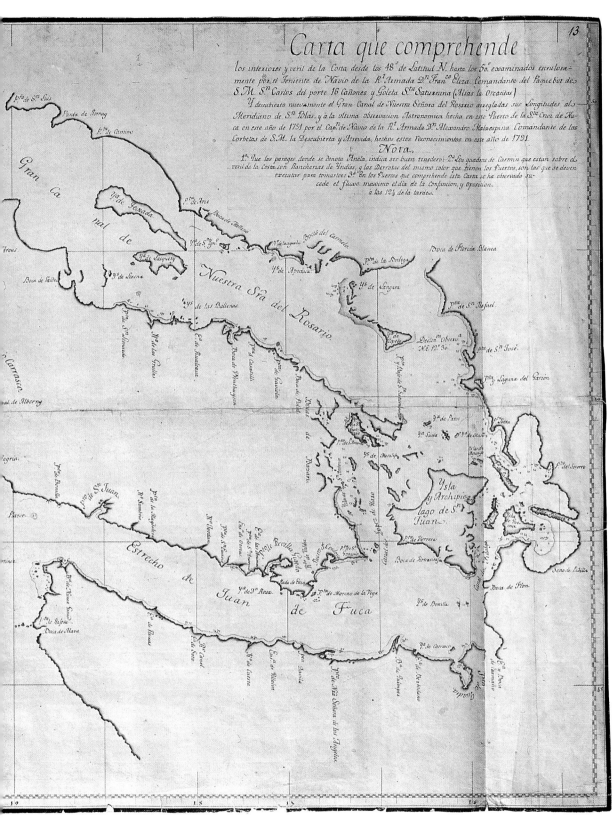

Carta que comprehende

los interiores y veril de la Costa desde los 48° de Latitud N. hasta los 50° examinados escrulosa-
mente por el Teniente de Navio de la R.ᵃ Armada D.ⁿ Fran.ᶜᵒ Eliza. Comandante del Paquebot de
S.M. S.ⁿ Carlos del porte 16 Cañones y Goleta S.ᵗᵃ Saturnina (Alias la Oracitas)

Y descubierto nuevamente el Gran Canal de Nuestra Señora del Rosario arregladas sus Longitudes al
Meridiano de S.ⁿ Blas, y à la ultima observacion Astronomica hecha en este Puerto de la S.ᵗᵃ Cruz de Nu-
ca en este año de 1791 por el Cap.ⁿ de Navio de la R.ᵃ Armada D.ⁿ Alexandro Malaespina Comandante de las
Corbetas de S.M. la Descubierta y Atrevida, hechos estos Reconocimientos en este año de 1791.

Nota.

1ª Que los parages donde se denota Anela, indica ser buen tenedero: 2ª Los quadros de Carmin que estan sobre el
veril de la Costa son Rancherias de Yndios, q̄ los Derrotas del mismo color que tienen los Puertos, son las que se deven
executar para tomarlos: 3ª En los Puertos que comprehende esta Carta se ha observado su-
cede el fluxo maximo el dia de la Confuncion, y Oposicion.
à las 12¼ de la tarde.

Chart of the coast studied by Francisco de Eliza
between 48° and 50° north latitude. Resurveyed
by Malaspina in 1791.
Museo Naval.

111

the maps produced by the expeditions to the Northwest; it is for this reason that Jacinto Caamaño, having completed his commission in 1792, hands over to Bodega, in Nootka, the results of his journies.

This must have been the usual way in which maps were produced at that time. The commandant of the 1779 expedition says in his accounts of the journey: "In this port (San Francisco) the captains, officiers and steersmen of both ships met and, having studied the ships' logs we decided to take the average values from both and in this way to produce the most accurate maps, thus avoiding the confusion that might arise as a result of the slight differences that existed between them" (sic). In summing up we may establish that the cartographic tasks of drawing up charts were entrusted to the steersmen, some of them very good, while the astronomical observations and location of harbours were the responsibility of the officers. These observations were almost always based on estimates as precision instruments were then unavailable. In this respect, Caamaño assures in his diary that the latitude is not over exact as it is the result of an estimate, and that it is decided upon at a meeting of officers and steersmen to contrast information. Only the Malaspina Expedition, which was sailing around the world on a scientific commission, was equipped with modern astronomical instruments of the highest quality, especially ordered from England and France for the occasion. The expedition undertaken by the schooners *Sutil* and *Mexicana*, which had the same apparatus as Malaspina's crews, was the only one, along with Malaspina's, to produce entirely reliable results, and the maps drawn during these two expeditions were of a very high scientific quality. The instruments carried by the schooners *Sutil* and *Mexicana*, which completed exploration of the entire Straits of Fuca and of the Island of Vancouver, are listed in the first chapter of the accounts of the journey, published in 1802, and were:

> One quarter circle.
> One pendulum.
> Two achromatic telescopes.
> One equator-locating instrument.
> One reflection circle.
> One chronometer.
> One longitude time-piece.
> Two barometers.
> Four thermometers.
> One eudiometer.

The corvettes *Descubierta* and *Atrevida*, seen from the stern. Fernando Brambila. Museo Naval.

IV. Problems of Navigation on the High Seas

We once more fall back on Juan Francisco de la Bodega y Quadra for an account of the problems encountered by the Spaniards at those inhospitable latitudes to which they were unaccustomed.

In a method of navigation for continuing the exploration of the northern coast of California Bodega recommends the month of January as the ideal time to set sail from San Blas towards the north, and the María Islands as the first stage. Once at these islands, it is necessary to gain latitude by steering 15º north-west to the west of San Blas and continue to gain longitude as far as 35º west of the same meridian or 200 leagues from the coast. From 50º latitude onwards care should be taken with adverse winds. Bodega recommends that the first landfall be made at 55º, in Bucareli Bay, to take on water and give the crew a rest, "from this place it is not necessary to sail out very far to find favourable winds". This same criterion of leaving the coast and sailing out onto the high sea until extreme latitudes are reached is expressed by the officers of the Sutil and Mexicana expedition when they state that to follow the coastline would be the ideal course for voyages of discovery and would simplify the taking on of provisions because of the opportunity to make several landfalls, however, as they point out, "this course (following the coastline) was found to be impracticable by many ships because of the currents and north to north-west winds that normally blow with great force; this has made it preferable to sail out onto the sea in search of north-east winds to later use the others to make land at higher latitudes".

Another, no lesser, problem was to do with the ships used on these expeditions, as they had to be vessels of a shallow draught, sufficient beam and very manoeuverable in order to allow the crews to sail up the channels and anchor off the coasts, which were full of small islands and very broken; at the same time the vessels had to be very tough and resistent in order to withstand the southwest winds that blew at those latitudes, and had to be tarred so as not to crack because of the ice. These demands could not be made of the few ships that were available at the San Blas Naval Station. Consequently, when the occasion presented itself to build ships expressly for the expedition of the schooners *Sutil* and *Mexicana,* we find in the first chapter of the accounts of the voyage that Alcalá Galiano lists the necessary qualities that these vessels should have: "let these vessels have the advantage of a shallow draught so that they may sail in shallow channels and be easy to free from the danger of running aground by sail or oar", "what we first noticed was the defect in the construction of the vessels in the narrowness of their beam", "the schooners had arrived from San Blas with a tackle that was something between a schooner's and a brig's".

V. Cartography of the Northwest Coast Engraved by the Depósito Hidrográfico: Cartographic Diffusion of the Explorations of Alta California

In 1797 the Hydrographic Survey was founded in Madrid; this institution was not only essential for Spanish nautical sciences in the XIXth century, but was also to make it possible to systematize and engrave the magnificent Spanish cartographic surveys of the last third of the XVIIIth century.

Consequently, and among others, the explorations of the Northwest Coast, from the very early expeditions of Vizcaíno to those of Malaspina and Galiano, were to see the light of day through the engravings made by the Depósito Hidrográfico, and thus be circulated in Spain and America as well as abroad.

Another of the Depósito Hidrográfico's tasks, of enormous value to nautical education in Spain, was to provide reliable maps for the nautical training colleges and to keep them informed of news of overseas navigation.

Between 1796 and 1825 the Depósito Hidrográfico of Madrid drew up twelve maps which included all of the Spanish explorations made in lower and upper California from the early expedition of Vizcaíno in 1602 to that of the *Sutil* and the *Mexicana* in 1792; production of these maps was directed by José Espinosa y Tello, and they were prepared for engraving by Bauzá; Ballester and Cardano.

Hull of the corvettes *Descubierta* and *Atrevida*.
Fernando Brambila.
Museo Naval.

In 1795 two spherical maps were engraved showing the explorations made of the Fuca Channel in 1792 by the *Sutil* and the *Mexicana;* these were produced with great urgency in order to gain priority over the English publications on that same coast.

In 1802, and for the Royal Printworks' edition of the *Sutil* and *Mexicana* voyage to the Straits of Fuca, the spherical maps of Vizcaíno's explorations in 1602 were engraved along with the 1782 explorations of the Bay of San Diego by Juan Pantoja, a speherical map showing the Spanish explorations of that coast between 1774 and 1792, and four more including the surveys made by the *Descubierta* and the *Atrevida* in 1791 of the Friendly Cove, Mulgrave Bay, "Puerto Desengaño" and Monterey Bay.

Finally, in 1825, the Dirección de Hidrografía engraved the spherical map of the coasts and gulf of California from Cape Corrientes to San Diego which corresponded to the surveys carried out by the Malaspina Expedition and others of the era.

Felipe Bauzá, 1764-1834.
Museo Naval.

Drawing box of Felipe Bauzá. XVIII c.
Museo Naval.

Continuation of surveys conducted on the Northwest Coast by Spanish ships from 1774 to 1792. Report on cartography of the Alaska coast at the conclusion of Spanish explorations in 1792. Museo Naval.

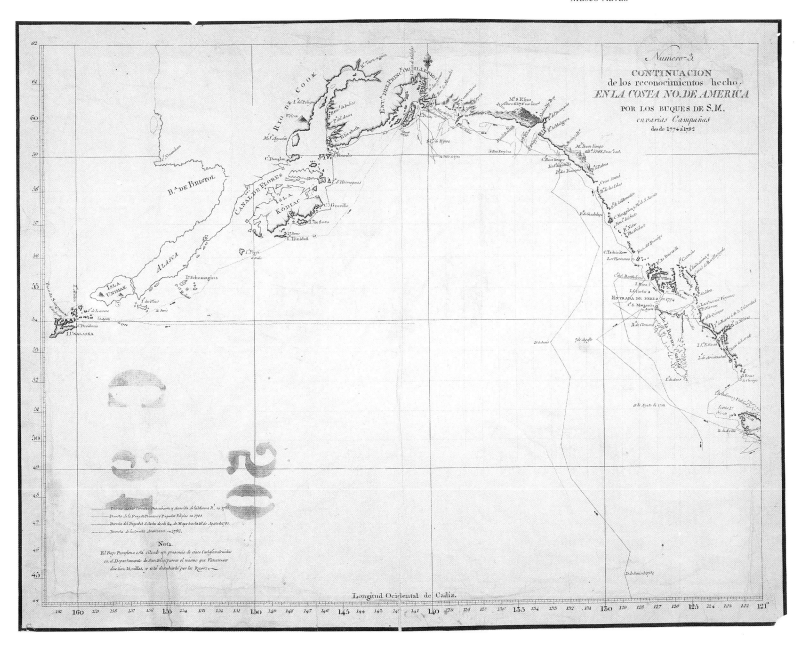

These maps were widely distributed, and some of them were used by the famous Humboldt, Espinosa y Tello having presented them, along with others of the Antilles, to this learned German during a visit to the Depósito Hidrográfico in 1799[15].

Summary

The explorations of the Northwest Coast carried out by the Spaniards from the first expedition to Alta California by Pérez to 1792, the year in which Galiano and Valdés surveyed the Straits of Fuca, constitute the most representative reflection of the great political-scientific effort made by Spain in the second half of the XVIIIth century in an attempt to recuperate her naval prestige and commercial and political role in the Pacific.

These explorations also significantly reflect the transformation that took place in the nautical training of the Spanish mariners and steersmen, as this lat epic deed of discovery was initiated by men like Juan Pérez and Estéban Martínez, representatives of the Colegio de San Telmo which was firmly anchored in the conceptos of the XVIIIth century, and culminated by others such as Malaspina, Alcalá Galiano, Valdés, Vernacci, Espinosa y Tello and Bauzá, who formed part of that great generation of enlightened and learned mariners that was trained by means of the courses of higher studies at the Astronomical Observatory in Cádiz in accordance with the most advanced scientific methods. It is to this generation of officers and to the constructional reform initiated some years earlier by Jorge Juan that the brilliant scientific and military revival of the Spanish Navy in the last third of the XVIIIth century is due.

Notes

1. According to Veitia and Linage *Norte de la Contratación de las Indias*, Sevilla, 1672.

2. The Universidad de Mareantes was an association of the owners, captains and steersmen of those ships that travelled to the Indies.

3. Vigón, Ana M.ª, *Los Colegios de San Telmo*, Documentary guide to the Alvaro de Bazán archives, Madrid, 1985, p. 450.

"Atlas Marítimo Español". Dirección de Hidrografía, 1789.
Archivo Histórico Nacional.

4. Ordenanzas Generales de la Armada (Naval Regulations), 1748.

5. Guillén Tato, Julio. *La Náutica,* in *Estudios sobre la Ciencia.*

6. Cedillo, Pedro Manuel. *Trigonometría aplicada a la navegación,* L. J., Seville, 1718.

7. Cedillo and Sánchez Reciente, both of the Colegio de San Telmo defended the scientific approach, while Moreno y Zabala and García Sevillano continued to champion in their books the values of practical experience.

8. Antonio de Ulloa. *Conversaciones de Ulloa con sus tres hijos* (Conversations between Ulloa and his threes sons) (...), Madrid, 1975, p. 10.

9. Carlier, Blanca. *El Cuerpo de Pilotos de la Armada* (The Corps of naval Steersmen). Revista general de Marina, August-September 1979, p. 169.

10. Lafuente, Antonio; Sellés, Manuel. *La Formación de los pilotos en la España del siglo XVIII* (The Training of Steersmen in the Spain of the XVIIIth Century). In *La Ciencia Moderna y el Nuevo Mundo.* Madrid, 1985, p. 164.

11. Ordenanzas de la Real Armada (Regulations of the Royal Navy), 1748. Heading I, article XXXIX, p. 173.

12. These courses of higher studies at the Observatorio Astronómico in Cádiz produced a group of exceptional scientific mariners, among which the following are worthy of special mention: Alejandro Malaspina, Alcalá Galiano, Ortiz Canelas, J. Vernacci, J. Espinosa y Tello, Felipe Bauzá (steersman) and Cayetano Valdés. This highly select group of officers, all of whom had come from the Escuela de Guardiamarinas in Cádiz (with the exception of the steersman Bauzá), participated during the period 1783-1788 in the production of the *Atlas Marítimo de España* under the guidance of Tofiño de San Miguel, and later played a leading role in the important maritime-scientific undertakings of the latter part of the XVIIIth century.

13. This place name is still used today, and refers to a stretch of water located alongside Prince of Wales Island.

14. *Diario del viaje de Bodega y Quadra* (Log of the journey by Bodega y Quadra). Anuario de la Dirección de Hidrografía, vol. III, p. 298.

15. Beck, Hanno. Alexander Von Humboldt. Mexico, 1791, p. 185.

The Culture of the Indians of the Northwest Coast

by José Alcina Franch

Universidad Complutense, Madrid

Although the search for the Northwest Passage was the constant concern of a great number of Spanish "explorers" and "geographers" in the new World from very early stages, and despite several journeys along the coast of California at equally early dates, it was not until the eighteenth century when the combination of economic, political and scientific interests made the Russians, Spanish and British take an interest in this most irregular coast we know as "The Northwest".

The Landscape

Very rarely has the natural scenery influenced so much the cultural configuration of the human population of a region as in the case of the Northwest. The structure and lie of the land of this coast which, on the other hand is strangely similar to the region of West Patagonia on the Chilean coast, is determined by the pacific Mountain System, which runs parallel to the coast, and by the Rocky Mountains, separated by the Fraser and Yukon Plateaus. This system, extended through the Aleutian islands covers a territory of almost 3000 km. lengthways, and ranges in width from 80 to 400 km. The whole coast is full of fjords, which make it very uneven, while in British Columbia the so-called Coast Mountains and the Island Range are separated by the Coast Depression.

The mountain system is cut across by many rivers, the majority of which rise in the Pacific Mountain System; only the *Alsek, Taku* and *Stikine* rivers which have their source in the plateaus lying between the mountains, cross the Coast Mountains to flow into the Pacific. Finally, the *Copper River*, which rises in a wide flat basin, crosses the *Chugach Mountains* winding along a narrow valley.

As in the Pleistocene period this region was an important focus of glaciation —The *Piedmont*— the landscape was modified by the action of glaciers, many of which still exist. However, the climate of the region, because of the action of the sea —the warm Kuroshio Current— has a temperature the variations of which are only moderate: 16.6º in the southern coast of British Columbia. At the same time, rainfalls are very intense all along the coast and in the northern regions fogs are frequent, these caused by the confluence of very cold masses of water coming from the north and other masses of warmer waters from the south of the Pacific. In any case, the heaviest rainfall occurs in winter, being much lighter in summer. On the coast of British Columbia rainfall ranges from 1500 to 1750 mm., but further north it is heavier: in *Sitka* it is 2200 mm. and 3325 mm. in *Dixon Entrance. Nutchek,* with 4750 mm. has the heaviest rainfall of the region.

The vegetation in the Northwest Coast is determined by the intense humidity of the ocean climate. All along the territory there are extensions of coniferous forests. On the coast and in Vancouver Island there are forests of Douglas fir, which may be 900 to 1200 metres high. Forests of Western red cedar are also quite abundant, while in Queen Charlotte Islands the dominat species is the *Sitka* pine tree and *Hemlock* fir.

The main wealth of the area, both at the present moment and when only the aboriginals lived there is the fauna; not only terrestrial but also marine and fluvial fauna. In the North Coast of British Columbia the *elk* abounds, and in this same region but in the interior the *caribou* lives in large migrating herds. It is frequent to find carnivorous animals like the black bear, lynx, wolf and fox in this region. However, marine fauna has been and still is of a greater economic importance than land fauna: the marine otter or kamchatka beaver, whose area stretches from Beringia to San Francisco Bay was one of the main attractions for Russian traders.

However, fishing is more important than sea hunting, not only along the coast but also in rivers. Salmon fishing is specially important, to the extent that for Indians life was exclusively based on it; this, according to Wissler, constitutes the economic and cultural area of salmon. "Salmon appear during spring on the coast, but large-scale fishing does not start till the end of July and then goes on till October. During these months large numbers of salmon invade the fjords and swim up river to the upper watercourses where, after egg-laying, they meet death" (Schmieder, 1946: 463-64). It is not as yet clear where the enormous banks of salmon which appear along the coast in spring and summer come from, but in any case their abundance is such that, as we shall later see, an entire economic system based on preserving this resource favoured the rise in the region of political systems which only rarely occur in fishing communities.

The Indigenous Groups

Along the coast the environmental characteristics of which we have just described, and in some other limited coast areas further south, in Washington and Oregon States, there settled several Indian groups that as a whole represent one of the most singular and homogeneous cultures of North America. Taking their language into account we can define a series of linguistic stocks which are well differentiated. The *Tlingit* and *Haida* groups —the southernmost of the area— together with the *Atapascos* form the linguistic stock *Na-dené*. The *Tsimshians* together with the *Chinooks* from Washington State belong to the great *Penutian* family. The *Kwakiutls* and *Nootkas* form the *Wakash* group. The remaining groups —*Comox, Cowichan, Klallam, Suuqualmi, Twana, Quileute* and *Quinault*— form the *Salish* group which, together with the Wakash group, constitute the great *Algonquino-Wakash* group (Pericot, 1962: 636-37).

The southernmost ethnos is that of the *Tlingit* Indians, which was made

Study of female head, Mulgrave Sound.
Diario de Tomás de Suria, 1791.
Beinecke Library, Yale University.

122

up of fourteen tribal divisions and is situated between Yakutat Bay and Cape Fox. The *Tagish* group, one of the smallest of the Tlingits offered a cultural pattern absolutely typical of inland rather than coast regions, in agreement with certain traditions which stated that these people came from the hinterland and reached the coast after a long and painful journey.

Further south we find the *Haidas*, who live in the southern part of Prince of Wales Island and Queen Charlote islands. Two main dialects of Haida language are mentioned, those called *Masset* and *Skidegate*. Certain Haida traditions assert that some of their ancestors, those belonging to the phratry of the Eagle, came from the mainland and joined the people who had been living there since the creation of the world.

The *Tsimishian* group lived in the mainland and the adjoining islands. This group was subdivided in three different sub-groups that spoke slightly different dialects. The first sub-group was the *Niska*, who lived near the River Nass; the second, made up of fourteen tribes, lived by the Skeena River and Lower Nass; and lastly the third sub-group, that of the *Gitksans*, lived in eight villages over the Skeena River Canyon.

South of the Tsimshians we find the *Kwakiutl* group, with three dialectal divisions: *Haisla*, near the Douglas and Gardner Channels in the North; *Heiltsuk* and *South Kwakiutl*. The Heiltsuk dialect was spoken by the *Xaihais* and the *Bella Bellas*, a confederation of originally independent tribes. The *Southern Kwakiutls* were made up of a great number of local groups and independent tribes which lived by the bays and islands surrounding Queen Charlotte Estuary and the northern end of Vancouver Island.

Between the two main groups of the Kwakiutl nation there were the *Bella Coolas* near the Dean and Burke Channels and in the lower parts of Bella Coola river. Their language is closely related to the Coast Salish groups, further south.

On the South-West coast of Vancouver Island we find the *Nootkas*, whose language is related to that of the Kwakiutls, forming the stock which linguist call Wakash. Internally, Nootka is divided in three main dialectal groups: Nootka proper and Nitinat and Makah, only slightly different from each other. The Nootka culture is a specialized form of the one that is common to the whole area: for example, they are the only inhabitants of the coast who hunt whales like the Eskimos.

A series of Indian groups of different names —Comox, Cowichan, Klallam, Suuqualmi, Twana, etc.— are known as Coast Salish and live along the coasts of the Strait of Georgia, near the Puget Sound, on a part of the Olympic Peninsula and in most western areas of Washington State.

Further South, on the coasts of Washington and Oregon and even in the North of California there are some Indian groups of lesser importance as the *Alseas, Siuslaws, Umpquas* and *Coos* and the *Tututnis, Tolowas, Yuroks, Karoks* and *Hupas* (Drucker, 1955: 18-19 and fig. 2).

Study of female head, Mulgrave Sound. Diario de Tomás de Suria, 1791. Beinecke Library, Yale University.

Though there are no systematic demographic data for all the Indian groups mentioned, using Swanton's information (1952: 394-95, 436, 543, 548, 573, 577, 588 and 607), for some of these groups we have been able to work out Table 1, where we can observe the process of depopulation, more or less intense in certain cases, as well as periods of recovery, all of which has affected the Indians of the Northwest Coast during the last two hundred years.

Table 1

Years	Tlingit	Tsimshian	Haida	Southern Kwakiutl	Nootka	Bella Coola	Salish	Quileute Hoh	Quinault
1740	10.000								
1780		5.500	9.800	4.500	6.000	1.400	600	500	1.500
1805									1.000
1835	5.850		8.325						
1839	5.455								
1861	8.597								
1884	6.763								
1889/90	4.583		2.500					64	95
b1895			593						
1902			739			311			
1904/06			687	1.257	2.159		557		
1907/09		1.840		2.090			598		196
1910	4.426		530				486	303	
1920/25	3.895		524						719
1930/37	4.462		588					284	1.228

Source: Swanton, 1952: 394-95, 435, 436, 543, 548, 573, 577, 588, 607.

Prehistory

Although the area of the Northwest coast is larger from the ethnographic point of view, as we have just seen, from the archeological approach the souternmost sub-areas provide scarce data. For this reason, we shall consider here, following Ames (1981: 793) only the northermost areas, North of Puget Sound. The *North Coast* includes the coast of British Columbia, North of Johnstone Strait and all the South-West coast of Alaska. The *South Coast* stretches from Johnstone Strait to Puget Sound. This is due to characteristic differences of the environment and to cultural and archeological features (Borden, 1975; Fladmark, 1975). The progress achieved since the 1940's when work on the region was started (Drucker, 1943) up to the present moment allows us to make a brief outline of the cultural evolution in these regions, which is in fact the background of the ethnographic cultures which the Europeans found in the eighteenth century.

The North Coast —less well-known than the South Coast— offers, however, a cultural sequence which can be defined to a certain degree of accuracy from the excavations carried out in Ground Hug Bay, Prince Rupert Harbour, Bluejacket's, Skoglund's Landing, Lawn Point and Namu.

The latter deposit offers a complete sequence, divided in six horizontal or cultural periods. The Namu I phase (7140-4000 B.C.) respresents a culture typically adapted to the sea; the Namu II period (2500-1400 B.C.) seems to look more, as far as patterns of subsistence go, to inland areas; in the next phase, Namu III (2400-800 B.C.) it can be seen that, though it is similar in general terms to the previous one, the bone industry is much more elaborate. The culture of the regions reaches its peak in the Namu IV period (140-1020 A.D.) when seasonal activities can be observed, the bone industry is simplified and there is a drastic increase of the hunting of pelagic mammals. A similar sequence has been discovered in the deposits of prince Rupert Harbor, period I (3000-1500 B.C.) offering a sets of artifacts simpler and smaller than in later periods. Period II (1500 B.C.-500 A.D.) is characterized by an increase in population and means of subsistence. Finally, in period III (500-1830 A.D.) the archeological records practically correspond to the ethnographic culture of the Northwest Coast.

The southern region of the Northwest Coast is comparatively better known than the northern one, and from earlier dates. The earlier occupations would be those of the hunters-gatherers who would cover and exploit a wide range of resources: salmon, shellfish, land mammals and plants. In the excavation of *Five Miles Rapids,* Cressman retrieved some 200.000 fish remains from sediment in deposits dated 9.785 ± 200 A.P. While some authors presume that salmon lost importance after the first intensive exploitation of this resource, others, like Kenneth M. Ames (1981, 796) think that it was continuously used in the last ten thousand years. The tradition we refer to is present on the coast in the *Glenrose* Component III (6200-3700 B.C.). The so-called Glenrose Component II is similar to another series of components which Borden (1975) includes within the Charles phase, of a wide regional distribution. These components dated between 2310 and 1970 in St. Mundo and between 2240 and 1280 in Glenrose.

The subsequent Marpole phase shows the beginning of the cultural pattern of the Northwest Coast in relation to subsistence, art and settlements. This phase is dated between 950/400 B.C. and 450/460 A.D. Still to be resolved is the continuity betwwen the Marpole phase or Locarno Beach phase (800-200 B.C.) and the ethnographic Coast Salish (Ames, 1981: 793-97)..

Ethnography of the Northwest: the Eighteenth Century

The ethnographic knowledge of the Indian population on the Northwest Coast is already history. We owe the first descriptions of those groups to European travellers —Russians, Spanish, French, British and North Americans— in the second half of the eighteenth century, though those descriptions continue during the nineteenth century to become, at the close of that century true ethnographic surveys. The first records not only have an unquestionable historical value but, to a large extent, are elements of doubtless worth because they described those societies under circumstances of obvious purity and lack of contamination in comparison with later culture processes resulting from their contact with Western civilization; at the same time they gathered the first collections of ethnographic items which are the most valuable objects of many museums of the Western world.

This volume includes a minute description of the earliest journeys along that coast, especially of those which took place in the eighteenth century, but we cannot but mention here some of the most important. The first was, undoubtedly, that of Dane V. Bering and Chirikov (1741-42), marking the beginning of Russian advance on the North-American coasts of the Pacific, but it is mainly from 1774 that exploration increases, with the first expeditions of the Spaniards Juan Pérez (1774) and that of Juan Francisco de la Bodega y Quadra, Bruno Hezeta and Francisco A. Mourelle (1975). The next would be those of captains James Cook and George Dixon (1778) and the second expedition of Juan F. de la Bodega, Ignacio Arteaga and F. A. Mourelle (1779); then those of G. Dixon and Captain Portlock (1785), Jean François Gallup, Count of La Pérouse (1786) and Shelikov, Billings and Sarichev (1788-91). The following years brought a great activity undertaken by Spanish sailors: in 1788 the journey of Esteban José Martínez to Nootka; in 1789-90 a new expedition of José Martínez; in 1790 that of Francisco de Eliza, Salvador Fidalgo and Manuel Quimper; in 1790 manuel Quimper and Jacinto Caamaño explore the Strait of Juan de Fuca, Núñez Gaona Bay, Quimper Port and Revillagigedo, Valdés and Bauzá Bay; in 1791 there is an expedition of Francisco Eliza and also in 1791 that coast is reached by the great Pacific expedition of Alejandro Malaspina; the process culminated in 1972-93 with the Comission of Limits led by Bodega y Quadra, which comprises the expeditions of Dionisio Alcalá Galiano and Cayetano Valdés, that of Francisco Eliza and Juan Martínez Zayas and the new expedition of jacinto Caamaño. At the same time there were the expeditions of Vancouver and Alexander Mackenzie (La Sota, 1985; Engstrand, 1981; Siebert-Forman, 1967 and Drucker, 1955).

All these expeditions not only provided detailed facts about the geography of the coast, but valuable ethnographic reports, the analysis of which has not as yet been tackled in a systematic and detailed way (Pino, 1982), in spite of some single instances as the survey of the Tlingit of Yacutat by Frederica de Laguna.

To illustrate the brief summary we offer about the culture of the Indians on the Northwest coast, in the following pages we shall preferably use texts from Spanish expeditions, objects sent to Madrid by the explorers (Vaughan-Crownhart-Palau, 1977; Cabello, 1983) and drawings, washes and watercolours of the artists that went along with the expeditionaries (Palau, 1980; Sotos, 1982) since the part played by the Spaniards in this process of discovery and scientific fact-gathering is, as we have just seen, is decisive in the last quarter of the eighteenth century, and specially in the last two decades.

Languages

The members of the Spanish expeditions to the Northwest Coasts, mainly naturalists, but also some navy officers interested in the study of the "habits" of their inhabitants, gathered a series of vocabularies as the first step towards the knowledge of the various languages and, therefore, as the essential means to get to know their social behaviour and culture. Those vocabularies belong to three regions: Mulgrave Sound or Yacutat (Tlingit), The Strait of Juan de Fuca (Salish?) and Nootka (Nootka Indians). Though the value of these vocabularies in not outstanding, a comparative use of them combined with what we know about the languages of these Indians at later periods can undoubtedly shed light on matters still not clear as far as their origin and relations go (Martin-Meras, 1984).

Though in certain instances the comments of our improvised linguists are picturesque, sometimes they quite approach an accurate phonetic description. That would be the case of Espinosa y Tello who, when referring to the language spoken in Mulgrave Sound by the Tlingits Indians reports that:

> *since there is no equivalente sound in Spanish, we have adapted the English sh and use it for those words which have that sound in the language. The pronunciation of h is much stronger and guttural than our aspirated sound. The k has been included in words where the pronunciation of c is much stronger, since the tongue touches the palate much in the same way as a stammerer does (Novo y Colson, 1885).*

Referring to the Indians of the same zone, Francisco Mourelle made a phonetic description of the language, which is of the utmost interest:

> *The difficult pronunciation of its words has been the great drawback that accounts for our not having been able to write down all the nouns they used in their answers to our questions, because they form the sounds in the throat, with a movement of the tongue against the palate, in such a way that we would need to use a great number of diphthongs; the women hardly use their lips which very rarely come together. However, we gathered that they only count up to ten, and*

then start again, though there was a woman who gave number 20 its own name (Mourelle, 1971: 253).

Sometimes, the remarks of the Spaniards of the eighteenth century go beyond what would be expected of people lacking specializaed training. Espinosa, for example, "keen observer of linguistic realities, noted the difference between the language spoken in Mulgrave and that of Prince William Sound and lamented not having enough time to compare them" (Martin-Meras, 1984: 67).

It is very interesting, in spite of its briefness, a vocabulary of 39 words from the Channel of Fuca, since it clearly established the differences between this language —possibly Coast Salish— and the relatively close Nootka (Martin-Meras, 1984: 68).

However, the region which most attracted the attention of the Spanish expeditionaries was Nootka. The Mexican naturalist José Moziño compiled a vocabulary which included 444 words, or 435 according to other copies kept in the Museo Naval in Madrid; but this same museum also has another vocabulary which is made up of 622 words.

Settlements and Material Culture

The peoples of the Northwest Coast, whose economy, as we shall see below, was based on fishing, mainly salmon, or whale- hunting, set up their villages by bays, coves and creeks or open beaches in the innumerable fjords of this region, over the line of the tali which border the beaches, with the typical totem poles, façades and house doors facing the sea.

From one of the earliest expeditions to the coasts of the Prince of Wales Archipelago, that of Juan Francisco de la Bodega, Ignacio Arteaga and Francisco A. Mourelle (1779) we have the description of a Tlingit o Haida village, by Mourelle:

The houses were built on the top of the hill and as it was not completely flat, they built passageways whose lower parts they raised with logs of wood; on top of them (they looked like false tables) they set up three thick logs on each end, the middle one being taller so that the stand between them provided support because the ones on both sides were shorter. These logs and stands were six yards long and its diameter was a quarter. All the houses had a corridor surrounding the four sides, so that seen from a distance that building was an inaccesible stronghold which we individually acknowledged (Mourelle, 1971: 236).

Winter house without roof at Mulgrave Sound.
José Cardero.
Museo de América.

There could be two types of houses. Those of the Haidas, Tlingits, Tsimshians and Northern Kwakiutls were rectangular, large and with double-sloped roofs. Big poles stuck into the ground were joined on their upper part by thick beams. The door, of oval shape, used to be at the lower part of the totem pole which had a central position in the house front. These houses are usually for more than one family, this accounting for their size, their large or very large dimensions, up to 160 metres in length. There is only one hearth, which has been dug in the central part, with a long bench surrounding it. The house is divided in three sections inside, and they are generally separated by mats or wooden partitions; in each compartment lived nuclear family akin to the other families grouped in one house. In the houses of the Haidas, the façade are decorated with bright colours, and so are the already mentioned totem poles.

Mulgrave Indian chieftain asking the corvettes
for peace. José Cardano.
Museo de América.

The second type of house is that of the South Kwakiutls, Bella Coolas and southern Nootkas. These houses are different from those of the North because of their enlonged ground plans, and single sloping roofs. The earth benches to sleep on run parallel to the axis of the house, near which they placed the different existing hearths.

Something similar happens with the building of vessels, where we find several types according to the region. The Tlingits, Haidas, Tsimshians, Kwa-

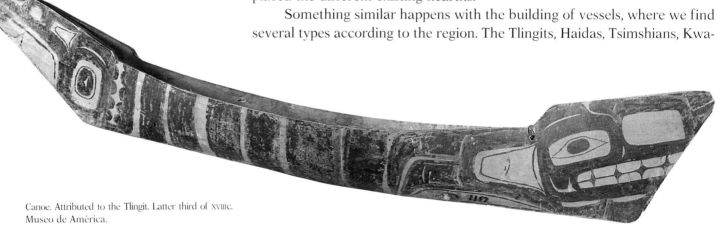

Canoe. Attributed to the Tlingit. Latter third of XVIIIC.
Museo de América.

kiutls and Bella Coolas had canoes with bows and sterns lifted by pointed pieces that were added to the vessel itself. This was made of a trunk of a cedar tree, hollowed out with fire, the gunwales were straightened by inserting crosspieces; both the inside and the outside were smoothed out. Bow and stern were usually decorated with paintings. Some of these canoes were very large —up to 20 m. in length— capable of holding a big cargo, or 50 to 60 men in war-time; in other cases they made smaller canoes but with the same design and proportions.

The first Spaniards navigating along the Northwest Coasts have left abundant and precise descriptions of numerous vessels. Referring to two canoes that Jacinto Caamaño saw in Lángara island, near Queen Charlotte Islands, and so within the region of the Haidas, he says what follows:

> ... the first one to sail in was that of the most important chief of the port (...) accompanied by 45 people including women and children, with eight oarsmen on each side; all were seated or kneeling, except the somoquet (which in their language means captain), who was standing singing one of their songs with the rest... (Caamaño, 1975: 206).

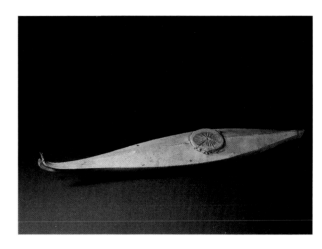

Kayak, used by the Tlingit. Northwest Coast.
Latter third of XVIII c.
Museo de América.

The Nootkas were canoe makers too. In this case the vessel has a totally different outlook, since both bow and stern are at a much lower level, and this makes them very adequate for the sea. They traded these vessels with their neighbours the Salish. When sailing on rivers they used much smaller vessels that were also less elaborate in their design and decoration.

In the northernmost region of the Northwest Coast, in the area of the Mulgrave, Yakutat and Cape Suckling, the Indians normally used their *kayak*. They are either Tlingits of Eskimos; Malaspina refers to them saying that they seemed little or not at all acquainted with the language of Mul-

Dance on the Nootka beach. Tomás de Suria.
Museo Naval.

131

grave Sound" (Malaspina, 1984: 272), which seems to point directly to the Eskimos; however, in his descriptions Mourelle states that the Indians using kayaks are the same as those who wore conical hats similar to the ones Tlingit Indians wore (Mourelle, 1971: 251) and makes a detailed description of a kayak (Mourelle, 1971: 260-61). The description of Ignacio Arteaga is equally precise and of great interest:

> *Their canoes was what caused great admiration in us because of the way they were made. They are small and fit to hold one man only; the deck is vaulted and it the middle there is a big hatch that, once inside, covers the man to the waist, and thus they sail with their paddle at a remarkable speed; they have two bows (...) and we noticed that the deck was covered with decorated leather.*

The industry of spinning, weaving and garment making combining weaving and leatherwork is one of the most important in the area that we are studying. "Its starting point is the manufacturing of blankets and rain cloaks, that the people living on the plateau know how to make out of twisted sage fibres, or leather stripes joined together by a double thread. On the coast, instead of sage they use the inner bark of cedar, sotened, once retted, with a bone tool similar to the Polynesian beater they use to prepare the so-called *tapa*" (Krickeberg, 1946: 78-79).

Francisco Mourelle, referring to Tlingit or Haida Indians makes a good description of this industry in the following paragraph:

Onalaska natives. Hogg, London.
Museo Naval.

... well-woven mats of several colours, furs of wolves and seals, otters, deer, bears and other smaller animals, some well tanned and others just pelts; wool blankets perfectly spun with brown and white patterns, well spinned (though these are scarce), sashes of the same fabric, clean wool which we compared to that of our mattresses (Mourelle, 1971: 253).

Nootka canoe. Malaspina Expedition.
Museo de América.

The main garments of the Indians of the Northwest Coast include the rain cloaks, the capes and a garment similar to a toga, made of two pieces of otter fur tied in a knot on the right shoulder. Their hats, which we will refer to later on have an Asiatic appearance, which is in agreement with other features of their material culture. The *shamans* use aprons and other ornaments or fur garments.

Among the most curious ornaments of these region we find the *labret* used by the women of the Tlingit, Haida and Tsimshian groups. Jacinto Caamaño describes them as follow:

The skin of the women is of the same colour as that of the men, and they are not less heavily-built than them, robust and of well-proportioned features, excepto for the mouth, because when they are born their lower lip is pierced with a wire which is left there and changed as they grow till finally they introduce a small oval piece of wood, the two fronts of which are concave, with a gorge in

133

Indian canoes. Diario de Tomás de Suria, 1791.
Beinecke Library, Yale University.

*its circumference, where the edge of the hole fits: in some of them
who are no longer young this hole becomes so big —due to
exercise— that they have to use bigger and bigger pieces, which
sometimes cover their noses when it is uplifted, and the whole chin
when it is lowered; making them look abominable with this
deformity... (Caamaño, 1975: 199).*

The Economic System

The economic system of the indigenous peoples of the Northwest Coast,
as may be inferred from the ecological conditions we described at the beginning of this study, was clearly focused on the sea —fishing and hunting
of marine animals— in contrast to the scant importance lent to the hunting
of terrestrial animals. The latter was of "little importance because, among
other reasons, a taboo existed prohibiting the simultaneous consumption of
the flesh of terrestrial animals and salmon, the main source of food; this taboo also existed in other regions of North America" (Krickeberg, 1946: 75).

Fishing, whether marine or fluvial, formed the basis of the economic
system of the group of Northwest Indians, especially *salmon* fishing, but also

that of *smelt,* a species of large trout, and *herring.* The schools of salmon that appeared annually along the coast of this area would travel far upstream along the numerous rivers to spawn. They multiplied to such an exent that the indigenous groups were able, or *required,* to preserve salmon for the following years, thereby regulating its use (Drucker, 1955: 37). The fishing of these species, and especially that of salmon, was conducted by means of various procedures: traps, harpoons and fishhoks. The traps —very complex and ingenious— helped to ensure an abundant catch through little effort and were widely used among the Kwakiutl Indians. The Nootka Indians distinguished themselves in the making of harpoons that were often equipped with a double point. Among the wide variety of fishhooks used in the Northwest, those with a V-shape for *hypoglossal* fishing used by the Tsimshians and Northern Kwakiutls are of particular interest (Drucker, 1955: 36-40).

Seafood gathering, a task performed mainly by women, was also an important element in the diet. Women, using digging sticks, would dig for crustaceans in the sand along the coast which were either consumed immediately or preserved by smoking.

In the southern area of the Northwest Coast, and especially among the Nootka, the hunting of sea mammals —the whale above all— had an importance comparable to that among the Eskimos. Many boats of the region were especially designed with this activity in mind. The chief harpooner not only occupied a special position in the boat but also enjoyed a privileged place in society: his job was hereditary, highly respected and carried with it the obligatory observance of various taboos and the performance of religious rites prior to departure on a hunt. "An entire fleet of canoes would attack a whale with harpoons of about 3 meters in length, whose tips, like those of the Eskimos, were loosely attached to the shaft of the harpoon and fixed to a seal skin float. The smaller harpoons, used for hunting dolphins, sea lions and seals, were fashioned with a double-tipped bifurcation at the front and, at the back section, a widened area with finger holes. This design, combining the harpoon with a propelling device, was not used by the Eskimos, who had a seperate tool for each purpose" (Krickeberg, 1946: 76).

Although, as stated above, the hunting of terrestrial animals was always less important than fishing or maritime hunting, it was nonetheless an ongoing activity. The use of deer-hunting traps by the Nootkas is an example of one of the most often used and ingenious practices of this group to increase the content of their diet.

The collection of edible plants rounded out their diet: sea weed, fern roots, kamas or clover, as well as berries and other plants. "While, for the rest, the Indians of the Northwest Coast were not familiar with farming, they nevertheless cultivated tobacco on a small scale. The leaves were crushed in stone mortars and chewed with lime, as the custom of smoking tobacco was unknown prior to the arrival of the first Europeans" (Krickeberg, 1946: 75).

Generally speaking, it can be said that, in addition to being diversified, the diet of the Northwest Coast Indians also offered a wide variety of culinary dishes. At the end of the XIX century, an indian woman reported no less than 150 cooking receipes to an anthropologist, apparently without exhausting her repertoire (Drucker, 1955: 54-55).

Socio-Political organization

Although the bibliography on the Northwest Coast Indians is very abundant (Murdock, 1960: 48-71), the most intensly studied group is the Southern Kwakiutl Indians, especially those living on Vancouver Island whom Franz Boas studied continually from 1886 for a period of fifty years. It should be recalled that at that time the region had already been in contact with Europeans for a hundred years.

Although we are unable here to enter into details regarding the theoretical impact of the study conducted by Boas et al of the Kwakiutl's social structure, and the reaction it provoked subsequent to the 1950's in American academic circles (Harris, 1978: 261-75), we should mention that Boas's position changed over time. At first (Boas, 1897), he maintained that the kinship groups of the Kwakiutl, that he called *clans* or simply *numwym,* were governed by a type of matrilineal relationship; he later stated that they had previously been governed by a patrilineal relationship. A transition had thus occured from patrilineal to matrilineal relationships. Around 1920, Boas's opinion underwent a further change when he affirmed that the *numaym* relationships were based on filiation with a preference of the paternal line.

"On the basis of this single, extremely insufficient example, the idea was gradually disseminated from Schermerhorn Hall in Columbia University like unquestionable dogma in lectures, conversations, articles and texts, that Boas had proven that it was just as likely that a patrilineal system had succeeded a matrilineal one as vice versa" (Harris, 1978: 264). This inverted evolutionist bilateral-patrilineal-matrilineal succession schema became a true *dogma* in American Anthropology. A review of the subject in the 1960's brought about an active analysis of the problem, revealing that in fact it was a bilateral filiation system in which individuals could join with the chief most able to offer security and sustenance.

Within the social system that we touched on in preceding paragraphs, the system of ownership of specific fishing grounds and land for the gathering of berries and roots should be situated in the same manner as the ownership of emblems symbolizing exogamous groups —ravens, eagles, wolves, beavers, etc. These "heraldic animals", whose most typical and popular representations are found on the well-known totem poles, could be installed on their property and had no true totemic value, because there was no taboo as to the species represented by the heraldic animal, nor did it denote any type of veneration or cult.

A very peculiar characteristic of the Northwest Coast Indians is that, as members of the gathering-fishing economic system, with hunting as a supplement, they were organized in a manner similar to a true "chieftain-ship" with a marked hierarchy of "ranks". In addition, being a society mainly based on kinship and therefore on the model of reciprocity, redistribution practices were applied. Testar (1982) explained this local situation, comparable to other cases around the world, as a particular form of evolution from a society of bands to one of a "chieftainship", concentrating its efforts on the preservation and accumulation of food, whether from agriculture, fishing or intensive gathering, as in the case of the Northwest Coast Indians.

Many characteristics of a "chieftainship" were apparent in these societies, where distinctions were made between a class of chiefs and nobles and a class of common people and slaves. The latter, who were normally not mistreated, and to the extent that they were the property of their owner, ran the risk of being sacrificied in one or another of the celebrations held to reaffirm or augment his prestige. These celebrations could take the form of a true potlatch, the founding of a house or the celebration of a secret society, or other reasons. In order to obtain slaves, the Northwest Indians would wage frequent and bloody wars, implying a certain level of proficiency in the field. Members of the first Spanish expeditions recorded excellent descriptions of their armor and breastplates. Caamaño wrote the following:

Armed Indian during War of Mulgrave Sound.
Diario de Tomás de Suria, 1791.
Beinecke Library, Yale University.

> To protect the body, they wore a breastplate and back plate that reached below the groin and over the shoulders, made of very round and smooth sticks as thick as a finger; they served as a woof for a series of cords that, forming the warp, constituted a fabric that is easily fitted and prevented damage by arms and even by a bullet at a moderate distance. The thighs were similarly protected and the entire armor was covered by a thick leather jacket as wide as a shirt; I know that they wore wooden helmets on their heads, although I have never seen them (Caamaño, 1975: 200).

Francisco Mourelle wrote a somewhat more precise description of offensive and defensive weapons:

> ...breastplate and back plate of the same width as the corsets used by the women of Europe, made of narrow slabs and woven together ty many cords, giving them a certain flexibility permitting a tight fit, but leaving the arms free for the handling of weapons. On the neck they wore a thick, wide gorget that usually covered the face up to the eye level and a helmet on the head usually in the shape of a ferocious

137

animal. From the waist down they wore an apron, also engraved, and on the back reaching to the ankles a beautiful leather jacket worn as a cape as a protection against arrows.

The offensive weapons they generally used were the bow and arrow, made with the same care as our best musical instruments, an 11-foot long lance with an iron barb, knives of the same material as long as our bayonets (...) and hatchets made of flint and another greencolored stone that is so hard it can cut wood without any chipping of the cutting edge (Mourelle, 1971: 252-53).

One of the long standing focal points of greatest interest in the socio-political system of the Northwest Coast Indians is the ceremony known by the name of *potlatch*, a Chinook term with variations that is known in the entire region. In the opinion of Boas *et al*, the *potlatch* was one of their most interesting characteristics, so much so that descriptions and interpretations of the potlatch have been disseminated and popularized by various intellectual media. According to Boas *et al*, the *potlatch* was an institution by which a chief confronted his rival in order to entrance his prestige. "There were two ways in which a chief could achieve the victory he sought. One was by confronting his rival, giving him more property than he could return with the requiered interest. The other was by the destruction of property. In both cases the offering compelled a response, although in the first case the wealth of the donor is augmented and in the second he is stripped of his belongings" (Benedict, 1971: 210).

For Ruth Benedict, the *potlatch* was a more effective and dramatic means of demonstrating the superiority of a *chief* over his rivals. This expression of inordinate self-glorification reached levels of megalomania as may be observed in some of the chants sung by the followers of a chief on such an occassion:

Detail of the proclamation of Princess
Ystocoti-Tlemoc. J. Guerrero.
Diario de Bodega y Quadra, 1792.
Ministerio de Asuntos Exteriores.

**"I am the great chief who puts the people to shame
I am the great chief who puts the people to shame
Our chief brings shame to the faces
Our chief brings envy to the faces
Our chief causes the people to hide their faces
He is continually performing his deeds in this world.
Holding repeated feasts of oil for all the tribes
I am the only great tree, me the chief!
I am the only great tree, me the chief!"**

(Benedict, 1971: 198)

This approach led Ruth Benedict to qualify the Kwakiutl culture as *dionysian*. In 1950, however, Helen Codera, analyzing the *potlatch* from a historical point of view, emphasized that these celebrations, in the era prior to the expansion of North America and thus prior to the downfall of the indigenous population around 1860, had not taken on the characteristics as analyzed by Boas and Benedict, namely, the decomposition of the Indian society, the fall in its numbers, the integration of the Indian economy into the American system. All this led to the formulation of the institution in the terms described by Boas and Benedict.

Tomb of the previous ankau of Mulgrave Sound.
José Cardero.
Museo Naval.

Finally, in the beginning of the 60's, Andrew Vayda and Wayne Suttles approached the *potlatch* from an ecological viewpoint "as a functional response to the problem of minimizing the effects that the seasonal and long term fluctuations had on the productivity of local groups. This was achieved by accumulating, on a relatively frequent basis, all the economic surpluses of a *numaym* under the auspices of their chief and redistributing them, also under the auspices of the chief, to the numaym that (...) were worst off" (Harris, 1978: 271). Consequently, the accumulation of wealth and its redistribution might allow or give rise to the development of a social stratification and the birth of a stable power concentrated in the *chief.*

This explains the fact that the first Spanish visitors regarded these societies as true *chieftainships,* an aspect noted with particular attention by one such visitor, Alejandro Malaspina, who stated, in reference to the Nootka:

> *...the number of inhabitants that lived in the area and constituted, so to speak, the society subordinate to Macuina, was approximately 4000, mainly subsisting on scarce fishing resources and alternating their abodes in accordance to this need, in the summer toward the seashore and in the winter toward the inland canals (Malaspina, 1984: 313)*

The System of Beliefs

The system of beliefs of the peoples of the Northwest Coast should be placed in a category below that in which Religion is normally classified: "absence of a systemized set of beliefs regarding creation, cosmology and the deities; a rather vague notion of an altruistic Supreme Being or Beings; a set of beliefs surrounding the immortality of certain economically important animal species, combined with a series of rituals designed to ensure the return of the creatures; and, finally, the concept of the possibility of a lifetime assistance from a personal, overseeing spirit" (Drucker, 1955: 153).
The performers of these propitiatory rites were the shamans or sorcerers who occupied a privileged place within the society but whose behavior was similar to that of the great "chiefs", as the confirmation of their privileges depended on their effectiveness as shamans, especially in cases concerning the curing of sicknesses.

In connection with *shamanism,* one should mention the secret societies of a sacred or secular nature. membership to these societies was hereditary, but at adolescence, each individual was requiered to personally acquire such a privilege by withdrawing to a nearby forest where he was "possessed" by one of the spirits of the secret society. Each participant of the celebrations, and especially of the dances held by these societies represented

Silvia la grabó.

TETACÚ,
Xefe de la entrada del Estrecho de Juan de Fuca.

Tetaku. Atlas from the schooners *Sutil* and *Mexicana,* 1802.
Biblioteca Nacional.

his spirit, wearing a number of masks, headdresses, helmets, etc., that we
will mention later. "All these traits clearly indicate that such a system of secret societies among the Kwakiutl and their neighbors was merely a system
of organized shamanism" (Krickeberg, 1946: 86).

During their performances, the shamans, besides using a number of
"tricks", wore masks of their guardian spirit and carried a wooden rattle in
the hand that represented the mythical raven, prior to performing the ap-
propriate acts designed to restore health to the patient.

Art

The artistic style of the Indians of the Northwest Coast was very distinctive and contrasted with that of other North American Indian groups. Their style did not extend to the entire region mentioned above, but rather to the area between Yakutat Bay and the Fuca Straits.

The characteristics of the Indian art found in the area are somewhat homogenous, distinguishing it from the art of other groups. Despite this stylistic homogeneity, significant regional differences may nonetheless be observed when an in depth analysis is conducted. Some authors state "that the most perfected expression of this art is that of the Northern group, especially that of the Tlingit and Tsimshian tribes and, to a lesser degree, the Haida" (Siebert-Forman, 1967: 38). In any event, one should consider Feder's proposal (1971: 280-81) of subdividing the area into three regions: north, center and south.

The northern area includes the territories of the Tlingit, Tsimshian and Haida tribes; although there are differences among them, they are quite closely related. The Tlingit and Tsimshian performed a refined, naturalistic and subtle art in which the fabric made by the women of the Chilkat branch of the Tlingit, as well as the totem poles of the Tsimshian, are among the most beautiful of the entire northwest Coast. The Haida, for their part, produced a more conservative and sacred art 'especially evident in the cedar wood monumental sculptures and in the very distinctive shale sculpture and relief work (Covarrubias, 1954: 168).

The central area of this Northwest artistic style includes the Kwakiutl and Bella Coola Indians whose sculpture was, broadly speaking, less refined than that of the Northern area. It is mainly noteworthy for the dramatic expression evident in its masks that were often characterized by eyes made of cylinders projecting outward. These striking masks are directly related to the extensive development of secret societies and the elaborate rituals performed during their celebrations, etc. (Feder, 1971: 281).

In the southern portion of the Northwest Coast, where the Nootka, Coastal Salish and Lower Chinook lived, sculpture appears to have undergone an autochthonous development, but with marked influences from areas further northward. The style of this region, especially that of the Nootka, is simpler and more mechanical with very limited sculptural activities (Covarrubias, 1954: 169).

While the art, and above all the sculpture, of the Indians of the Northwest Coast were made known through "historic" ethnographic studies subsequent to contact with the Europeans (after 1774-93), their "pre-historic" roots in phase III of Prince Rupert Harbor (500-1830 a.d.) were not pinned down until very recently. Consequently, some authors feel that this art "appears very recent, depending on the introduction of iron for its complete ve-

Detail of the funeral pyre and tomb of the family of the present ankau. Fernando Brambila. Museo Naval.

Helmet. Attributed to the Tlingit. Latter third of xviiic. Museo de América.

lopment" (Holm, 1965: 3). Other authors, however (Adam, 1936; Barbeau, 1950), focused their work on the striking similarities to Asia and primitive Chinese art, in contrast to the few traits in common with other North American Indian cultures. Covarrubias (1954: 189-90) mentions no less than nine aspects in common between the two regions and other authors (Heyerdahl, 1952) have used this type of comparison to suggest possible transpacific contacts. The theory that art as we know it may have had an extensive local history and development has been raised by Gunther (1962: 40) and Duff (1956: 104-10; 1964: 84-94; Holm, 1965: 3).

Feder (1971: 279) stated that "it is perfectly demonstrable that the artistic style of the Northwest Coast enjoyed a flourishing tradition before the arrival of the Europeans", however, with their arrival and the introduction of iron instruments, production was intensified of objetcts that are today considered artistic and that fill the storerooms of the most important American museums —The Field Museum of Chicago, The American Museum of Natural History of New York, The National Museum of Man of Ottawa and the provincial Museum of Victoria. The introduction of tools stimulated the *potlatch* system, causing a greater production of totem poles, masks, fabrics, boxes and instruments for use by shamans (Feder, 1971: 16). This boom in production may have reached its height in 1910, after which the breakdown in community relations was accelerated to the extent that it may be said today that this art is practically dead (Inverarity, 1950: 40).

The causes behind such a high production of objects with artistic value, as indicated above, may no doubt be found in the aristocratic desire to be ostentatious and competitive, characterized by the *potlatch* and reaching extreme proportions (Covarrubias, 1954: 167).

Franz Boas, to whom we owe one of the first and best analyses of Northwest Coast art, identifies two styles: "man's style expressed in the art of carved wood and in painting and related activities; and that of women as observed in fabric, basketry and embroidery. The two styles are fundamentally different. The first is symbolic, the second, formal. Symbolic art possesses a certain degree of realism and is full of meaning. Formal art has, at most, a number of patterns but lacks meaning of any importance" (Boas, 1947: 181).

In the opinion of George C. Vaillant (1939: 43-44) Northwest art is identified by two social conditions: the distinction of rank —chiefs, nobles, common people and slaves— on the one hand, and, on the other, the "religious conception of a totemic spirit or guardian that protects the members of the clan". However, the conventional aspect of art equally effects religious and secular art, although the first offers a dynamism and dramatization that contrasts with the placidity and serenity of the examples of secular art (Jonaitis, 1983: 129). The conventionalized and completely formal rules of design may be considered analogous to the equally conventionalized and formal rules os social conduct that governed interaction among the chiefs. The passive and restricted quality of many works of secular art is similar to the dignified and self-controled behavior particular to the elite" (Jonaitis, 1983: 131).

Robert B. Inverarity (1950: 42-43) defined Indian art of the Northwest Coast as "exact, intellectualized and symbolic (...) symmetrical and curvilinear". Wood was the principal medium through which this artistic style found its expression. This was true to such an extent that when other materials, such as stone, bone, metal, etc., were used, they were treated as though they were wood. In addition, color was applied to these materials.

144

The main colors were red, black, yellow and blue-green, without any type of symbolization having been observed in their use. The chief forms were round, oblong, circular, curvilinear, etc., but these forms were always organized taking into account the workmanship of the object to be decorated or sculptured (Inverarity, 1950: 43).

Franz Boas (1947: 199-200) summarized in a list the characters and designs used to symbolically represent the numerous animals that made up their real and magic world. Some of their body parts are emphasized, while others are left unused:

"1.　The **beaver:** large incisors; a large and round nose; a scaly tail and a stick held in the front paws.

2.　The　**hogfish:** two points rising above the mouth and a continual dorsal fin.

3.　The **sparrow hawk:** large, curved beak, whose point is turned back so that it touches the face.

4.　The **eagle:** a large and curved beak whose point is turned down.

5.　The **killer whale:** large, long head; large and elongated nostrils; round eye; large mouth with teeth; large blowhole and a large dorsal fin.

6.　The **shark** or **dogfish:** an elongated and round cone rising from the forehead; mouth with depressed angles; a series of curved lines on the cheeks, representing gills; two circles and curved lines on the decoration rising over the forehead, representing the nostrils and wrinkles; round eyes; numerous filed teeth and a heterocercal tail.

7.　The **bear:** large paws, a large mouth with teeth; projecting tongue; large, round nose, sharply turned up from the snout to the forehead.

8.　The **sea monster:** the head of a bear; claws of a bear with added natatorial membranes, gills and the body of a filler whale with several dorsal fins and other combinations of bear and killer whale.

9.　The **dragonfly:** large head, thin and segmented body and wings.

10.　The **frog:** wide mouth without teeth; flat nose, no tail.

11.　The **budding horn of a stag** personied: similar to a bear with the mouth depressed in the corners like that of the dogfish.

12.　The **snail:** long snout with a sharp downward turn."

As stated above, the raw material most widely used by the Nortwest Coast Indians was wood. They mainly used *red cedar* for the building of houses, totem poles, canoes, boxes, masks and other ceremonial equipment and for innumerable, smaller objects" (Harnoncourt, 1941: 162).

They also used yellow cedar, Sitka fir, yew, alder, maple and American fir (Siebert-Forman, 1967: 35).

While wood was the main medium in artistic work in the Northwest, paint was used "to emphasize details and underscore the artistic effect" (Sie-

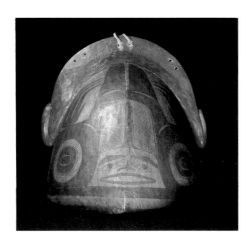

Helmet with copperwork. Attributed to the
Tlingit. Latter third of XVIII c.
Museo de América.

Nootka mask. Latter third of XVIII c.
Museo de América.

Mask, with silver and copperwork. Northwest
Coast. Latter third of XVIII c.
Museo de América.

bert-Forman, 1967: 36). paints, mainly of a vegetable origin, were crushed and mixed with salmon eggs to form a smooth paste.

Among the Tlingit and Tsimshian, soft and moderate tones were preferred, the stronger tones being reserved for the decorating of masks and helmets with representations of evil spirits and supernatural beings. The Kwakiutl, on the contrary, were more given over to the use of brillant colors. When industrial paints became available, they developed a very particular style, highlighting the colors' pure and violent foce.

It is well known that the so-called "art" of the Northwest Coast indians

Helmet. Northwest Coast. Latter third of XVIII c.
Museo de América.

is present in any type of object, utilitarian or other. Among those of a nonu-tilitarian nature we should mention the totem poles, masks, helmets, neck rings, dance headgear, rattles, shaman amulets, etc.

The most ostentatious of the Northwest art are the *totem poles* and the paintings that decorate the façades of Indian houses, known and remembered by all. There are several types of totem poles: those that possibly represent the oldest or most traditional form are the ones that are considered tombs or graves of ancestors. Within this category there are two varieties: those with two columns and a large coffin for two persons and those with a sort of vertical coffin. Some authors suppose that these types of totem poles with obvious funeral characteristics evolved into the tall and thin type of pole, sculptured with genealogical and legendary motifs, and into those that are the central pole of the Haida houses, in the old style with an oval orifice that serves as a door (Covarrubias, 1954: 181). In modern times, with a view to exports and sales to visitors, Indians fashion small scale models of totem poles in ivory, bone or shale.

Among the most notable work by the Northwest Coast Indians from the artistic viewpoint, are above all the *Masks*. Masks were made for three specific ocassions: for representing high-level ancestors and chiefs; for presenting dances of a mythical nature; and for shaman-related activities (King, 1975: 5). "As regards those masks in the shape of animal heads, animals with human heads or, as was the custom, of fantastic beings, all the coastal tribes made them. The difference consisted in the details of style" (Siebert-Forman, 1967: 38). The uniqueness and brilliance of this type of object explains the fact that they are among the most abundantly represented in museum collections and, consequently, in art books (Holm, 1983: Cat. Num.: 28-47; Inventary, 1950: Cat. Num.: 59-79 and 87-96; Newton-Boltin, 1978: 70; Siebert-Forman, 1967; Cat. Num.: 1-15 and 22-27). Some of these pieces were collected in the XVIII century, such as the one from Yakutat Bay, Alaska, and included in the collection of the Museo de América in Madrid and supposedly collected by Alejandro Malaspina in 1791, although some of its details —eyes and the application of a pelt for the moustache— suggest it originated further south, perhaps in the Nootka area (King, 1979: 48, fig. 42).

In addition to painting, very important in the making of masks, which, along with headgear, were "decorated with *haliotis* shell incrustations and other decorations made of pelts, human hair, sea lion whiskers and feathers" (Siebert-Forman, 1967: 40).

Besides the masks, but within the same class of objects as the shaman paraphernalia, one should note the *headpieces* and *helmets,* used at times with masks (Inverarity, 1950: Cat. Num. 96-99; Siebert-Forman, 1967: Cat. Num. 37-51), the *frontlets* (Siebert-Forman, 1967: Cat. Num. 16-21), the *neck rings* (Siebert-Forman, 1967: Cat. Num. 52-53) and, above all, the *dance headgear* (Holm, 1983: Cat. Num. 1-11; Inverarity, 1950: Cat. Num. 81-86; Newton-

Mask. Attributed to the Tlingit. Latter third of XVIIIc. Museo de América.

Boltin, 1978: 211; Siebert-Forman, 1967: Cat. Num. 28-36). The ritual nature of all these objects, or their relation with rituals, necessarily implies that one must be familiar with the many legendary and mythological accounts of these peoples, where mythical or spiritual figures abound, such as *"Tsono-qua"*, the Wild Woman of the Woods, *Neugase,* the Bear Woman, or animal spirits, such as *Wasco,* the sea monster in the form of a wolf, and *Sisiutl,* the two-headed serpent" (Covarrubias, 1954: 169).

Rattle. Attributed to the Tlingit. Latter third of XVIIIc. Museo de América.

The long-standing special interest shown by Lévi-Strauss in masks of the Northwest Coast Indians brought about structuralist methodology-type analyses of this kind of artistic creation, as if it were truly a matter of myths (Lévi-Strauss, 1968: 221 & following and 1981).

The so-called *"rattles"* or "raven rattles", another fundamental utensil in the shaman dances of these peoples in which the figure of the *raven* (ancestor of a phratry of the Tlingit Indians and hero of innumerable myths) or other birds or animals were represented in very fine carvings and are equally interesting (Holm, 1983: Cat. Num. 12-26; Inverarity, 1950: Cat. Num. 109-113, 115, 117-26; Siebert-Forman, 1967: Cat. Num. 54-60).

Rattle in the shape of a bird. Nootka. Latter third of XVIII c. Museo de América.

Ivory and bone work, a longtime tradition among the Eskimos, was also an important contribution to the art of the Northwest peoples. They made objects from the tusks of the walrus and the long teeth of the bear (for the shamans' amulets) or from the horns of goats or mountain sheep, all to adorn small plates, spoons and larger spoons. They would carve the latter in designs so complicated that at times they would appear more like small totem poles" (Siebert-Forman, 1967: Cat. Num. 82-86; Inverarity, 1950: Cat. Num. 160-68).

Among the most widely known and valued objects are the famous blankets or capes. They were made of mountain goat hair with vegetable fibers. The *chilkat* capes, created by a tribe of that name of the Tlingit group, are especially valued. These capes are "made of white wool, with motifs in black, yellow and blue-green. The extraordinary beauty of these blankets is explained by the symbolic and stylized ornaments mentioned above, namely, the characteristic decoration of artistic objects fashioned by men. Men drew the figures in wood and the women in charge of weaving would copy the designs" (Siebert-Forman, 1967: 43; Harnoncourt, 1941: 163, fig. 77; Holm, 1983: Cat. Num. 81-88; Siebert-Forman, 1967: Cat. Num. 93-95).

Female activities extended to the making of basketry articles. Hat-making was an especially noteworthy part of this activity by the Haida and Nootka Indians.

Some old hat shapes of the Nootka, of which splendid examples have been conserved in the collection of the Museo de América in Madrid, were no doubt brought by the Malaspina expedition (Feder, 1971: illustration 186). Hats, headgear, and baskets with other decorative designs and different shapes are included in most collections (Holm, 1983: Cat. Num. 48-80; Siebert-Forman, 1967: Cat. Num. 89-92).

Three basketry hat styles have been identified: the Kwakiutl Indian type, consisting of a shortened and inverted cone, profusely decorated with paint; the type used by the Nootka is also conical in shape, but the upper section is crowned with a type of dome ending in a point; finally, the hats of the Haida have an inverted basket shape. Mourelle, referring to these hats, wrote:

On their heads they wear well-woven hats of pieces of tree bark,
whose shape is the same as the wide part of a funnel (Mourelle, 1971: 251).

In the economic system described above the accumulation of goods —cloth and other possessions— had a great deal of importance. The Indians of the Northwest Coast, in order to accumulate and preserve these goods, would build heavily decorated and beautiful chests and boxes of wood (Harnoncourt, 1941: 178; Holm, 1983: Cat. Num. 98-111; Inverarity, 1950: Cat.

Bird bone. Brought back from Nootka by Juan Pérez in 1774.
Museo de América.

Hat. Attributed to the Tlingit. Latter third of XVIII c.
Museo de América.

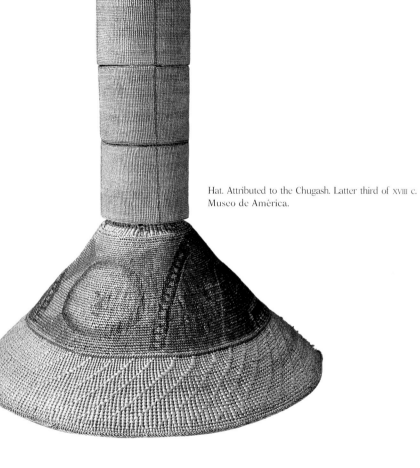

Hat. Attributed to the Chugash. Latter third of XVIII c.
Museo de América.

Chief's hat. José Cardero.
Museo de América.

Hat. Nootka. Latter third of XVIII c.
Museo de América.

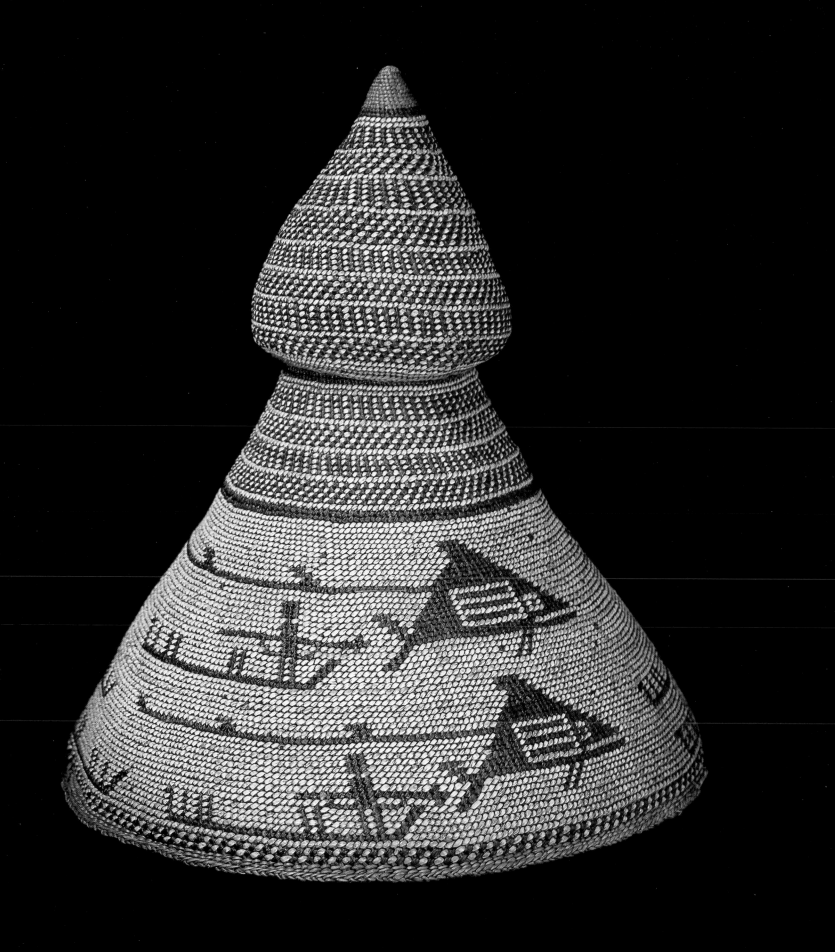

Num. 19-25; Siebert-Forman, 1967: Cat. Num. 61-67). Mourelle also referred to these boxes and trays in the following paragraph:

> *... rather pretty wooden trays, small canoes painted in several colors nearly always including in its motifs heads with all their parts. Frogs of wood, perfectly copied, that open in the same way as powder boxes, concave on the inside; they used them to store their small belongings; plank boxes measuring 24 cubic inches, heavily decorated with designs on the outside representing various animals, the tops of which were made in the same way as the tops of Flemish bottle cases with their edge and overhanging fitting over the body of the case (Mourelle, 1971: 253-54).*

A very unusual style found only among the Haida Indians is shale sculpture. This material, an exquisite carboniferous material, intense black in color is called *argillite*. It is found only on the Queen Charlotte Islands and has been used to make numerous objects such as boxes, totem pole models, very elaborate pipes, models of canoes, human figures, etc.

This style, that flourished in the middle of the XIX century, was at first oriented toward export and for sale to Europeans (Covarrubias, 1954: 183 and Siebert-Forman, 1967: 41). While some examples indicate Russian influence, most known objects are assigned to the second half of the XIXcentury (Holm, 1983: Cat. Num. 170-88; inverarity, 1950: Cat. Num. 169-73 and 191-95; Siebert-Forman, 1967: Cat. Num. 79).

The silverwork of the Tlingit and Haida Indians underwent a similar process. After being introduced in 1774 by the Spaniards of the Pérez expe-

Box containing the Nootka chief. José Cardero. Museo Naval.

Wooden plank found in the Channel. Atlas de las goletas *Sutil* y *Mexicana*, 1802. Biblioteca Nacional.

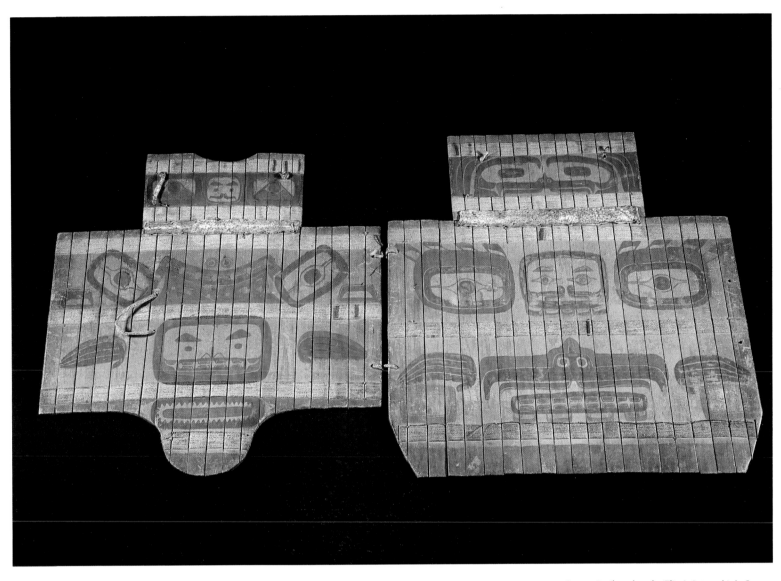

dition, at first it was not appreciated by the Indians who held copper and iron in higher esteem, but later on silverwork became a widespread craft (Harris, 1983: 132; Holm, 1983: Cat. Num. 207-16; inverarity, 1950: Cat. Num. 155-56 and 159).

Although stone, in contrast to wood, is not abundantly present in art collections of the Northwest Coast, it was nevertheless put to use (Inverarity, 1950: Cat. Num. 40-54). Several objects brought back by Captain Cook in 1778 and preserved in the British Museum bear witness to its use at that time (Covarrubias, 1954: 183). "The sculptures most invariably represent men, animals, birds or fish. Their favorites were the Bear, the Wolf, the Beaver, Cetaceans, the Raven, the Eagle and the Hawk. Nonetheless, fish and insects, such as mosquitos, can be found among the carvings" (Siebert-Forman, 1967: 38; Wingert, 1949).

The collections of objects and instruments of Northwest Coast Indians include a multitude of artefacts of scant artistic value, but of great utility, such as hachets, hammers, hoes, polishers, crushers, scrapers, projectile tips, fishnet wieghts, mace, perforated disks, earrings, etc. (Stewart, 1973) and beautifully decorated *spoons* (Holm, 1983: Cat. Num. 134-48; Inverarity, 1950: Cat. Num. 127-31; Siebert-Forman, 1967; Cat. Num. 87); *harpoons* (Holm, 1983: Cat. Num. 149-51; Siebert-Forman, 1967; Cat. Num. 72-730); *canoe models* (Holm, 1983: Cat. Num. 154-59); numerous examples of the so-called *"coppers"* (Holm, 1983: Cat. Num. 162; Inverarity, 1950: Cat. Num. 151, 153-54); *clubs* (Holm, 1983: Cat. Num. 166-69; Siebert-Forman, 1967: Cat. Num. 100 and 102); *war shirts* and shaman aprons (Siebert-Forman, 1967: Cat. Num. 96-99 and 103-04) or *weapons shields* (Siebert-Forman, 1967: Cat. Num. 101).

The extensive list included in the preceding paragraphs is one of the most important contributions to the world's cultural and ethnographic heritage, a work of one of the most unusual, and at the same time most creative, indigenous groups that has ever existed on the face of the earth.

Wodden bust. Attributed to the Chugash.
Latter third of XVIII c.
Museo de América.

Hatchet. Northwest Coast. Latter third of XVIII c.
Museo de América.

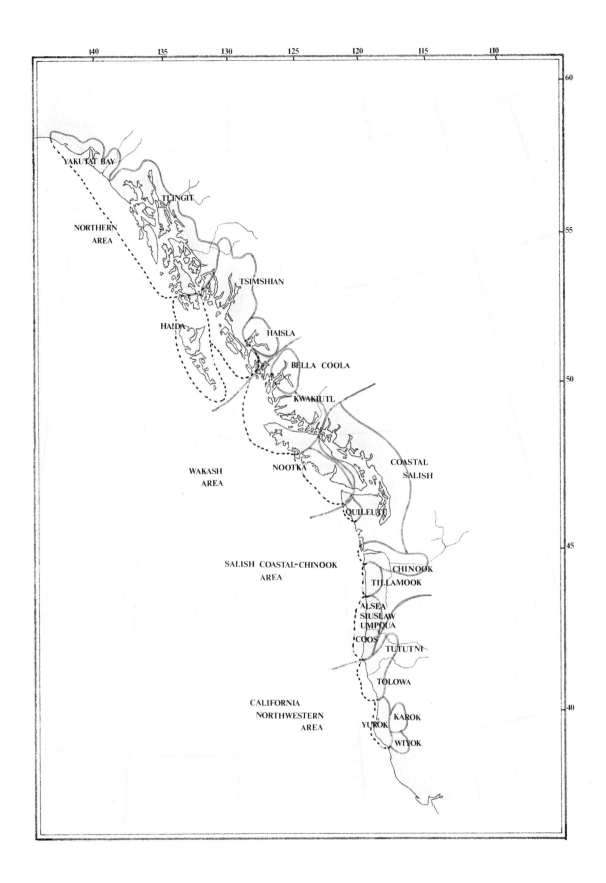

YAKUTAT BAY

TLINGIT

NORTHERN
AREA

TSIMSHIAN

HAIDA

HAISLA

BELLA COOLA

KWAKIUTL

WAKASH
AREA

NOOTKA

COASTAL
SALISH

QUILEUTE

SALISH COASTAL-CHINOOK
AREA

CHINOOK

TILLAMOOK

ALSEA
SIUSLAW
UMPQUA
COOS

TUTUTNI

TOLOWA

CALIFORNIA
NORTHWESTERN
AREA

KAROK
YUROK
WIYOK

Faces in the Forest :
Moziño's Noticias de Nutka

by Frederic V. Grunfeld, F.R.G.S.

Nootka Sound, on the west coast of Vancouver Island, was first visited by Europeans in 1774, when the Mexican-based Spanish frigate *Santiago* anchored offshore and was greeted by a party of canoes bearing nearly 150 astonished Indians. "At first the sight of this ship filled the natives with terror", writes the botanist José Mariano Moziño, who lived among the Nootkans in 1792 and heard the story from the Indians themselves. "They were seized with fright as soon as they saw the huge machine appear on the horizon and approach their coast little by little. They thought that Qua-utz [the Creator] was coming to pay them a second visit." Only the most intrepid Nootkans actually paddled out to examine this ocean-borne monster; to their great relief they soon realized that the visitors were men, not gods, and "with great admiration they examined all the new and extraordinary objects to be seen on the ship". The Spanish captain, Juan Pérez, distributed a number of gifts, and in return received some sea otter skins, but did not attempt to explore the region.

That task was undertaken four years later by Captain Cook, who entered the Sound and anchored in the harbor still known today by the name he gave it Friendly Cove. He also perpetuated a misunderstanding by calling ing the nearby Indian village Nootka[1], under the mistaken impression that this was the Indians' own name for it— though in fact, as Moziño later pointed out, "what Cook called Nootka had always been called Yuquatl by the islanders". The inhabitants of Yuquatl —henceforth to be known to the world as Nootkans— were, in fact, Indians of Wakashan stock (as modern anthropologists call them), and members of the Moachat confederacy —the name means "People of the Deer". It was the crew of Cook's *Resolution* and *Discovery* who later made the electrifying discovery that the soft, lustrous pelts of the sea otter which they had traded against trinkets and bits of hardware could be sold in Canton for a hundred dollars apiece. As a result, Nootka suddenly became a potential El Dorado and acquired a political and commercial importance out of all proposition to the size of its population, which numbered about 2,000.

Both Britain and Spain had reason to consider Nootka part of their American empire, and a violent confrontation over the issue was only narrowly averted by intense diplomatic negotiations that took place in Madrid. The agreement between His Catholic Majesty (Carlos IV) and His Britannic Majesty (George III) signed at the Escorial on October 28, 1790, stipulated that subjects of either crown were free to fish, trade or settle in those parts of the northern Pacific coast which were not already occupied.

Meanwhile, in 1789, the colonial government of New Spain had established an outpost at Nootka and began the extensive effort of mapping and exploring the region. The most notable of the scientists sent from Mexico to make observations at Nootka was the naturalist Moziño, who spent more than four months at Friendly Cove classifying the local plants and animals in accordance with the Linnean system[2]. At the same time he learned the Indians language and took extensive notes on what he had seen and heard of their way of life —"it became easy for me to learn some of the customs of the natives: I believe I was the first to obtain certain information about their religion and system of government, having learned their language well enough to converse with them". He was indeed the first outsider to study the Indians of the Pacific Northwest in any depth, and thus ranks as the first "foreign correspondent" to report on one of the most remarkable civilizations on the face of the earth.

An eighteenth-century Rationalist might have described Moziño's experience as a symbolic encounter between "the noble savage" and a man of modern science whose very mission as a writer and classifier was characteristic of the sophisticated script culture of Europe. The Nootkans and their neighbors were in fact almost unknown to the outside world and still living in what Jean-Jacques Rousseau would have called the "state of nature". According to Rousseau and the philosophers of the Enlightenment, the "friendly and flowing savage" was, most definitely, a paragon of the natural virtues —a healthy, happy and sovereign creature, much as the poet John Dryden had painted him a century earlie:

> I am as free as nature first made man,
> Ere the base laws of servitude began,
> When wild in woods the noble savage ran.

What Moziño could not know, and what has been established only recently thanks to archeological excavations, is that the society on which he had come to report was as ancient and in many ways as sophisticated as his own. A buried "Nootka" village at Cape Alava, south of Cape Flattery, which was inundated by a mudslide some four hundred years ago, had evidently been inhabited for at least fifteen centuries before its destruction —and has yielded an incomparable treasure of works of art and archeological information. The mudslide occurred at night, and caught the inhabitants asleep: by keeping everything damp for centuries, it preserved the contents "as the dust of Vesuvius preserved Pompeii", in George Woodcock's words. Among the marvels of this buried village were a wooden sculpture of a killer whale's fin inlaid with seven hundred sea otter teeth in the shape of a thunderbird, and a fourteen-foot wooden screen painted with the image of a whale. In the first four houses to be excavated, archeologists unearthed some forty-five thousand items of local manufacture or intertribal trade.

Woodcock makes the point that two important facts emerged from the discoveries at Cape Alava: "that the material culture and artistic fertility of the Coast Indian culture, as it was seen by early anthropologists in the later nineteenth century, had not resulted merely from the influx of goods and

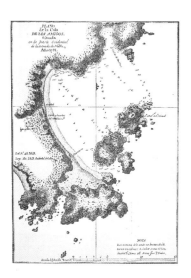

Map of the Friendly Cove at the entrance of Nootka, 1791. Atlas de las goletas *Sutil y Mexicana,* 1802. Museo Naval.

Detail of sardine fishing. Tomás de Suria.
Diario de Bodega y Quadra, 1792.
Ministerio de Asuntos Exteriores.

of metal tools through the establishment of the fur trade", and that "iron knives and chisels had reached the village in small quantities at least two hundred and possibly four hundred years before the arrival of the first European traders". The iron known to the prehistoric Nootkans may very well have been produced in Asia and have been traded across Bering Strait and down the coast, along the same route that the Indians' ancestors had once traveled.

Moziño was among the first but also, unfortunately, one of the last to see this enigmatic and fascinating civilization while it was still intact, before its essential patterns of culture had been disturbed by the fur trade and its

View of Nootka settlement and Sound.
[Fernando Brambila].
Museo de América.

Nootka Indian. Malaspina Expedition.
Museo de América.

aftermath. A few thousand Indians, scattered in small settlements along an immensely long coast, produced wooden houses of great beauty, wooden totems of imposing height, and a vast range of smaller objects in wood, bone, stone and sea ivory, all magnificently carved and decorated. Per capita, as it were, theirs may well have been the most art-conscious and artistically creative civilization that has ever existed.

The Coast Indians' achievements had escaped the notice of earlier explorers and adventurers largely because their treasure chests contained not even a promise of gold and silver. Equipped with the simplest of tools, they made objects that are now almost beyond price in the auction houses where works of art are sold: cedarwood boxes inlaid with haliotis shell, spruce root rain hats, whale's tooth amulets, dance rattles, feather-light totemic spoons carved of mountain-sheep horns... and, most magnificent of all, elaborately carved dance masks and potlatch dishes. While it lasted, it was a society in which (strange as it may seem to us, living in the era of the rusty tin can) *everything had style*. "Everything they have", wrote the astonished Cook in 1778, "is as well and ingeniously made, as if they were furnished with the most complete tool chest... Their invention and dexerity, in all manual works, is at least equal to that of any other nation".

Moziño, fortunately, realized that these were not a "primitive" people, and he was sufficiently sensitive not to write his *Noticias* from a purely ethnocentric point of view. Though of Spanish parentage, he had been born in Mexico —at Temascaltepec, in 1757; had been trained both in medicine and theology, and had received the finest botanical education then available in the New World. His teachers were the naturalists of the Royal Botanical Expedition, headed by Martín de Sessé, which had been established in 1786 by Carlos III for the purpose of conducting a far-ranging botanical survey of New Spain, which then extended from Central America to Alaska. Moziño had studied Nahuatl, and though there was no connection between the language of the Aztecs and that of the Nootka, it had at least prepared him mentally for the difficult task of learning a non-European language in a very short time. Above all, he was a sympathetic observer of Indian folkways at a time when most of the mariners who came to this coast regarded the natives merely as illiterate savages with highly exploitable skill as fur trappers.

The botanist, on the other hand, admired the marvelous flexibility of a way of life that was ideally adapted to a difficult environment; the Nootkans' nomadic habit of moving from one settlement to another, for example, "according to the scarcity of fish in one area or its abundance in another". The immense ornamented framework of their "great houses" would be left standing in all of their alternative villages, since the yellow cedar logs would outlast a man's lifetime even in the rainy weather of this coast. But they would take the side boards with them on their sea voyages from one fishing ground to another, for thin boards represented an immense investment of time and effort in a society without proper saws: "In order to move their houses from one place to another", Moziño noted, "they unite three or more canoes with the planks that are used as walls, and on these they are usually able to transport all their furniture in one voyage. On the land they leave behind all that remains are the supporting stakes and the beams that serve as the skeleton of the building".

Equally impressive to a scientific observer was their custom of taking new names to mark the successive stages of life, which played an important role in the lives of the *taises* (chiefs): "When the prince is more than a month old, all the nobles assemble and he is given his first name. This allegorical christening is performed either by the father or by another responsible person whom he delegates to do it. The new name is celebrated with feasts, songs, and dances, during each of which the provident *tais* makes presents of sea otter pelts, copper, shells and as many precious objects as he can to the nobles who have come to congratulate him."

This, of course, was the famous potlatch of the Coast Indians, the marathon ceremonial feasts at which the hosts traditionally attempt to "flatten" their guests with the weight of their gift-giving. Moziño counted up to thirty-six different dishes —including fish, birds and animals, roasted and boiled, and numerous vegetables, fruits and berries found wild in the forest— that were served to visiting chiefs at potlatch banquets. But in his day potlatches had not yet turned into the orgies of conspicuous consumption and destruction they were to become in the nineteenth century, when commerce had upset the traditional status relationships of the coast —prompting an uncomprehending government to enact a law prohibiting anyone from celebrating,

Carlos III, King of Spain. 1716-1788. Museo del Prado.

163

encouraging or engaging in "the Indian festival known as the «Potlach» [*sic*] or the Indian dance known as the «Tamanawas»".

In the process of growing up, a Nootka prince would trigger a fresh potlatch with every change of name, for "names are changed in accordance with the varying stages of each age, and, in this matter, each new stage is celebrated with more extravagance and magnificence than the first". Moziño cites the case of one youth who was called Tlu-pa-nia-pa in infancy, Na-na-fa-mitz in childhood, Gu-gu-me-ta-tzautlz in his puberty, Quia-sechiconu as a youth and finally, "having been accorded the privileges of manhood, at the moment that he entered into the dignity of the *tais*", he received the name Quio-comasia, meaning "excessively liberal prince".

Moziño was fortunate in being present at the puberty ceremony of the daughter of the principal chief, Macuina; her name had been Apenas:

> The savage pomp with which they celebrated this occasion is worthy of note. At one corner of the house situated at the edge of the forested Coti mountains they built a platform as high as the roof which was supported by four column-like posts. On top they constructed a sort of balcony enclosed on all sides by wooden planks. The balcony and the columns alike were decorated with various large, poorly-designed figures, painted white, yellow, red, blue and black and also adorned with mirrors of various sizes. Two sculptures in the corners with open arms and extended hands were meant to symbolize the magnificence of the monarch. At the foot of the columns was a leveled arena surrounded by a wooden fence.

> Inside the house, seated on newly woven mats, was the young princess. She was dressed in the finest materials made from cedar bark, and covered with countless necklaces of small beads made from some species of Venus shell (dentalium shell), that when carefully and evenly cut have a splendid shine and look like glass. Her hair was evenly parted down the middle and held together tightly at the ends with several well-polished copper rings, like those hanging from ears. The weight of these could not have been less than one Castilian pound.

> Macuina took his daughter by the hand and led her to the center of the balcony. There, he remained to the right of her, and at her left was his brother Quatlazape. A profound silence fell over the asembly of natives occupying the arena and the beach. The chief then directed his voice to the crowd: 'Now my daughter Apenas is no longer a child; she is a woman. From now on she will be known by the name Ystocoti-Tlemoc, that is the great taisa of Yuquatl'. With one voice they answered: 'Hua-cas, Hua-cas, Macuina,

Indian man and woman, Nootka chiefs.
[José Cardero].
Museo de América.

Hua-cas-Ystocoti-Tlemoc', an expression which is the equivalent of our viva. The greatest measure of praise and friendship among these people is always conveyed by the word Hua-cas.

Then the taises *and other nobles began to dance and sing, and each received a special gift that Quatlazape threw from the balcony in the name of Macuina and of the princess. One of the principal games in this ceremony was the athletic contest for which the arena had been leveled. The prize presented to the winner was a shell. Twenty or thirty naked athletes entered the field to vie for the honor of victory. From the platform Quatlazape threw down a small wooden ring which they struggled to catch in their hands, fighting among themselves, using all their strength to get a hold of it and keep it in their possession, until the strongest or the most cunning of them gained the final victory, either by wearing down his opponents' resistance. Our sailors took part in this contest and the prizes which their champions received were always more valuable than those given to the natives, since the latter only received shells, while the former were given fine sea otter pelts. Macuina was exceedingly grateful to us for having participated in the festivities, and later continued to remind me of the satisfaction he had felt when one of the chaplains and I danced before the princess, his daughter.*

After the ceremony was over —several days having been dedicated to public celebration— Macuina ordered Ystocoti-Tlemoc to descend from the platform: leading her to one of the looms in the best corner of the house, he said, 'Now, my daughter, you are a woman, and you should only dedicate yourself to the obligations of your sex.' From that day on, the tender young woman began to spin and weave, her hard work serving as a reproach to all young ladies who think that nobility is an excuse for laziness...

Nootka Taisa. Marchena. Diario de Bodega y Quadra, 1792.
Ministerio de Asuntos Exteriores.

When Alexander von Humboldt came to Mexico in 1803 to write his *Political Essay on the Kingdom of New Spain* —"the first modern regional geographic essay", as Douglas Botting calls it— he studied Moziño's notes at the Royal Botanical Garden and was impressed by the "great number of curious facts" which the 'eminent doctor" had collected. Humboldt, imbued with German rationalist ideas, was particularly fascinated by Moziño's account of the struggle between Qua-utz and Matlox, the powers of good and evil that rule the world an Indian version of the eternal conflict between *Geist* and *Ungeist* that played such a prominent role in Goethe's thinking and in the works of the German romantic philosophers. He was also intrigued by what Moziño had heard of the Nootkan creation myth:

Proclamation of Princess Ystocoti-Tlemoc. José
Guerrero. Diario de Bodega y Quadra, 1792.
Ministerio de Asuntos Exteriores.

They say that God created a woman whom he left completely alone in the dark forests of Yuquatl, in which lived deer without antlers, dogs without tails and ducks without wings. This isolated woman wept day and night in her loneliness, not finding the slightest means to remedy her pitiful situation, until Qua-utz, sympathizing with her tears, allowed her to see, on the ocean, a resplendent copper canoe, paddled by many handsome young men using paddles of the same metal. The island woman was astonished by this sight and stood stunned at the foot of a tree, until one of the paddlers told her that it was the All-Powerful who had been kind enough to visit this beach and to provide her with the company she longed for.

At this, the lonely and melancholy woman redoubled her tears —her nose began to run, and she expelled the disgusting fluid onto the sand. Qua-utz then ordered her to pick up what she had sneezed out, and to her amazement she found the small, palpitating body of a man that had just been formed. She picked him up in a shell his size, as the god had commanded, and was told to keep moving him into larger shells as he grew.

This done, the Creator reembarked in the canoe, having allowed even the animals to share in his generosity, for just as the deer saw antlers growing on his head, the dog began to wag his new tail and the birds flew up with the wind to try out their new wings. The man began to grow little by little, moving from one cradle to the next until he began to walk. He left his childhood behind and his first proof of early manhood was to impregnate the woman who had raised him, and whose firstborn began the lineage of the taises, *while his siblings began that of the common people.*

Natsapi, Nootka chieftain. [Tomás de Suria].
Museo de América.

Nootka woman. [Tomás de Suria].
Museo de América.

Many of Moziño's observations, indeed, run exactly contrary to what Rousseau expected of the "state of nature". Far from enjoying a kind of primitive democracy, the Nootkans were ruled by hereditary chiefs presiding over an iron-clad system of class distinctions: the high chief, Macuina, "simultaneously carries out the duties of father of the families, king and high priest". The commoners, or *meschimes,* moreover, lived in squalor, had neither political nor property rights, and sometimes were obliged to do without a wife, "because not being the owners of the fruits of their labors, except in a very small part, they can never collect the dowry, so that many die without marrying, and the few who have better luck must content themselves with only one wife, given to them by their princes as a reward for their services". The *taises* and nobles, on the other hand, "consider the buying and keeping of several wives a sign of greatness." When the *taises* died, they went to join their ancestors in glory in the realm of Qua-utz-while commoners were destined for a kind of Hell called Pin-pula, ruled by a prince named Iz-mi-tiz. So much for the unfettered freedoms of the noble savage! Still, there was none of the elaborate servility that made life at European courts a nightmare of protocol. Despite their veneration for the chief, "the *meschimes* present themselves any which way before him; they will sit down indiscriminately, lie down and push each other around in his presence, seemingly showing no signs of submissiveness, except that they will not behave this way beside the chief, and will instantly obey whatever order is given, even leaving their meal if at that moment he orders them to do something".

Detail of the interior of Macuina's house.
Diario de Bodega y Quadra, 1792.
Ministerio de Asuntos Exteriores.

Moziño recorded a number of revealing asides, as when one of the chiefs hears the foreign sailors sing their ballads and asks, "Don't the Spanish or English sailors have a God, since they only seem to celebrate fornication and drunkenness? The *taises* of Nootka sing only to praise Qua-utz and ask for his help." Yet it turned out that the chiefs did attend the commoners' pantomime performances, "the most lascivious that one can imagine", though as aristocrats they took care "not to mingle their voices in the obscene songs". Moziño had an ear for Indian music, poetry and rhetoric, which he found exemplary, and an appreciation of the Nootka dances: "Sometimes they disguise themselves with bear and deer skins and heads, or with wooden masks which represent a huge image of some aquatic bird. They try to imitate the movements of each animal, as well as those of the hunter who snares it. The bear caught up in a net, its death, or the death of the deer whose heart is pierced by an arrow —these are events that the people show so naturally and so rhythmically in time with the music that they cannot help but excite admiration".

Northwest Coast Indian. [José Cardero]. Museo de América.

Yet Moziño had a blind spot when it came to the very thing that we now admire most about the vast "potlatch culture" stretching from Vancouver Island to Yakutat Bay —its painting and sculpture. He describes their painting as crude and their totemic carvings as *mal diseño* —"poor design". The "large figures of poor design" he saw at Ystocoti-Tlemoc coming of age were the superb totem sculptures of the Nootka, whose paintings Moziño also dismisses as "very crude".

Cook, too, spoke of the "enormous deformity" of the totem poles. Indeed, none of the visiting Europeans were able to comprehend that they had encountered an art that could bear comparison with the best of Peru or ancient Egypt. The artists who accompanied the eighteenth-century mapping and scientific expeditions had all been taught to serve as "cameras" and to produce accurate renderings of what they saw. The most gifted of them —such as Atanasio Echeverría, who went with Moziño to Nootka— were able to draw flowers, birds, insects with breathtaking verisimilitude. Yet they were strangely unable to "see" Indian art or to draw even the most rudimentary reproductions of how the Indians painted and carved their decorations. They had been trained in European schools that stressed the Greek ideal of *physeos mimesis* —the imitation of nature— and though they were sent on these expeditions to record everything as accurately as possible, they could not reproduce on paper what their minds were incapable of comprehending.

The Nootkans and their neighbors were motivated by a very different way of seeing and perceiving nature. Theirs was an art of faces and eyes that went far beyond the tyranny of appearances, yet even the most abstract of the totem faces convey a remarkable sense of having been sculptured *d'après nature*. The artists who produced them were among the greatest

Epilobium undulatum

Notha

epilobium

The plant «Epilobium undulatum» (Willow-herb).
Nootka.
Hunt Institute for Botanical Documentation,
Pittsburgh.

171

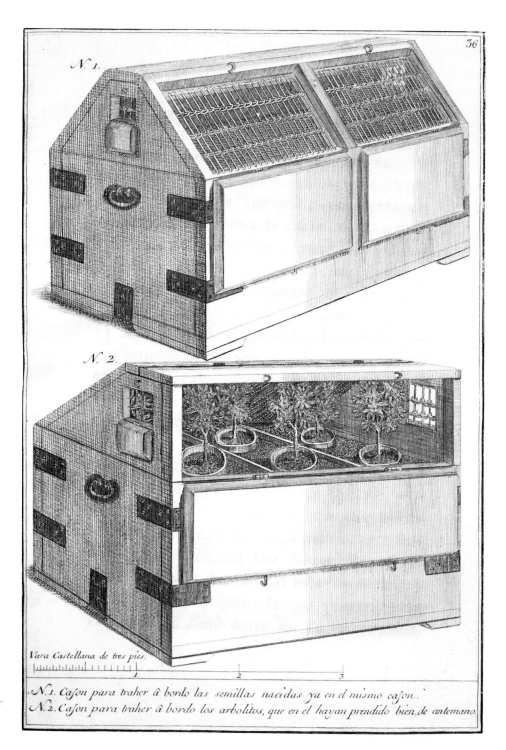

Boxes for transporting plants aboard ship.
«Instrucción sobre el modo más seguro y
económico de transportar plantas vivas por mar
y tierra a los países más distantes». D. Casimiro
Gómez Ortega. Madrid, 1779.

wood sculptors of all time, and —as we now realize— among the most gifted depictors of the human face in the history of art. They prized faces and heads of people and animals, but cared relatively little for the body. For the most part they simply dissected it, and an artist could pass with perfect equanimity (and without a break in line) from showing the outside of the whale —fins, eyes, mouth, tail— to the inside, with a cross-section of the bone structure and a catalogue of the contents of the stomach. Having invented this kind of X-ray vision it was only natural that they should return again and again to the symbolism of the eye. It is one of the dominant motifs of Coast Indian sculpture: everything they used bore the eyes and faces of art —their cooking boxes, amulets, dance rattles, canoes, weapons, "soul catchers". But the splendor of these designs, which has dazzled and inspired so many artists of the twentieth century, escaped the artists of the Age of Reason.

Moziño, Echeverría and the third man on his team, the naturalist José Maldonado, left Nootka in September, 1792, having gathered and classified more than two hundred plants, animals and birds, and produced a splendid series of botanical and zoological plates to illustrate the descriptions. But Moziño's later history is one of confusion and disappointment. After further work in Mexico he accompanied Martín de Sessé to Madrid with the collected results of fifteen years' work of the Royal Botanical Expedition, including some ten thousand herbarium specimens and more than two thousand drawings. But the times were not propitious for the great botanical compendium Sessé hoped to publish in Madrid: Carlos III was dead; Spain had become a pawn in the Napoleonic game and was soon to suffer the *Disasters of War* illustrated by another great documentary artist, Francisco Goya. Under the short-lived regime of Napoleon's brother, Joseph Bonaparte, the Mexican naturalist became director of the Royal Museum of Natural History, but during the French retreat from Spain Moziño was among the *Afrancesados* —the collaborators— who were forced to flee the country. He took the precious drawings with him in a handcart and deposited them for several years with a Swiss botanist who made copies of about half of the watercolors. Eventually, in 1817, Moziño brought them back to Spain —this time to Barcelona, where the original drawings disappeared into a private library for more than a hundred and fifty years. They finally came to light again in 1981, when the entire collection —a great buried treasure of art and science— was purchased by the Hunt Institute for Botanical Documentation at Carnegie-Mellon University in Pittsburgh.

Moziño's *Noticias de Nutka* remained in manuscript until 1913, when they were published in Mexico City by the Sociedad Mexicana de Geografía y Estadística —though of course without the missing illustrations. I know of at least one Indian cultural society in the Vancouver island region that uses the English translation of his *Noticias* as a kind of reference handbook and guide to half-forgotten folkways. He himself could not have foreseen the ex-

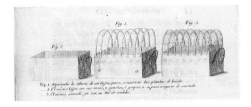

Box for preserving plants aboard ship. «Instrucción sobre el modo más seguro y económico de transportar plantas vivas por mar y tierra a los países más distantes». D. Casimiro Gómez Ortega. Madrid, 1779.

tent to which the Indians' way of life would soon be affected by contact with the English and the "Boston men", but he realized that the coming of the Europeans was a tragedy for the Indians, even on the most basic human level. "Many of our officers went alone and without arms to visit certain villages, carried in the Indians' own canoes, and they always returned quite taken with the affection and gentleness they observed in everyone. What a shame that the Indians cannot, in general, say the same about us! Our sailors, either because of their brutal upbringing, or because they were jealous of the humane way that the commandant and other officers treated the natives, would insult them; they crippled some, wounded others, and didn't fail to kill a good number. Humanity is the greatest quality of civilization. All the arts and sciences are worth nothing if they only serve to make us cruel and haughty".

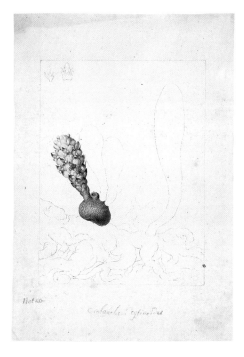

The plant «Orobanche? cytinoides» (Cancer root). Nootka.
Hunt Institute for Botanical Documentation, Pittsburgh.

The plant «Pyrus? Crataegus? Mespillos?». Nootka.
Hunt Institute for Botanical Documentation, Pittsburgh.

The plant «Mimulus notkanus» (Monkey-flower). Nootka.
Hunt Institute for Botanical Documentation, Pittsburgh.

Notes

1. As Iris Higbie Wilson (now Iris Engstrand) points out in her indispensable modern edition of Moziño's account, *Noticias de Nutka*, Cook's men, using sign language, had asked the Indians what the port was called, and the reply they received probably included the word *noot-ka-eh*, a verb meaning "to go around". Cf. p. 67, José Mariano Moziño: *Noticias de Nutka*, Translated and Edited by Iris Higbie Wilson, Toronto and Montreal, McClelland and Stewart, Ltd., 1970.

2. The system of binomial nomenclature by genus and species had been introduced in 1753 by Carl von Linné, the great Swedish pioneer of modern systematic botany, who later extended it to the classification of animals as well. Significantly, Carlos III —then perhaps the most enlightened and scientifically minded monarch of Europe —invited Linné to settle in Spain in 1755, but for a variety of reasons his pupil Löffing, to whom he had dictated his *Fundamenta Botanica*, was sent instead.

The plant «Andromeda glandulifera» (Moorwort).
Nootka.
Hunt Institute for Botanical Documentation,
Pittsburgh.

A Personal View of
the Northwest Coast :
The Journal of
Tomas de Suria (1791)

by Catherine Poupeney Hart

Université de Montréal

Introduction

While the elite of Europe were reading with pleasure and interest the travel journals of their contemporaries such as Bougainville and Cook, to name only two, the Spanish journals —even those which would have contributed so much to the prestige of Spain— were victims of a "policy of silence". Buried for centuries in archives, these texts have finally been read and rightly extolled as precious sources of information permitting the reconstitution of realities which have long since disappeared. Moreover, these writings are worthy of attention in and of themselves.

Typical of such texts are those resulting from the North American branch of the Malaspina Expedition which had been officially dedicated to finding the Northwest Passage. In effect, a remarkable variety of journals and logs took note of this expedition. Following the tradition of the Spanish navy, officers and pilots were obliged to maintain written records of the full details of navigation particulars. Although this obligation imposed a rigid framework allowing little expression of personal views, it did not prevent most authors, however, from acquitting themselves with elegance.

To this group of writings must be added a personal journal which was written on the individual initiative of the civilian Tomás de Suria, an engraver temporarily associated with the undertaking. These circumstances alone, quite rare in the case of Spanish expeditions justify further examination of his work. in addition, the fact that this lively journal is illustrated with several sketches, offering a totally unique point of view, adds to its exceptional character.

In addition to relating the same adventure, these different journals possess common characteristics which we shall firstly identify. Then, in a second step, we shall examine more closely the original aspects of Suria's contribution.

The Text

Suria's text is brief, all the more so that the original manuscript, presently kept in the Beinecke Library at Yale University, is unfortunately incomplete. It is composed of 46 folios recto verso, 14 of which contain ink sketches consisting essentially of portraits of Indians of Mulgrave Sound (Yakutat), the scene of a confrontation between Spaniards and warriors at the same spot, a plan of Nootka, the portrait of a soldier of the Monterey garrison and various studies (hands, faces, etc.).

As Suria himself admits, this text only constitutes a working draft whose contents he intends to organize "without terror or undue inconve-

Common Mulgrave woman.
Diario de Tomás de Suria.
Beinecke Library, Yale University.

nience" upon his return to Mexico[1]. The pagination of the booklet makes reading difficult. The journal begins at folio 4 with the arrival of the engraver at Acapulco and his integration into the expedition, initially as an assistant to Antonio Pineda, who was in charge of the natural history section, and subsequently on board the corvette *Descubierta*. Rather than the voyage to the North (folios 4 (verso) to 11), the largest part of the text concerns the sojourn at Mulgrave Sound (folios 11 (verso) to 26, and 29 to 32) and the search for the Northwest Passage (folios 34 to 35). Accordingly, it is the stopover at Nootka (folios 46, 28, 2 and 3) and especially the return to San Blas —with a further stopover at Monterey— which suffer from the fragmentary character of the manuscript.

The confusion is not limited to the arrangement of the text: pages containing drawings are themselves often laden with notes. This muddled impression, accentuated by the presence of words scratched out and of ink and seawater stains, nevertheless contributes in part to the charm of the document and renders it all the more vivid.

It remains possible, however, for the English reader discouraged by the obstacles contained in the original manuscript to refer to the translation and edition of the text produced by Henry Raup Wagner[1]. It would be a pity, nevertheless, for the Spanish reader to satisfy himself with the adaptation of Justino Fernández taken from the English version[2].

The Author

As a replacement for the sketcher José del Pozo, who had been discharged at Lima, Suria was considered as a temporary solution while awaiting the arrival of the painters Juan de Ravenet and Fernando Brambila who had been hired in Italy. As a result, Suria merely participates in the single Northwest voyage and the completion, upon his return, of the sketches resulting therefrom.

This thirty year old Spaniard, living in Mexico since 1778, thus joins the occupants of the *Descubierta* and the *Atrevida* for a period of six months. previously employed at the Mexican Mint as an engraver, it is an honour for him to have been chosen by the Viceroy to fill the vacant position and to frequent in this fashion the elite of the Spanish navy during an excursion to a barely explored territory which has become the object of sudden interest by powerful European nations.

Conventional Characteristics

Despite their contrasts in personal involvement which result from entirely different motivations for writing, the journal of Suria and those of the officers and pilots of the expedition contain certain common fundamental characteristics which make them appear to the modern reader as part of a very broad group of travel literature. To the same extent as the works of James Cook, George Dixon, or Lorenzo Ferrer Maldonado, so frequently referred to during the expedition, these journals may be inserted into a sub-category, the sea diary, whose characteristics are clearly defined.

A sea diary is presented as an authentic record of the movement of a boat and its navigation particulars which is signed and given in chronological order by one or several of its occupants. The sea diary is furthermore distinguished by the alternation between the narration of events, on the one hand, and descriptions and synthesis of informations on the other.

We thus encounter in Suria's journal the following passage which characterizes a phenomenon which is common to all the others: "The 27th dawned cloudy and rainy. At 7 in the morning, we found ourselves at the mouth of the Bay of the Puerto de Mulgrave. This port had a very wide entrance. On the port side, the coast continues with a range of mountains, very steep and rough and black from the foot halfway up" (246).

At other times it can be noted that upon departure, the narrator forms a synthesis of the information accumulated on the place of landing and its inhabitants. This is the type of order to which Suria refers when he writes of his first contacts with the inhabitants of Mulgrave Sound: "The commander had various conferences with them, all amusing, which will be told when their character, dress, and religion are described" (248). He in fact does it some pages later.

Mulgrave Indian.
Diario de Tomás de Suria.
Beinecke Library, Yale University.

Discord with the native of Mulgrave.
Diario de Tomás de Suria.
Beinecke Library, Yale University.

Officers conversing with Indians. Detail of the tomb of the previous ankau of Mulgrave Sound. José Cardero. Museo Naval.

Any writing of this kind contains as its basis a certain information contract entered into between the narrator and the entity for whom he is writing, such as a political authority. This contract is the counterpart of another "real" contract, consisting of the general mission orders given to the navigator and the imposition of ordinances to prepare "the chronicle and make the synthesis of that which they might see or find and all that which might occur to them in the discovered territory"[3].

In the case of Suria, this contract is voluntary and unilateral: "Being desirous of writing down an individual account of all the incidents of this voyage in technicological nautical terms, as they are so fruitful and interesting, principally in matters of geography, and deal with the navigation of the Northwest Coast of America, and in view of the fact that few come to these parts, I proposed to myself on my departure from Acapulco to keep a diary with the greatest formality" (260).

This statement of intent presents very explicitly the scope of the reality which the engraver seeks to encompass —"all the incidents of this voya-

ge"— and specifies the degree of accuracy which his description hopes to
attain. In effect, he laments the spirit of cooperation which is absent in the
pilot who shares his cabin and the "mysterious and studied silence of the officials and the pilots" (265) insofar as he is concerned. But the result is to
highlight the conciseness and the sharpness of his own contribution: "(...) my
journal does not proceed with all the exactness possible in the realm of geography. Nevertheless, I will endeavor to gain information with sagacity and
astuteness. At the same time I shall omit what I know to be useless and what
only interests the pilots. I do not do this with the information regarding the
Indians as these are more interesting generally and I have endeavoured to
observe all their actions and movements and as this is so much part of my
business it is easier for me to gain the information than for the others. To
this may be added my understanding the character of the Indians through
a period of thirteen year's residence in Mexico" (261).

By undertaking to provide information on a reality which is external
to the text, the sea diary is submitted by that simple fact to a test of verifi-

Este de este cubie...to de pieles descalzos de
un senbrero y des... ...do desdel mas
lo al pie y lo se ... de su guidado

Common Mulgrave man.
Diario de Tomás de Suria.
Beinecke Library, Yale University.

cation. The instructions leave no doubt on this subject. The descriptions contained in the diaries must, orders the Viceroy Revillagigedo, be sufficiently similar to reality in order to allow other navigators to recognize places that they may see for the first time:

> *I hope that, from the departure from San Blas, you as well as the pilot will keep circumstantial diaries where the discoveries of the voyage may be found, well observed and marked with every clearness so that every navigator may recognize without any mistake those places marked on your maps which you may have discovered*[4].

But the diary will not be a simple carbon copy of an external reality. A selection of pertinent features and an ordering (notably by way of synthesis) of that wich is perceived as chaos are accordingly rendered necessary without losing view, however, of the imperative of faithfulness to nature.

In his desire to give the most truthful image possible of the world, the author of the diary must call upon extremely varied means. He will thus attempt to seize any given reality as closely as possible, either as Suria does by reducing as much as possible the time between the event itself and the time of writing ("It is eight o'clock at night and the sun is setting. The rays shine straight through the porthole of my cabin and give me light to write at this hour" (244)), or by textually repeating instructions, passages from diaries, or translations of native speeches. Moreover, and most importantly, he will make use of a system of signs which imitates reality, visual images. "Without this assistance'», Malaspina confesses to his friend Greppi, "the descriptions of the voyage would be entirely weak"[5]. On two occasions Suria even includes in his work sketches completing his description, including a plan of the Port of San Lorenzo de Nootka (verso 46) surrounded by the words: "The port is not the most capacious and the entrance as stated above is very narrow. (...). It makes a figure similar to this [rough pen and ink sketch of the port] aside from the many islands and farallons which are close to the coast" (273).

In their broad outlines then, some of which are described above, there is a great overlap in the work of Suria and that of the officers whose destiny he shared during a few months. The difference, however, is found at other levels.

The Originality of the Journal

In the environment characterized by hierarchy and compartmentation which is found on the corvettes, Suria must satisfy himself with the role of punctual assistant as a result of his absence of scientific or military background and, probably, his social origin. As we have seen, he complains of his isolation from official sources of information.

That which might from a certain point of view limit the scope of his contribution —the absence of a model to which he might refer at any time— permits him to have a new look on things and allows him to express himself with a freedom which we appreciate today as readers.

Everything is new and worthy of interest for Suria, who appears to be animated by an open and rather jovial disposition. With respect to a period of bad weather he mentions: "On the 12th the wind was stronger (...). The ship rolled heavily from port to starboard. The 13th the wind increased still more and the main top gallant masts were taken down and reefs were taken in the topsail, the foresail and the foretopsail. The meals were something to laugh about because the plates kept dancing about and everything else rolling around so that mobody could hold them" (244).

Since he is not writing for specialists, he does not hesitate to give all sorts of details, such as the usual preparations for bad weather: "It rained and all the portholes on the leeward side were closed, as the water would enter them, on account of the list of the ship. This operation is always practiced on such occasions, as well as that of covering with tarred strong linen the window in the quarter deck and which opens on the cabin. Chairs, tables, and other necessary utensils were strongly tied" (243).

Where the officers would satisfy themselves with rapid and general notes regarding the living conditions on board, Suria gives us this very graphic description: "I will only say that, stretched in my bed, my feet were against the side of the ship and my head against the bulkhead, which what they call the timbers which enclose the cabin. From my breast to the deck, which was my roof, the distance is only three inches. This confined position does not allow me to move in my bed and I am forced to make for myself a roll of cloth to cover my head, although this suffocates me, but this is a lesser evil than being attacked by thousands of cockroaches which are such a great pest that you see some individuals with sore on their foreheads and bites on their fingers" (260).

He is cold, he is hungry, he appreciates good food and good wine and does not fail to note: "The cold is increasing but with it comes the desire for eating and for drinking good wine. The common wine on board is of San Lucar", or else "The saint's day of Quintano was celebrated with the fine and spiritual wine of Malaga kept in reserve from Spain for such occasions. This wine had attained at Cape Horn a degree of excellence which is unexplainable" (244-243).

With these records of sensations and emotions, we are a considerable distance from the often disembodied and purely intellectual personality of the narrators of the other versions.

An essential difference between these two types of diaries is also found
at another, more intellectual, level. The origin of this difference is found by
comparing the professional and scientific backgrounds of the official narrators against the relative ignorance of Suria with respecto to major currents
of modern thought.

The practical necessity of constantly observing the sea, the sky, and possible signs of danger on the face of things and people, when added to the
classical notion of the eye as a privileged instrument in the discovery of the
world, explains the small regard that these navigators have for any senses
other than that of sight. The reality which is invoked is thus, at the outset,
somewhat curtailed. To that are also added, of course, the limitations imposed by that model of all science which is, in the XVIIIth century, natural
history. As Michel Foucault very clearly reminds us: "From the XVIIth century on, observation, a knowledge based on the senses, is accompanied by
systematically negative conditions. Taste and flavour are excluded (...) because with their uncertainty, with their variablity, they do not allow a univ-
ersally acceptable analysis as distinct elements. The sense of feel is narrowly
restricted to designating only certain contrasts which are rather obvious,
such as smooth and rough; sight is granted an almost exclusive privilege as

the sense describing what is manifest and extensive and, as a result, permits a "partes extra partes" analysis, accepted by everyone"[6].

Accordingly, in the official version of the expedition, for instance, fruit has no flavour and flowers have no odour, but simply characteristics which allow nature to make, through them, contributions to the conservation or re-creation of man. There is practically no mention of the sense of feel and only a very general reference to the bad odour of certain women at Mulgrave Sound and to the somewhat brackish taste of the waters in the Bering Bay.

Insofar as sounds are concerned, there is no trace of any effort made to note the songs or voices of the natives other than a few very brief re-marks regarding certain phonemes which are peculiar to the natives and which are inserted as an appendix to the Spanish-Mulgravian lexicon.

The sole voice presenting any sort of developed sensuality is that of Suria who evokes the sweet and sour taste of a berry and particularly often notes in detail the striking aspects of voices, songs and the accent of the natives such as the following example: "At the end of each song they finished with a kind of laugh which jointly and in measure they maintained on this sound, Xa Xa Xa Xa Xa. In others they ended with another sound which can-not be described but it's like the barking of a dog" (258).

Suria is also the only one to take advantage of any sense other than that of sight as an instrument of knowledge. Consequently, his sense of smell allows him to determine the origin of the grease that the natives use to coat their hair and he records the following: "Their hair is very thick and flaccid without any dressing or care, loose in the wayward natural manner, and co-vered with the greatest abundance of red ochre and grease, which accord-ing to the odour must be deer grease" (247).

By not taking into account of the recent scientific promulgations, the engraver emerges also as a defender of the old order in his interpretation of the objectives of the voyage.

As far as Malaspina's inquiry about the existence of the Northwest Pas-sage is concerned, his decision is quickly taken, as early as July 28, 1791, as he writes much later to the Minister Valdés: the principal objective of the voyage is fulfilled inasmuch as the passage does not exist or, if it does exist, it is impracticable since it is situated too far north. Rather than waste pre-cious time trying to verify the theories of a Parisian geographer, the com-mander prefers to devote himself to tasks which are more immediately use-ful to the advancement of science. The navigators thus undertake the comple-tion, insofar as possible, of marine surveys begun by their predecessors. They devote themselves to experiments on the form of the earth and to a study of savage man which will be placed in the philosophical account of the of-ficial version of the voyage. All of these things should be looked upon with interest by enlightened readers.

Inhabitants of Mulgrave Sound.
Diario de Tomás de Suria.
Beinecke Library, Yale University.

Dance on the Nootka beach. Tomás de Suria.
Museo Naval.

Tomás de Suria, however, remains insensitive to the criterion of utility while the notion of glory seems to him a much more valuable objective. He allows himself to express his point of view on several occasions, criticizing openly the negligence of the commander: "In this space we should explore carefully, foot by foot, for the desired Strait of Ferrer Maldonado. Even if we were not successful in finding it there would still be left the complete satisfaction that no one in the future could carry off this glory. Such considerations brought much grief to the pilots and some of the officers, among whom there exists a true appreciation of the honour and glory of the nation. The commander was also inspired by the same sentiments but he was whimsical and had formed the opinion that there was not and would not be any such Strait. For this reason he did not wish to persist in scrupulously examining this piece of coast" (267).

This liberty, here used to express his indignation and to echo the discontent of "even the humblest sailor" (264) would be unthinkable in a professional version of the voyage. It is an aspect which we can appreciate all throughout Suria's modest work. The existence of such discrepancies between Suria's version and that of the others contributes in more than a small part to rendering the study of these works stimulating and less austere.

Mulgrave woman.
Diario de Tomás de Suria.
Beinecke Library, Yale University.

Notes

1. "Journal of Thomas de Suria of his Voyage with Malaspina to the Northwest Coast of America in 1791". Translated by Henry Raup Wagner. *Pacific Historical Review*, vol. 5 (Sept. 1936), p. 275. We refer systematically to this edition of Suria's journal in the following pages by indicating the page number between brackets.

2. *Tomás de Suría y su viaje con Malaspina*, México: Porrúa Hnos. Cía, 1939.

3. Quoted by H. Martínez Montero, "Prólogo" *Diario de viage* de Francisco Xavier de Viana —Montevideo, Ministerio de Instrucción pública y Previsión Social, 1958— I, XVII (Our translation).

4. Instruction to Mourelle, 1791. Translated and published by Henry R. Wagner, *Spanish Explorations in the Straight of Juan de Fuca*, Santa Ana, California: Fine Arts Press, 1933.

5. Carlo Caselli, *Alexandro Malaspina e la sua spedizione scientifica in torno al mondo con documenti inediti*. Milán: Edizioni Alpes, 1929. (Our translation.)

6. Michel Foulcault, *Les mots et les choses*, Paris: Gallimard, 1966. (Our translation.)

Soy un Principe... tari ycs...

Vnprincipe

Jefe del Puerto de Mulgrabe nombrado
Ankaiui

Ankaiui, Chief of Mulgrave Sound.
Diario de Tomás de Suria.
Beinecke Library, Yale University.

Nootka :
The Crisis of 1789

by José de la Sota
Historian, Madrid

Since the second half of the seventeenth century, knowledge of world geography had been added to little by little. At the same time, the weight of the new territories and that of the former colonies over the relations between European States, was growing[2].

The Treaties of Utrecht of 1713 enshrined a new international equilibrium which reflected this increasing influence of the territories beyond the continent.

As far as Spain is concerned, the eighteenth century is marked by the rivalry with Great Britain for supremacy at sea and, in particular, for the defence of the territories and exclusive commercial dominion in America. Utrecht meant that "the American presence in Spanish life was to become much more powerful", marking the beginning of an "Atlanticisation" of the Spanish monarchy[3].

It was Carlos III who was to define his overseas policies in an intimate relationship with the Americas. Throughout his reign, both the development of the Third Family Pact with France[4] and the continuous confrontations with the English (entry into the Seven Years War, the question of the Falkland Islands —1770— support for United States Independence —1779— as well as innumerable incidents at sea) point towards the attempt to sustain the "colonial balance" which arose from Utrecht. This balance was based on the containment of the undeniable naval power of the English.

The American preoccupation, a key factor, as we have seen, in the policies of the Bourbons, was to pass into second place behind the European events, in France, which broke the patterns of the international politics of Carlos IV who had inherited those of his father.

In the incident of the Nootka Sound, we shall see the development of the last confrontation between the Spanish and English Crowns under these assumptions, astride the events of the French Revolution. If it began under the spirit of the policies of Carlos III (in 1789), it developed and ended under the pressure of the new international situation of 1795.

The diplomatic development of this crisis brought with it the continued presence of Spaniards on what is now Vancouver Island between 1789 and 1795. The Limits Expedition, which brought together there Commander George Vancouver, on the English side, and Captain Juan Francisco de la Bodega y Quadra, made it possible to complete the intense cartographic and scientific work which had been undertaken by the Spanish since 1774.

I. The Background

Although the study of the Spanish expeditions to the Northwest Coast has been carried out in another chapter of this book, it is necessary to set out the background to the Spanish presence there in order to better understand the Spanish attitude in the crisis of Nootka Sound.

In Spanish expansion northward from the Viceroyalty of New Spain, undertaken since the very beginning of the court conquest, there are a number of constant factors. On the one hand, there was the search for a northern passage connecting the North Sea, or Atlantic Ocean, with the Southern Sea or Pacific Ocean, like the Strait of Magellan; on the other hand, there was the presence of foreigners on the northern Pacific coast.

During the eighteenth century, this expansion was organised by land expeditions for Lower California (Constanzó, Anza, etc.) and, from 1774 onwards, with sea expeditions from the recently created San Blas Department for Upper California, a region which was ill-defined, and whose northern limit was according to the distances reached by the different expeditions. Part of the plans were thus accomplished of the Visitor General Gálvez, the great organiser of the Viceregal expansion northwards[5].

Soldier from Monterey. [José Cardero].
Museo de América.

It is possible to divide the sea expeditions of this time into two clearly defined periods. The first of these covers the 1774, 1775 and 1779 expeditions, while the second covers those from 1788 until 1795.

Juan Pérez's Expedition in 1774 was organised with the basic aim of discovering as exactly as possible the Russian possessions in Alaska. For a number of reasons, of which the main one was the seasonal delay (the subsidies having had to be got to the strongholds at Monterey and Santa Barbara), the expedition was a relative failure. Pérez showed that the coast did not deviate significantly either to East or to West. He was, moreover, the first Westerner to enter Nootka, fixing its position and dealing with the natives. Some of the silver teaspoons which were stolen from him were found by Cook when he put into this port. Pérez's pilot was Esteban José Martínez who was entrusted with taking possession of the port in 1789. As far as the Russians were concerned, he was able to do little as he did not make contact with them[6].

The following year, six new officers were posted to the Northwest Coast expeditions. Using almost negligible resources, this group of officers carried out intensive cartographical work throughout the length of the coast. The expeditions of 1775 and 1779 were intended to reach as far north as possible, surveying the coast, mapping it, and taking possession of the most suitable ports. These expeditions are of the greatest interest, not only for the personal valour demonstrated by those taking part (we should remember that the schooner *Sonora* had a length of barely ten metres yet reached as far as 56º latitude North), but also because of the cartographic results, which provided the basis of subsequent expeditions.

With the outbreak of the war with Great Britain for the Independence of the United States, the expeditions were suspended, and the officers involved were posted to other departments. A further influence was the verification of the distance of the Russian establishments, which did not threaten the Spanish holdings.

II.   The Nootka Incident

A number of different factors coincided with the resumption of the expeditions to the northern coast of America in 1788. On the one hand, there was the attempt by the crown to stabilise the Viceregal Government, with the appointment of Manuel Antonio Flórez, a Sevillian seaman of wide experience in administration in the Americas, as Viceroy. Since the death of Viceroy Bucareli (1779), there had been a succession of interim governments who had failed to undertake organised labour. While his mandate was also short, he did manage to reorganise the Viceroyalty militarily. One other factor was the "Russian alert" which arose once again as from 1787. These factors coincided with the desire of the Spanish governors in Madrid to complete their surveys of the colonies. To this end, Alejandro Malaspina's expedition was organised in 1789 in order to examine the political, economic and social system of the American colonies and to complete the hidrographic maps in order to improve navigation. As far as the Northwest Coast was concerned, Malaspina's expedition, and those generated by his presence led to the most exact maps of the epoch[7].

Following the voyages of James Cook to this coast, the presence of English vessels increased, especially from 1785 onwards, so that a new nation was added to the dispute for its possession.

James Cook. 1728-1779.
Biblioteca Nacional.

View of the entrance to Nootka at a distance of 3 leagues. Gabriel Gil. Diario de Bodega y Quadra, 1792. Ministerio de Asuntos Excteriores.

Reception of the Count of La Perouse.
Tomás de Suria.
Museo Naval.

In 1787, news of the presence of Russians on the continent, given by the French seaman the Count of La Pérouse[8], along with the publications of Cook's diaries[9], provoked considerable disquiet in the Madrid Court. The order to resume the expeditions was given immediately, even prior to the new Viceroy's taking possession[10].

Thus, on March 8th 1788 the expedition left San Blas commanded by Sub-lieutenant Esteban José Martínez and the pilot Gonzalo López de Haro, in the frigate *Princesa,* of one hundred and eighty-nine tons, and the packet-boat *San Carlos* of one hundred and ninety-six tons.

This was an important expedition, since it reached as far as 61º latitude North, and entered the port of Onalaska "an island where the Russians have their main establishment and factory, not far from the continent..."[11]. This was, therefore, the first contact between Spanish and Russians in this part of the continent. The upshot of this was to establish that the Russian establishments were not a threat to the Spanish possessions; however, an expedition was prepared, to the port of Nootka, for the following year. This news led to the 1789 expedition, to convert Nootka into the northernmost port of Spanish Northern California. No doubt, Martínez also got news from the English vessels which traded in the zone. The expedition was organised in no more than two and a half months, as against the six months normally required, especially because of the scarcity of internal resources of the port of San Blas.

Detail of Nootka Sound from the beach of the
Spanish settlement. José Cardero.
Diario de Bodega y Quadra, 1792.
Ministerio de Asuntos Exteriores.

When Martínez was anchored in Nootka on May 5th 1789, he met with two American ships, from Boston, the *Columbia* and the *Lady Washington*, under the command of John Kendrik and Robert Gray. The *Iphigenia Nubiana*, sailing under the Portuguese flag, was algo present.

Martínez had clear orders on how to act should he come upon foreign vessels. As far as the Russians were concerned, given the good relations between the two crowns, he was not to act with excessive firmness, but rather to remind them of Spanish rights in those waters. This was to be done as well with American vessels. The real danger was thought to come from the English vessels given over to fur trading. This was why, throughout the conflict, Martínez's posture was to prevent them from entering.

The first incident on Martínez's arrival occurred with the *Iphigenia Nubiana* which, although sailing under the Portuguese flag, was owned by an Englishman. At this time, Portuguese vessels had an exclusive hold on trade with China, the main market for furs from the northwest coast.

The owners of the *Iphigenia* were the "Merchant Proprietors" formed by English traders in Canton and India. John Meares, one of the promotors of this company, had been on these coasts in 1785 with the brig *Terrible* and, in 1786, with the packetboat *Nootka*. In 1788, two ships of this Company were put under his command for a new expedition; these were the *Iphigenia* and the *Felice Aventurer*. The ships left China in January 1788. When Meares anchored in Nootka in May, he put a small cabin up for trade with the Indians. At the same time, he built a small frigate, the *Northwest America*, in the following months dedicating himself to the exploration of the

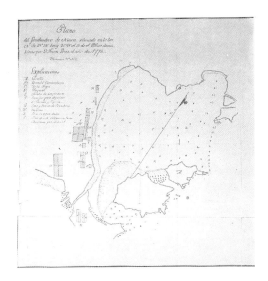

Map of the Nootka anchoring ground, discovered by Juan Pérez in 1774.
Diario de Bodega y Quadra, 1792.
Ministerio de Asuntos Exteriores.

View of Nootka settlement in which the letters A B designate the site occupied by Captain Meares. Francisco Lindo. Diario de Bodega y Quadra, 1792. Ministerio de Asuntos Exteriores.

Strait of Juan de Fuca and to trade with the natives of this region. Later, he was to claim that he had bought a strip of land from Macuina, head of the Nootka settlement. Towards September, he left for China with a substantial cargo of furs, while the *Iphigenia* and the *Northwest* headed for the Sandwich islands in order to winter over, after the cabin put up by Meares had been taken down.

This is the background to the presence of John Meares's vessels in Nootka. In the winter of 1789, the *Iphigenia* and the *Northwest* embarked upon a new voyage, in the hope of meeting up with the new vessels being commanded by Meares.

Martínez arrested the *Iphigenia* as long as it did not explain why it was in Nootka. The fact that it was sailing under the Portuguese flag led Martínez to release it, but not before having obliged Douglas, the ship's purser and owners' representative, to sign a document in which he undertook to "pay in Macao the assessed value of the said vessel, should His Excellency the Viceroy of New Spain declare them fair prisoner"[12]. Thus he confiscated the *Northwest America* in payment of the aid received by the Spanish. When this vessel reached Nootka, it was seized and sent to San Blas, where it was added to the Spanish Navy with the name of *Santa Gertrudis*.

The following incident with the vessels of the "Merchant Proprietors" was the detention of the *Princess Royal* and *Argonaut*, which reached Nootka on June 5th and July 2nd. This must have made Martínez think that a real English offensive was being mounted, so that he hardened his attitude. The refusal by Colnett, the Commander of the *Argonaut*, to show his papers, as well as his haste to leave the port, made Martínez suspicious of the instruction which Colnett had. Meares had organised the occupation of a port on this coast as a factory for the company, which is why he sent these two vessels along with Chinese colonists.

Following a verbal confrontation in which, without doubt, a determining factor was the bad temper of both captains and their excessive attachment to alcohol, Martínez arrested Colnett.

The Spanish officer's reasons for acting as he did were as follows: 1) The fear that, if Colnett were left in liberty, he might set up in another port from which it might be difficult to dislodge him, "there would continue to be a bad neighbour and, in a war, a very close enemy, leaving Old and New California, because of their limited defences, exposed", and, 2) the London Court should not have news of the event without the Spanish Court having been advised first[13].

Colnett's version is to be found in a memorandum which was drawn up by the Viceroy on September 12th of that year. He claimed that he was tricked into entering the port against his intentions. The real reason for his detention was to rob him, and he sets out a list of objects from the vessel, to a value of 5196 *pesos fuertes*, a vast sum for the period[14].

Macuina, Nootka chief. Tomás de Suria. Museo de América.

The fish «Cyprinus Americanus». (Carp).
J. Castañeda. Diario de Bodega y Quadra, 1792.
Ministerio de Asuntos Exteriores.

Count of Revillagigedo.
Biblioteca Nacional.

In the meantime, the head of the Viceroyalty changed, and Flórez was replaced by the Count Revillagigedo. The position of the former had been to fully approve Martínez's actions, coinciding as they did with his instructions. The Count was more cautious, aware of the possible reprecussions of the incident.

The two English ships were sent to San Blas, where Viceroy Florez received them correctly, making inventories of their cargoes and careening their hulls.

Once the detention had been completed, it was decided to consolidate the port. To this end, Bodega y Quadra, Commander of the San Blas Department organised an expedition with the frigate *Concepción*, the packetboat *San Carlos* and the schooner *Princesa Real*, under the command of sea captains Francisco Eliza, Jacinto Caamaño and Manuel Quimper. The instructions given them[15] contemplated the possibility that they might find Nootka occupied, since Martínez had abandoned it for lack of provisions, in what was a serious tactical error. Article 21 ordered the fortification of the port, with a battery of 20 cannon, and the *Compañía de Voluntarios de Cataluña*, under commander Alberni[16]. Exploration was ordered to continue as far as 59º, with examination of the fauna and flora, as well as of the character, temperament and numbers of the Indians, and with orders to establish good relations with them. The most advantageous ports were to be possessed, in accordance with a formulary accompanying the instructions.

These are the facts which led to a serious crisis between the Spanish and English crowns in the confines of the Americas. Alexander von Humboldt said of these lands "A few huts on the beach, a miserable bulwark defended by a handful of stone slingers, some cabbages planted inside a fence, were on the brink of provoking a bloody war between Spain and England"[17]. In fact, somewhat more than that stated by Humboldt was at stake. We shall next try to perceive the significance of this crisis in international politics in the last and transcendental quarter of the eighteenth century.

III. Diplomatic Developments

News of the event did not create excessive concern in Madrid, given the numerous incidents of this type which occurred in the Pacific[18]. Normal diplomatic mechanisms were used i.e. the Ambassador in London (Marquess of Campo) was notified of the facts so as to raise a formal protest, demanding guarantees that a recurrence would not take place.

Naturally, and given the international situation, it was not the intention of the Spanish crown to create a diplomatic crisis in this case. This protest was lodged on February 10th 1790, to the Duke of Leeds.

However, the English response was extremely hardline. Not only were no explanations given, but (it) "made it necessary for His Majesty to require satisfaction of this injury, previous to entering into other discussion"[19]. For a few months previously, English public opinion had been attracted to the Northwest Coast of America. The logs of the navigators who had explored it spoke of its riches in furs and fish. As well, John Meares carried out an intense campaign in which the Spanish crown was made to appear lord and tyrant of the southern seas. On the other hand, Spain's international position had been much weakened by events in France so that, in Madrid, it was feared that the incident might be used by England to claim greater freedom for its vessels in America. Spain had always defended its exclusive rights in the southern seas although, for two centuries, it had been sufficient to do so on paper, since no other country was making incursions of any significance.

Wagner, a historian who is fundamental to the history of the Northwest Coast informed of a plan on the part of the British crown to make a settlement there in 1790, in other words, after the events of the Nootka Sound became general knowledge[20].

The arms

From this moment on, an "escalation" began of the tension between the two nations, which was reflected in the arms of the two fleets. The Count of Floridablanca, Minister of State to the Spanish Crown, initiated the preparations of the Navy as early as April 1790, while the English did the same with two fleets, one destined for the Baltic and the other for the Atlantic.

Nootka Taisa with a child in cradle. M. García.
Diario de Bodega y Quadra, 1792.
Ministerio de Asuntos Exteriores.

England's maritime supremacy was beyond doubt, notwithstanding the intensive efforts carried out in Spain since the reign of Fernando VI and, in particular, under Carlos III. In 1790, theoretically, there were 69 ships and 39 frigates; and two factors were essential for this fleet to be effective. There needed to be sufficient resources with which to bring it up to combat capacity, and France would have to provide another fleet of similar characteristics. In point of fact, the force which sailed out of Cádiz on July 30th was of 30 ships, 11 frigates and 4 smaller vessels[21].

To put a naval fleet on a war footing involved an enormous burden on the public treasury. It is calculated that, for the London Court, more than three million pounds were involved. This meant that even the Bank of England would refrain from discounting naval ions. Such costs, all but unsupportable in peace time, naturally shot up on the outbreak of war, making them factors which acted in favour of swifter settlement of conflicts.

The international background

Spain's overseas policy throughout the eighteenth century swung from the Mediterranean rivalry with the Austrian empire to that of the Atlantic, with England, in the times of Carlos III. It was for this reason that an alliance system was forged with France, the so-called *Third Family Pact* which, far from being a mere union amongst the Bourbon family, was the only resource for containing the relentless increase in English influence. The pact was based on the equality of the two crowns and was of relative use as long as the internal cohesion of France made it possible to fulfill its provisions. From the Falklands crisis of 1770, the alliance entered a crisis. As Professor Rodríguez Casado has explained, the final scuttling of the Pact occurred with the Nootka incident[22], and it is true that, in the negotiations, it played a fundamental role. It was thus the French Revolution which finally brought to an end the system of European alliances inherited from Utrecht.

At the same time there was, from Carlos III on, an attempt by the Spanish Crown to open up towards the Nordic powers and the Russian Empire. This policy did bear fruit, especially with Russia, but without practical reality during the Nootka crisis.

The English situation was much more favourable. During the century, England had, in general, benefited from the numerous wars and their subsequent periods of peace. Even the Peace of Paris, of 1783, did not involve a serious internal crisis, since the European enclaves were upheld. The alliance with Holland continued, as did the influence over Portugal, while vigilance was maintained as the French Revolution loomed.

By way of continuation, we shall see some of the details of this situation, and their implication in the development of the Nootka crisis.

On April 15th 1790 the Count of Fernán Núñez, the Spanish Ambassador to France, wrote to the Count of Floridablanca, the Minister of State, of

Carlos III.
Ministerio de Hacienda, Madrid.

the conversation held with the French minister Montmorin: "... he added to my impression that the sad situation in France was the cause of which the English spoke with such arrogance..."[23]. At that moment, France was being transformed, the King and his ministers, true to the maintenance of the alliance with Spain, confronted with the National Assembly, many of whose members had great sympathy for the English system.

In this situation, in a letter dated June 4th, the Count of Floridablanca asked Fernán Núñez to petition the French court unequivocally to make a stand, from which the negotiation with England would depend, "... thus we will know what they think and do in order for us to handle the English... to which end you will understand that we will not be left alone and will not be taken in by courtly words if they are not accompanied by very clear and positive acts"[24].

The answer, on the application of the Family Pact, articles 5, 10, 12, 13 and 16 referring to the arming of a fleet and troops in defence of the petitioning nation, was delayed until August 1st, when Spain and England had already reached an agreement in principle. Louis XVI ordered the arming of 30 ships, the maximum permitted under the Constitution. In the National Assembly, Mirabeau defended the Spanish claim in payment of Spain's numerous interventions in the defence of France throughout the century. The Assembly debated between the need to maintain good relations with England and that of providing the world with an image of respectability, upholding the international treaties, the revolution notwithstanding. The rhetoric of Mirabeau was abble to combine all these factors. He pointed out that aid to Spain and the Third Family pact were not only dynastic, but also national questions. The Assembly rose above the question (and evaded it) taking a double decision and arming fifteen vessels more (to make a total of forty-five), at the same time declaring its renunciation of "all wars aimed at reducing the freedom of other peoples"[25].

A few words must be devoted to explaining Spain's situation in relation with the other powers. As far as the Russian Empire was concerned, Floridablanca was hoping to reach an agreement which would put the brakes on English ambitions. To do this, he had to back Russia in the Mediterranean and in its war with the Turkish Empire, which was not possible except on the base of significant subsidies, which were not available.

The Dutch alliance with England, and the strength of the party in power, pro-English, made neutrality difficult. Nevertheless, Floridablanca wrote to the Spanish representative in The Hague: "Your Excellency must make it understood that the King considers that England's allies are not in the *casus foederis* as that country claims"[26].

The alliance was also sought with the United States of America, but the concessions demanded on the navigable Mississippi "opening to them the doors of Mexican trade and its contraband"[27] were not acceptable to Flori-

Carlos IV. Goya.
Museo de Bellas Artes, Córdoba.

dablanca. On the other hand, within the United States, the neutralist current began to take a strong hold. Some writers locate here the real birth of the Monroe doctrine. For the United States, the Nootka incident involved its entry into international affairs as a nation, as well as the neutrality option, which it was to apply later, during the Napoleonic wars.

This was, in very summary form, the international situation when, in May 1790, Alleyne Fitzherbert arrived in Madrid as plenipotentiary ambassador to negotiate the solution to the crisis.

The diplomatic action

Fitzherbert (1753-1839) is a good example of eighteenth century English diplomacy. Educated at Derby, Eton and St. John's College Cambridge, he entered the diplomatic service very early, occupying a post in the English Embassy in Brussels. In 1783, he was appointed plenipotentiary in the peace negotiations with France and Spain in Paris. That same year, he was appointed special ambassador to the Court of Catherine of Russia. In 1787, he was Secretary to the Marquess of Buckingham in Ireland, from which post he was transferred to Madrid as special ambassador for the negotiations for the peace following the Nootka incidents. As a result of his action, he was appointed Baron of St. Helens. His diplomatic career culminated as Ambassador to The Hague and in the Court of Alexander (April 1801). He died in London in 1839. This brief biographical summary reveals the wide diplomatic experience which he had when he reached Madrid. He was thoroughly gamiliar with Franco-Hispanic relations and the situation in Europe, and was able to keep up the pressure on the Spanish Crown as long as the internal French crisis made this possible. Until he arrived, the negotiations had been handled by the official in charge of English affairs in Madrid, Merrit, whose work was centred on the negotiation of mutual disarmament.

The Spanish minister proposed three conditions in order to reach an understanding: 1) to seek an international arbiter from amongst the Kings of Europe to rule as to whether there had been injury to the English flag; 2) to refer in the conversations only to proven facts and 3) Spain's satisfaction would not suppose waiver of her rights[28]. In principle, these were not acceptable to Fitzherbert, but it was agreed to delay the discussion on the two nations' rights. Finally, on July 24th, there was a drawback from war, although the two Fleets remained at sea for some months more.

The legal arguments of the English were based on the application of private law, claiming that English subjects had been *forcibly* dispossessed of their possessions at Nootka. It was claimed that, as John Meares had, for a few sheets of copper, purchased a strip of land from Macuina, chief of the settlement of the port of Nootka, the Spanish officer had committed an offence of usurpation. The issue as to whether or not Meares had bought the land was to be argued by the two commissioners sent to Nootka in '92. Ano-

Luis XVI.
Museo Lázaro Galdiano, Madrid.

ther of the points taken into account by the English was the nature of the northern lands, which they considered to be free terrain, subject to the natural law of *prima ocupatio.*

The Spanish posture was precisely based on the Treaties of Utrecht, where the limits of the Spanish colonies had been fixed, given England's fear that the new Bourbon dynasty would favour French interests. For the Spanish Crown, the northwest coast was included within its possessions for two reasons. The expeditions during the seventeenth century to Lower California, and the acceptance of this principle by the Russians in the years from 1774-1779. The English Ambassador did not accept this argument, claiming that the possession is carried out when done *de facto* and not *de jure.* The Spanish presence prior to the incident could not be demonstrated (Juan Pérez's expedition 1774), so that it would be necessary to seek an agreement promoting freedom of trade and of navigation.

On September 16th, Floridablanca presented a new plan, based on four points. Freedom of entry for the two nations into the Nootka Sound, freedom of fishing and trade with the natives of the area, with rigorous control of possible contraband and negotiated settlement of any possible incidents. A series of proposals and counter-proposals followed this plan, clearly not to be detailed here, but which were the base for the future agreement. The English position advanced, throughout the conversations as a whole, was the generalisation of the scope of application of the agreements to the Americas as a whole[29].

Catalina II of Russia, 1729-1796.
Museo de Bellas Artes, Chartres.

The Convention of October 1790

On October 28th 1790, in El Escorial, the final agreement was signed. The negotiations had been handled personally by Floridablanca, although he had created a Board of State to examine the question. This Board was against the signing of the agreement, given the concessions made to England in America, and was rather in favour of war.

This Convention can be considered to be a transition agreement. On the Spanish side, it meant ceding important rights, defended since the very moment of the Spanish conquest. To England, it opened the doors on colonial trade and the possibilities of territorial expansion in the North of America. None of this took place, since the pressure of events in Europe rendered its articles null and void.

As already pointed out, the concessions made by the Spanish Crown under the Convention were significant[30]. In the first place, the foundation was limited of new settlements in America, so closing the possible expansion of the Viceroyalties; new settlements were to provide freedom of entry to both nations (Article V). The English subjects were permitted to form temporary settlements in places not occupied by the Spanish, and were allowed to trade with the Indians (Article VI). At the same time, freedom of naviga-

View of Nootka settlement. Malaspina Expedition.
Museo de América.

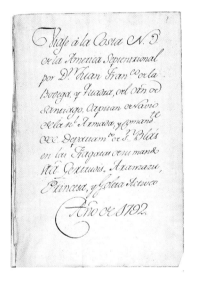

«Viaje a la Costa Noroeste de América
septentrional por Juan Francisco de la Bodega y
Quadra», 1792.
Ministerio de Asuntos Exteriores.

tion was provided for at ten leagues from the coast of all continents (Article IV). Therefore, the heavy restrictions defended by the Spanish crown during the previous three centuries before in relation to the possession of establishments, navigation and trade by other nations was abandoned under this treaty. Its provisions promoted contraband, an endemic evil of Spanish colonial trade.

From the English side, we find only vague promises to restrict and control contraband.

But the convention had the political virtue of ambiguity, in its scope of application, in the definitition of terms such as occupied territory, town, settlement..., in the role of the commissions which were to fix a dividing line separating exclusive Spanish territory from those of free circulation.

For Floridablanca, the Convention signified the delay of the war, and it was possible to concentrate on the French "evil", save the life of his King and prevent the "contagion" of revolutionary ideas.

IV. The Limits Expedition

In order to comply with the Articles of the Convention referring to the concession of territories and to fix the dividing line, two commissions were set up to meet in Nootka.

For the Spanish side, Juan Francisco de la Bodega y Quadra, head of the San Blas Department, sea captain, was appointed Commander of the expedition. Bodega y Quadra is a key figure within the history of the North-west Coast, with which he was linked for twenty years. As a naval officer, he took part in the expeditions of 1790 and 1792, and took part in the preparation of numerous maps made during these expeditions. At the same time, he promoted the investigation of the flora and fauna, and the study of the customs of the natives. All this forms an important document, which is essential to the historical study of the Northwest Coast. In the 1775 expedition, he travelled as far north as 56º with the small schooner *Sonora,* of ten metres length and a crew of ten men. The navigation took 250 days, during which several men died of scurvy. He took possession of some ports, and was attacked by the Indians, losing seven men. Thanks to the reinforcements provided by the frigate *Nueva Galicia* with which he was navigating in reserve, he was able to achieve the objectives proposed. The 1779 expedition was formed by the frigates *La Favorita* and *La Princesa,* with a crew of 195 men. They sailed from San Blas on February 11th, and reached 60º on July 22nd. They took possession of the ports of Santiago, Santa Cruz and Bucareli. The cartographic results of this expedition are housed in the Museo Naval in Madrid.

The English, for their part, commissioned George Vancouver (1758-1798), a seaman of wide experience, who had entered the Navy at the age of 13. He took part in James Cook's voyages to these coasts. The purpose of his expedition was to survey the Northwest Coast between 30º and 60º North. The vessels under his command, the *Discovery* and the *Chatham* were to survey and date the European settlements and to take possession of such lands as were discovered. The voyage was undertaken around the Cape of Good Hope and through New Zealand, Tahiti and the Sandwich islands. On April 17th 1792, he divided the Northwest Coast at Cape Mendocino. On May 2nd, he entered the Strait of Juan de Fuca, and laid up there for a long time. He took possession of the lands to the north, and christened them New Georgia. In the strait, he met up with Valdés and Caliano, Spanish commanders of the vessels *Mexicana* and *Sutil,* with whom, for a number of days, he explored the entrances to the strait. Finally, they went their separate ways, having exchanged maps. Vancouver entered Nootka on August 28th.

The talks between the two commissioners began immediately, following a splendid ceremony (given the circumstances) in which thirteen salvos were fired in honour of the two sovereigns. This was repeated for as long as the talks continued[31].

Most of the negotiations were carried out by letter, so that there would be a record, and a total of thirteen were exchanged between the commanders. This correspondence was complemented by some talks on shore.

Without going into the details of the discussion, we can attempt to define the two postures.

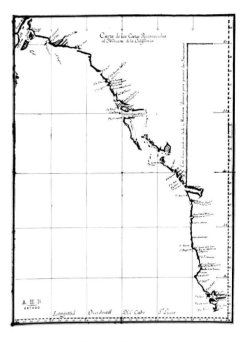

Chart of the northern California coast from Monterey to the entrance of Prince Charles. The demarcation line was to prevent penetrations further inland, 1791.
Archivo Histórico Nacional.

CONVENTION between His *Britannick* Majesty and the King of *Spain*. Signed at the *Escurial*, the 28th of *October*, 1790.

CONVENCION
ENTRE EL REY NUESTRO SEÑOR
Y EL REY DE LA GRAN BRETAÑA,
TRANSIGIENDO VARIOS PUNTOS
SOBRE PESCA, NAVEGACION Y COMERCIO
EN EL OCÉANO PACÍFICO Y LOS MARES DEL SUR,
FIRMADA EN SAN LORENZO EL REAL
Á 28 DE OCTUBRE DE 1790,
CUYAS RATIFICACIONES
SE CANGEARON EN EL MISMO REAL SITIO
Á 22 DE NOVIEMBRE SIGUIENTE.

DE ÓRDEN DEL REY
EN MADRID, EN LA IMPRENTA REAL.

Nootka convention. San Lorenzo de El Escorial, October 18, 1790.
Archivo Histórico Nacional.

Bodega sought from the beginning to explain the background of the convention, justifying Martínez's actions and showing the presence of the Spanish on these coasts to have been much earlier than that of Meares's ships and, with testimony from Macuina, a denial of the purchase of land by Meares[32].

Vancouver's stance was not to accept any discussion of the events which led to the Convention, and limited himself to meeting his orders to receive the establishment from Spanish hands.

As to the dividing line, the appearance in London of a map fixing it at San Francisco caused the Spanish position to harden, with Bodega seeking to have the Strait of Fuca as the southern limit of Upper California. Naturally enough, this was not accepted by Vancouver.

The Spanish Commander, satisfied that Vancouver was not going to accept, remitted the matter once more to the two Courts. By so acting, he coincided with the opinion of the new Spanish minister, the Count of Aranda, who had been a severe critic of the signing of the Treaty.

Without these initial stands having been altered, the conversations ended. The island where Nootka is located was named Vancouver and Quadra Island in honour of the two men and of their mission.

During his time in Nootka, Bodega organised a series of expeditions with the other ships from the department. Jacinto Caamaño[33] went northward by Queen Charlotte Island while Salvador Fidalgo explored the Strait of Juan de Fuca.

The two commissions still had to be met, since Vancouver went to the port of San Francisco and, later, to Monterey[34]. He corrected the English maps of these two ports. The Viceroy admonished Bodega for having allowed Vancouver to enter the two ports, since he was able to gather precise information on them[35].

The commander of the *Chatham,* Broughton, travelled to England through Veracruz, with Vancouver's papers, while he headed for the Sandwich islands to winter over, since he was planning a new campaign for the following year.

V. The Final Solution of the Conflict

Having failed to reach an agreement at Nootka, the two commissions were received very differently in the Courts of Madrid and London. While in Madrid this was seen as a "happy contingency", and the new Minister of State hoped to delay the taking of a decision until the situation was more favourable[36], in London it was suspected that Bodega was following some sort of secret orders to cause the mission to fail. We have already pointed out that this was not the case. Thanks to the common ground between Bodega and the new Minister, Bodega was given a commandery in the Order of Santiago, of which he was already a member, and a gratification of a year's salary.

The replacement of Floridablanca as minister and that, later, of Aranda, were dictated by the changing circumstances in France. The obsession of the Spanish King, Carlos IV, was to save the neck of Louis XVI, which is

Manuel Godoy. Príncipe de la Paz. Carnicero. Museo Romántico, Madrid.

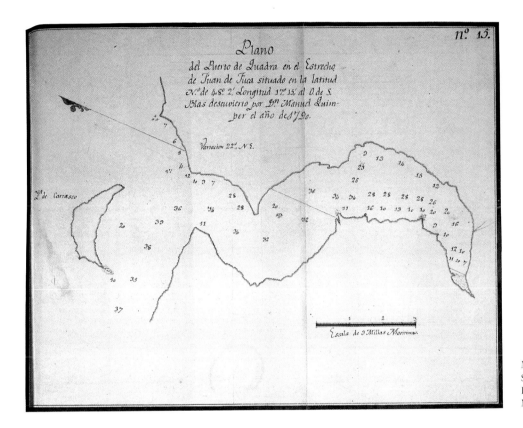

Map of the Port of Quadra in the Juan de Fuca Strait, discovered by Manuel Quimper in 1790. Diario de Caamaño, 1792. Ministerio de Asuntos Exteriores.

why he replaced the intransigent Floridablanda for the esteemed friend of the enlightened French, the Count of Aranda. When the situation improved an unbiased person was sought to take the initiative which the King lacked. The unhappy choice fell to Manuel Godoy[37].

Godoy's posture in respect of the Convention was never defined. France's declaration of war on England, then on Spain (March 7th), meant an Indian summer in the relations between the two nations. This was the moment used to settle once and for all the already too long Nootka incident.

Alleyne Fitzherbert, now Baron of St. Helens, was once more sent to Madrid.

Nootka had lost its strategic value once the coast had become better known as a whole. Given the fear that the talks might be prolonged indefinitely, the Baron proposed that both nations be allowed freedom of movement in the port, and ceded on the question of sovereignty. Thus a situation similar to that of a condominium was reached[38].

Under these assumptions, on January 11th 1794, the final agreement wqs signed, and the ceremony was detailed so as not to produce a new delay. The same commissioners as in 1792 were appointed, but, before they received the pertinent orders, Bodega died and Vancouver returned to England. The Spanish appointed Brigadier Alava and the English Lieutenant Pearce.

After demolishing the fortress at the entrance, the Spanish flag was struck and the English banner hoisted. Also struck, the two commissioners left the port in the same Spanish vessel.

Nootka was restored to its solitude, being visited by little more than the occasional hide hunter. Even in 1818, Macuina, the Indian chief of the settlement, remembered the presence of Spaniards and Englishmen, and his friendship with Bodega. In the Adams-Onís Treaty of 1819, Spain ceded its rights to the North of the 42nd parallel to the United States.

Detail of the Nootka Sound. [José Cardero].
Museo de América.

Sardine fishing. Tomás de Suria. Diario de
Bodega y Quadra, 1792.
Ministerio de Asuntos Exteriores.

Conclusion

Thus we come to the end of the examination of an incident, in the most
literal sense of the word, which took place at the end of the eighteenth century within the confines of the known world of that time. With this, our aim,
apart from fulfilling historical science, through which all the past is worthy
of familiarity, has been twofold. In the first place, and for the history of the
Northwest Coast, the continued presence of these vessels for almost two decades made it possible for its inclusion in the Western world to be carried
out by means of "scientific expeditions". This was, without doubt, lucky. It
made it possible to incorporate in a series of documents a large amount of
information on the flora and fauna, as well as on the native population, which
it is difficult to find in other zones of earlier colonisation. The men of the

Interior view of Macuina's house.
Diario de Bodega y Quadra, 1792.
Ministerio de Asuntos Exteriores.

eighteenth century who went there did so with their eyes open, and prepared to classify and order everything that came before them. Of this there is sufficient evidence in this book. On the Spanish side, a tradition was followed uninterrupted since the times of Felipe II, of the *conquistadors* being accompanied by missionaries and perhaps some scientists. During the eighteenth century, the Spanish Crown organised more than seven purely scientific expeditions and, from 1775, there were, to all intents and purposes, eleven which coincided. It is logical to think that the sailors who travelled to Nootka were immersed in the same spirit. During Bodega's time in Nootka, more than four hundred species of fauna and flora were classified and, as well, a number of vocabularies were prepared of the language of the natives of Nootka[39].

Peace chant. Haenke, Malaspina Expedition, 1791.
Museo Naval.

The study of the Nootka incident has enabled us to understand, as well, the international situation at the end of the eighteenth century. The system of alliances, the "colonial balance", the colonial wars, are all concepts which emerged during this period and which had an assured future in the following epoch.

For Spain, the Nootka incident was to remain as the last colonial move in which it would have some triumphs on its side. Just a few years later, as from the War of Independence, Spain's situation in the world was to have changed radically. Loss of the majority of the overseas possessions, international isolation, economic crisis and internal division mark the following stages, for us the period of "Spanish decadence". This stage, however, is subsequent to the Nootka incident.

Notes

1. *Viaje científico y político a la América Meridional, a las costas del Mar Pacífico ...en los años 89, 90, 91 y 93 por D. Alejandro Malaspina y D. José Bustamante*, Madrid, 1984.

2. This was a gradual process. Jover Zamora has pointed out, for example, the scant attention paid by the Emperor Carlos V to the Indies, in relation to his European policies. Only in respect of its undoubted influence on Spanish revenues would America have increasing importance. *Carlos V y los Españoles*, Madrid, 1985, p. 45.

The bird «Tetrao Californica». (Heath-cock)
Cerdá. Diario de Bodega y Quadra, 1792.
Ministerio de Asuntos Exteriores.

3. Jover Zamora (ed.): *Historia de España*, vol. XXIX, Madrid, 1985, p. 433.

4. Palacio Atard, Vicente: *El Tercer Pacto de Familia*, Prologue, Vicente Rodríguez Casado, Madrid, 1945.

5. Priestley, H. I.: *José de Gálvez, Visitor General of New Spain, 1765-1771*, Berkeley, 1916.

6. There were six Russian estableshments, with 422 men, Onalaska being the one closest to the continent. One study of this expedition was made by Barreiro Meiro: "El primer encuentro entre españoles y rusos en América; *Revista General de la Marina*", Madrid, April 1962.

7. Wagner, H. R.: *The Cartography of the Northwest Coast of America to the year 1800*, Amsterdam, 1968, p. 254.

8. The Count of La Pérouse (1741-1778?), French seaman who, from 1783, made a voyage to complete those of Cook. On the Northwest Coast, he studied the fur trade with China and Japan. He disappeared in 1788, and his remains were found on Vanikoro Island.

9. In 1784.

10. The order is dated 12/2/87, and Flórez took possession on August 17th.

11. *Diario de navegación* in "Colección de diarios y relaciones para la historia de los descubrimientos", vol. 1, Madrid, 1964, p. 70.

12. Idem, p. 87.
13. AHN Estado, leg. 4289, cp. 2, doc. 16.

14. Idem, cp. 5, doc. 2.

15. Idem, cp. 5, doc. 4.

16. "Relacion de la fuerza que se haya en este puerto de Nuca (sic)", MN ms. 330 f.86v. A total of 76 men, of which 31 were in Nootka.

17. Humboldt, Alejandro von: *Ensayo político sobre el Reino de Nueva España*, 5 vols., Mexico, 1941: Pol. 2, p. 359.

18. "De Chile a Nutka", AHN State, leg. 4291, cp. 1.

19. Idem, doc. 14.

20. Wagner, R. H.: op. cit., p. 239.

21. AHN Estado, leg. 4291, cp. 1, doc. 9.

22. In Palacio Atard, op. cit. Prologue, p. XIV.

23. Quoted by Mariñas in "El incidente de Nutka" in *Revista General de Indias*, Madrid, 1967, July-Dec.

24. Letter from Floridablanca to Fernan Nuñez (4/6/1790), in AHN Estado, leg. 4291, cp. 2, doc. 6.

25. Franklin, L. Ford: *Europe 1780-1830*, Madrid, 1973, p. 126.

26. AHN Estado, leg. 4291, cp. 2, doc. 27.

27. Idem.

28. Idem, doc. 10.

29. All the documentation on the talks is contained in the dossier already quoted.

30. The text of the Convention in AHN Estado, leg. 4290.

31. Bodega y Quadra's log in MAE, mss. 145 and 146.

32. AHN Estado, leg. 4287. This dossier contains copies of all the declarations taken.

33. Copy of Caamaño's log in MAE, mss. 10 and 11.

34. There are numerous documents which show the friendship which sprang up between the two commanders. Vancouver considered Bodega to be "my very esteemed and cordial friend", AHN Estado, leg. 4288, cp. 1.

35. AHN Estado, leg. 4290, cp. 2, doc. 3.

36. Idem, cp. 2, doc. 11.

37. Anes, Gonzalo: *El Antiguo Régimen: Los Borbones*, Madrid, 1981, p. 417, and, in addition, the Introduction to the *Memorias de Godoy*, Biblioteca de Autores Españoles, Madrid, 1965.

38. "... the British Court recognises that the restitution stipulated in Article 1 of the 1790 Convention of the provisions and plots of land belonging to its subjects has not given that Crown any right of sovereignty or exclusive possession of the whole port", AHN, Estado, leg. 4291 (2), cp. 3, doc. 12.

39. "Catálogo de animales y plantas que han reconocido y determinado por el sistema de Linneo los facultativos de mi expedición D. José Mozino y D. José Maldonado", in Bodega's log of the 1792 expedition, in MAE, mss. 145 and 146. As to the dictionaries compiled by the scientific expeditions, a sample is that of the article by M.ª Luisa Martín-Merás, *Revista de Historia Naval*, no. 6, Madrid, 1984.

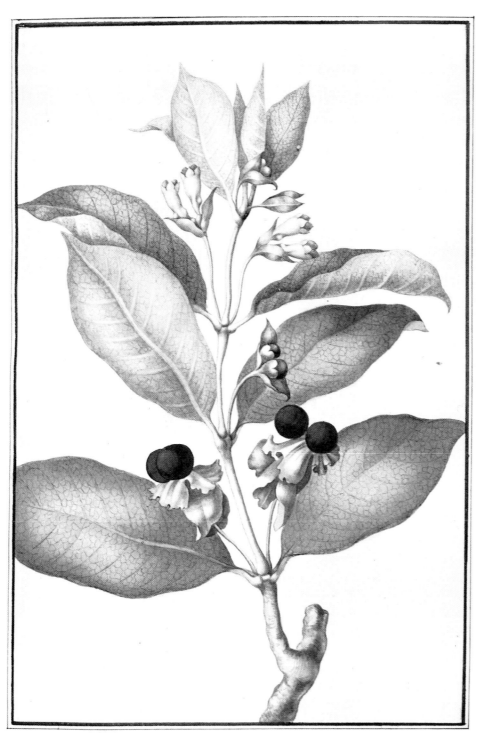

The plant «Campanula Linearis» (Harebell).
Castañeda. Diario de Bodega y Quadra, 1792.
Ministerio de Asuntos Exteriores.

The plant «Lonicera Nutkensis» (Honeysuckle).
Miguel Albián. Diario de Bodega y Quadra, 1792.
Ministerio de Asuntos Exteriores.

The plant «Lilium Kamschatkense» (Lily).
Miguel Albián. Diario de Bodega y Quadra, 1792.
Ministerio de Asuntos Exteriores.

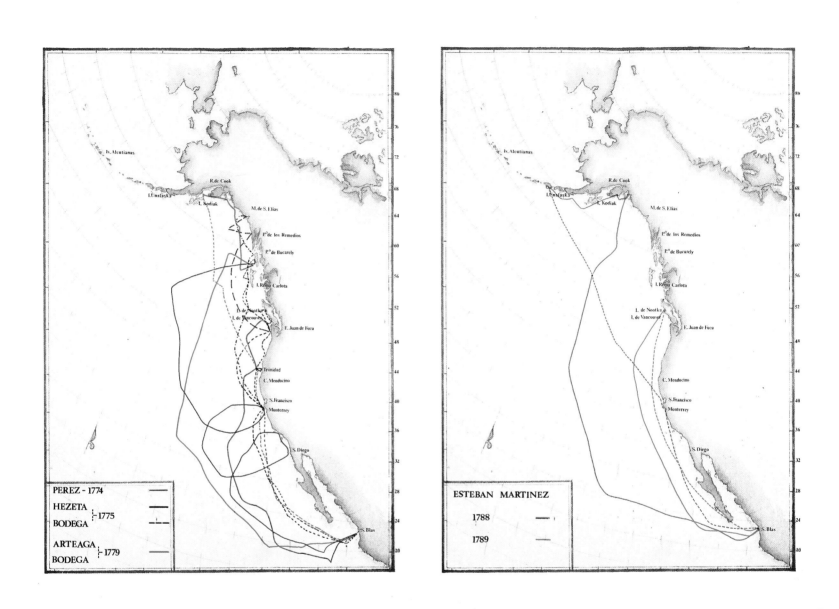

Sea-going Expeditions (1774 – 1792)

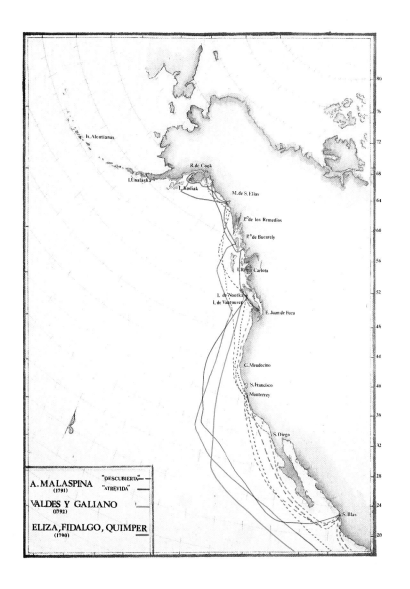

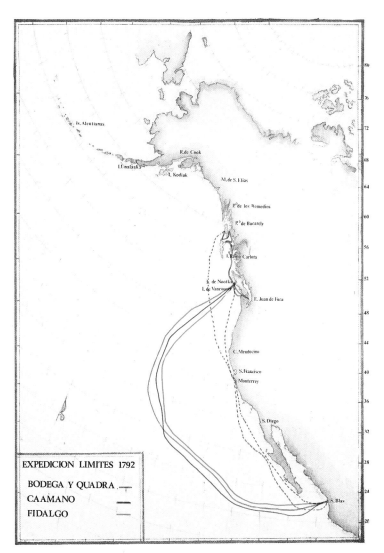

Documentry Appendix

The following list of diaries and their copies of the Spanish
Expeditions to the Northwest Coast, have been compiled from the
files of the Museo Naval de Madrid, and the systematic research
from the catalogues of the American section of the Biblioteca
Nacional, Biblioteca del Palacio Real, Archivo Histórico Nacional and
Archivo del Ministerio de Asuntos Exteriores of Madrid; Archivo
General de Indias de Sevilla. The references from the Archivo
General de la Nación de México have been extracted from the article
by Carmen Sotos Serrano.
The published diaries appear in the bibliography with their respective
author.

1774: Juan Perez Expedition

Juan Pérez:

"Primera exploración de la costa septentrional de California hecha por el Alférez de Fragata graduado D. Juan Pérez con la fragata *Santiago* en el año de 1774"
MN ms. 331, fol. 1.
Continuación del Diario que formó el Alférez graduado de Fragata D. Juan Pérez con la titulada *Santiago* alias la *Nueva Galicia*... que comprehende su salida de Monterrey a explorar la costa septentrional y su regreso a este puerto en 26 de agosto de 1774"
AGI Estado, 38-3

Esteban José Martínez:

"Copia de lo que el segundo piloto del Departamento de San Blas, D. Esteban José Martínez expresa en su diario de navegación sobre las exploraciones de la costa septentrional" (1774)
AGI Estado, Audiencia de México, 20-10
"Copia de lo que el segundo piloto D. Esteban José Martínez expresa en su diario de navegación referente al 20 y 21 de julio" (1774)
AGI Estado, 20-11
AGI Estado, 38-3

Fray Tomás de la Peña:

"Diario del viaje en la fragata *Santiago* por orden de Fr. Junípero Serra, en el viaje de D. Juan Pérez" (1774)
MN ms. 332, fol. 137 and Bancroft Library

Fray Juan Crespi:

"Diario de Fray Juan Crespi, misionero del Colegio de Propaganda Fide de San Fernando de México, del viaje que en compañía de Fr. Tomás de la Peña, realizó en la fragata de S. M. *Santiago*, desde el puerto de Monterrey hasta los 60º Norte"
(6 june-27 august 1774)
AGI, Estado 43-10

1775: Bruno de Hezeta and Juan Francisco de la Bodega y Quadra Expedition

Bruno Hezeta and Juan Francisco de la Bodega y Quadra:

"Segunda exploración de la costa septentrional de California en 1775 con la fragata *Santiago* y la goleta *Sonora* mandadas por el teniente de navío D. Bruno Hezeta y el de fragata D. Juan Francisco de la Bodega y Quadra desde el puerto de San Blas hasta los 58º"
MN ms. 575, doc. 8
MN ms. 331, fol. 46
MN ms. 127, fols. 226-271

Bruno Hezeta:

"Copia del diario de navegación que hizo el teniente de navío D. Bruno Hezeta en la fragata *Santiago* alias la *Nueva Galicia*, que fue a los descubrimientos de las costas septentrionales de California desde el Departamento de San Blas, del 16 de marzo a 20 de noviembre de 1775"
AGI Estado, 38-11
AGN Hist., 324
AHN Estado, leg. 2314

Juan Francisco de la Bodega y Quadra:

"Navegación hecha por D. J. F. Bodega y Quadra, teniente de la goleta *Sonora* a los descubrimientos de los mares y costas septentrionales de California" (1775)
MN ms. 622, doc. 1. See Bodega y Quadra, 1943
BP mss. de América, 324
"Comento del Diario de Navegaciones, Descubrimientos y demás particularidades desde la Latitud en que se encuentra el Departamento de San Blas de 27 grados 30 minutos hasta los 58º, todo inspeccionado por el Teniente de Fragata D. Juan F. de la Bodega y Quadra, Capitán de la goleta *Sonora* de 18 codos de quilla y 6 de manga, tripulada por un piloto, un contramaestre, un guardián, tres marineros, un sangrador, un cocinero, un paje y el criado del dicho comandante" (1775)
AHN Estado, leg. 4291, cp. 2, doc. 10
AGN California, 324
"Carta-relación de D. Juan Francisco de la Bodega y Quadra al virrey de Nueva España D. Antonio M.ª de Bucareli". (1775)
AGI 20-21

Antonio Mourelle:

"Relación de los descubrimientos hechos en el viaje que D. Antonio Mourelle emprendió en la goleta *Sonora* a las órdenes de D. Bruno Hezeta para las costas de California en 1775, por mandato de D. Antonio Bucareli, Virrey de Nueva España"
MN ms. 575, doc. 5. See Landin Carrasco; 1978
"Extracto de la relación de..."
MN ms. 332, fol. 156
"Copia del diario de la navegación hecha por el segundo piloto de la Armada D. Antonio Mourelle en la goleta *Sonora* del mando del Teniente D. Juan Francisco de la Bodega y Quadra a los descubrimientos de las costas y mares septentrionales de California del 1 de enero a 20 de noviembre del año 1775, por orden del Virrey de Nueva España D. Antonio María de Bucareli y Ursua"
AGI Estado, 38-5
"Navegación a las costas de California por el piloto D. Antonio Mourelle en la goleta *Sonora* al mando de D. Juan Francisco de la Bodega y Quadra. Año de 1775"
BP ms. de América, 299
AGI Estado, 38-5

Fray Benito de la Sierra:

"Diario de la expedición de Hezeta" (1775)
Ms. belonging to G. R. G. Conway, Mexico City, traslated by A. J. Baker, and printed with notes by H. R. Wagner in *Quarterly* of California Historical Society for September, !930

1779: Ignacio Arteaga and Juan francisco de la Bodega y Quadra Expedition

Ignacio Arteaga and Juan Francisco de la Bodega y Quadra:

"Exploración hacia el Norte hasta los 60º 14'. Expedición de D. J. Arteaga y con D. J. F. Bodega y Quadra en las fragatas *Nuestra Señora del Rosario* alias la *Princesa* y *Nuestra Señora de los Remedios* alias la *Favorita*. Año de 1779"
AGN Historia, vols. 63 y 64
MN ms. 331, fol. 89 y ms. 575 bis, fol. 2

Ignacio Arteaga:

"Diario de navegación que con el favor de Dios y la Virgen de la Regla espera hacer el teniente de navío D. Ignacio Arteaga mandando la fragata de S. M. nombrada *Nuestra Señora del Rosario* alias *la Princesa* desde el puerto de San Blas... hasta los 70º de la misma especie" (1779)
MN ms. 622, fol. 47 y ss. See Arteaga; 1975
AGI Estado, 38-13

Juan Francisco de la Bodega y Quadra:

"Navegaciones y descubrimientos hechos por orden de su majestad en la latitud en que se halla el Departamento y puerto de San Blas de 21 grados 30 minutos hasta los 61 grados, por el teniente de navío de la Real Armada, D. Juan Francisco de la Bodega y Quadra del orden de Santiago y Comandante de la fragata de S. M. *Nuestra Señora de los Remedios* alias *la Favorita* de 39 codos de quilla y 13 de manga, calada de popa en 14 pies y de proa en 13. Año de 1779"
BN ms. 19266, fols. 134-165. See Noticias y Documentos..., 1959
MN ms. 332, fols. 11 y ss. y fols. 38 y ss.
"Comento de la navegación y descubrimientos hechos en los viajes en la costa septentrional de California por Juan Francisco de la Bodega y Quadra" (1779)
MN ms. 2012

Antonio Mourelle:

"Navegación hecha por el Alférez de Fragata D. Antonio Mourelle destinado de segundo capitán de la fragata *Favorita* de 40 codos de quilla, 14 de manga, calada de popa de 14 pies; ídem de proa de 13, desde el puerto de San Blas que está en la latitud de 21º 30' N. al Occidente de París 107º 6' en longitud, a los descubrimientos de la Costa Septentrional de California que se extendieron hasta la altura de 61º al Occidente de París 158º"
MN ms. 332, fols. 93 y ss. See Landin Carrasco; 1978
AGN California, 8

Juan Bautista Aguirre:

"Diario de navegación que trabajó el segundo piloto de la fragata *Nuestra Señora de los Remedios* alias *la Favorita*, D. Juan Bautista Aguirre
AGI Estado, 38-18

José Cañizares:

"Navegación que hace el Alférez de fragata graduado y primer piloto D. José Cañizares desde el puerto de San Blas en 21 grados 30 minutos de latitud Norte a los descubrimientos de la Costa septentrional de California en la Fragata de S. M. *Nuestra Señora de los Remedios* alias *la Favorita*... de la que es comandante el Teniente de Navío de la real Armada y Caballero del orden de Santiago, D. Juan Francisco de la Bodega y Quadra... Año de 1779"
AGI Estado, 38-17

Fernando Bernardo de Quirós:

"Diario de navegación... que espera hacer el Teniente de Navío de la Real Armada y segundo Comandante de la Expedición de Altura D. Fernando Bernardo de Quirós, embarcado en la Fragata *Nuestra Señora del Rosario, la Marinera* alias *la Favorita* del mando del de la misma clase D. Ignacio Arteaga a cuyas órdenes va también la Fragata *Favorita* mandada por el de igual grado D. Juan Francisco de la Bodega y Quadra, con órdenes una y otra de llegar en conserva a los siete grados de latitud al Norte de California y venir desde ellos reconociendo la Costa y tomando cuantas posesiones se puedan" (1779)
AGI Estado, 38-14.

José Camacho:

"Diario de navegación que... pretende hacer el Primer Piloto del número de la Real Armada D. José Camacho, embarcado en la Fragata de S. M. *Nuestra Señora del Rosario* alias *la princesa*... mandada por el Teniente de Navío D. Ignacio Arteaga"
AGI Estado, 38-16.

Juan Pantoja and Arriaga:

"Diario de Navegación que principia hacer D. Juan Pantoja y Arriaga segundo Piloto de la Fragata de S. M. *Nuestra Señora del Rosario* alias *Princesa*" (1779)
AGI Estado, 38-19

1788 and 1789: José Esteban Martínez and Gonzalo López de Haro Expeditions

José Esteban Martínez and Gonzalo López de Haro:

"Diario que llevaron las fragatas *Princesa*, mandada por el Alférez de Navío D. José Esteban Martínez y el paquebot *San Carlos*, mandada

Walrus. Diario de Esteban José Martínez.
Archivo General de Indias.

por el primer piloto D. Gonzalo López de Haro, 8 de marzo, 1788"
MN ms. 331, fol. 137

José Esteban Martínez:

"Noticia de lo acaecido en la fragata *Princesa* y paquebote *Filipino* en su expedición al reconocimiento de los Establecimientos rusos en el año de 1788 por el mar del Sur, al mando del primer piloto de la Real Armada D. José Esteban Martínez"
MN ms. 330, fol. 7
"Relación de la entrada de San Lorenzo de Nittka (sic) formada por los individuos de la expedición que de orden de Carlos III salió de San Blas el año 1788 del puerto de San Blas en la fragata *Princesa* (Geografía, fauna, flora, religión y vocabulario de las lenguas nutkeña y de Sandwich)"
BP ms. América, 329
"Extracto de una carta escrita en el puerto de San Lorenzo de Nootka sobre lo ocurrido en la expedición de la fragata el *Rosario* alias la *Princesa* y el paquebot *San Carlos, el Filipino* al mando del Piloto D. José Esteban martínez que salió de San Blas para dicho puerto el 18 de octubre de 1789"
MN ms. 330, fol. 40. See Martínez; 1964
"Expedición de San Lorenzo de Nutka, 1789, por el piloto D. José Esteban Martínez y noticias sobre el descubrimiento del estrecho de Juan de Fuca"
AGN Historia, vol. 65
"Noticias relacionadas con el apresamiento de los buques ingleses *Argonauta* y *Princesa Real* en Nutka" (1789-1790)
AGN Historia, vol. 66

1790-1791: Francisco Eliza, Salvador Fidalgo and Manuel Quimper Expeditions

Francisco Eliza:

"Extracto de la navegación y reconocimientos hechos por el Teniente de Navío D. Francisco Eliza" (1790)
AHN Estado, leg. 4288
"Relación del viaje de D. Francisco Eliza remitida a D. Juan Francisco de la Bodega y Quadra el 5 de julio de 1790"
AHN Estado, leg. 4289, cp. 5, doc. 6
"Segunda expedición a Nutka al mando del Teniente de Navío D. Francisco Eliza con la fragata *Concepción,* el paquebot *Filipino* y la balandra *princesa Real*" (1790)
AGN Historia, vol. 68, exp. 1, 3, 5
"Extracto de la navegación y reconocimientos hechos en la costa septentrional de California en el año 1791 por el paquebot *San Carlos* y la goleta *Santa Saturnina* al mando del Teniente D. Francisco Eliza"
MN ms. 332
"Extracto de la navegación hecha en la goleta *Santa Saturnina* del puerto de Santa Cruz de Nutka a los reconocimientos de la costa Sur de dicho puerto y llegada al Departamento de San Blas" (1791)
AGN Historia, vol. 44. See Wagner; 1933

Salvador Fidalgo:

"Extracto del diario del Teniente de Navío D. Salvador Fidalgo comisionado para pasar a Nutka y continuar el reconocimiento del Príncipe Guillermo y Río Cook para saber si se hallan establecidos los rusos en aquellos parajes" (1790)
NM ms. 271, fol. 104 y ms. 331, fol. 169

"Noticias y apuntes sobre el viaje de D. Salvador Fidalgo a la exploración de California septentrional y a los establecimientos rusos en América" (1790)
MN ms. 575 bis, doc. 4
"Noticias sobre el viaje del Teniente de Navío D. Francisco Eliza de Nutka a Príncipe Guillermo, Rivera de Cooke, Isla Corza"
AGN Historia, vol. 68, cp. 6 a 11
"Viajes de descubrimiento de D. Francisco Eliza a bordo de la *princesa Real* y la fragata *Concepción*" (1790)
AHN Estado, leg. 4287

Manuel Quimper:

"Segundo reconocimiento de la entrada de Fuca y costas comprendidas entre ella y la de Nutka hecho en el año de 1790 con la balandra *Princesa Real* mandada por el alférez de navío D. Manuel Quimper" (1790)
MN ms. 331, fol. 193
"Noticias del viaje del Comandante D. Manuel Quimper al estrecho de Juan de Fuca y escrituras de toma de posesión de la bahía de Núñez Gaona, de Quimper y Revillagigedo, rada de Valdés y Bauzá" (1790)
AGN Historia, vol. 68, exp. 12 a 17

1789-1793: Alejandro Malaspina Expedition

D. Alejandro Malaspina:

"Viaje científico y político a la América Meridional, a las costas del Mar pacífico y a las Islas Marianas y Filipinas verificado en los años de 1789-94 a bordo de las corbetas *Descubiertas* y *Atrevida*... por los capitanes de navío D. Alejandro Malaspina y D. José Bustamante y Guerra"
MN ms. 753
See Malaspina; 1885 y 1984

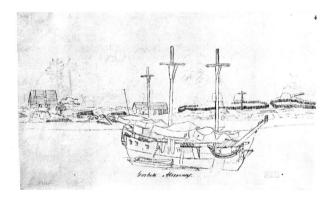

A corvette in Nootka. Malaspina Expedition.
Museo de América.

D. José Bustamante y Guerra:

"Viaje de las corbetas *Descubierta* y *Atrevida* a Montevideo, Chile, Perú, Acapulco y Filipinas" (1789-93)
MAE ms. 13. See Bustamante; 1868 and Malaspina; 1885

D. José Espinosa y Tello:

"Diario de Cádiz a Veracruz, Méjico y Acapulco, de este puerto de San Blas con la *Atrevida*, reunión de ambas corbetas en Acapulco y continuación del viaje a la costa NO Pacífico, Filipinas... y regreso al puerto del Callao" (1790-93)
MN ms. 95, fols. 1-320 and 320
Mss. 140 y 562, fols. 84-290

Arcadio Pineda:

"Fragmento del diario de navegación de la *Atrevida* de Acapulco a San Blas y acontecimientos en este puerto; regreso a Acapulco y estancia en dicho puerto" (1791)
MN ms. 92 bis, fols. 120-128v
"Noticias de San Blas"
MN ms. 127, fols. 250-251v

Francisco Javier Viana:

"Diario del Teniente de Navío D. Francisco Xavier de Viana trabajado en el viaje de las corbetas de S. M. *Descubierta* y *Atrevida* en los años de 1789 al 1793..."
MN ms. 92 bis. See Viana, Francisco Javier; 1849 y 1958

Tomás de Suria:

"Diario de Tomás de Suria"
The original in the Colection Beinecke. Library of the University of Yale. Pub. Wagner, Henry: "Journal of Tomas de Suria of his voyage with Malaspina". PHR. The Pacific Historical Review, september 1936, 234-276

Antonio Tova y Arredondo

"Diario del viaje del segundo comandante de la *Atrevida* D. Antonio Tova y Arredondo" (1789-1794)
The original in the Biblioteca Pública Municipal de Santader
See Sanfeliu Ortiz; 1944

1792: Dionisio Alcalá Galiano y Cayetano Valdés Expedition

Dionisio Alcalá Galiano y Cayetano Valdés:

"Relación del viaje hecho por las goletas *Sutil* y *Mexicana* en el año de 1792 para reconocer el Estrecho de Fuca, con una introducción en que se da noticia de las expediciones ejecutadas anteriormente por los españoles en busca del paso del Noroeste de América"
See Relación..., 1802 y 1958
"Copia del extracto del diario de la Campaña ejecutada por las goletas *Sutil* y *mexicana* al mando de los Capitanes de Fragata D. Dionisio Alcalá Galiano y D. Cayetano Valdés por el estrecho o canal de Juan de Fuca" (1792)
AHN Estado, leg. 4287, cp. 3, doc. 11
"Viaje de las goletas *Sutil* y *Mexicana* al reconocimiento de la entrada de Juan de Fuca" (1792)
AHN Estado, leg. 4290, cp. 2, doc. 44

Dionisio Alcalá Galiano:

"Expedición de las goletas *Sutil* y *Mexicana* al reconocimiento de la entrada de Juan de Fuca en el año de 1792"
MN mss. 143 y 619

1792: The Limits Expedition

D. Juan francisco de la Bodega y Quadra:

"Viaje a la costa NO de América septentrional por D. Juan Francisco de la Bodega y Quadra del orden de Santiago, Capitán del Departamento de San Blas en las Fragatas de su mando *Santa Gertrudis, Aranzazu, Princesa* y goleta *Activa*. Año de 1792"
MAE mss. 145 y 146

Mariano Moziño:

"Descripción de la isla de Mazarredo" o "Noticias de Nutka"
MN ms 468, fols. 114-164 y ms. 143. See Moziño, Mariano; 1804, 1913 and Wilson; 1970

Jacinto Caamaño:

"Diario del año 1792. Extracto del diario de las navegaciones, exploraciones y descubrimientos hechos en la América septentrional por D. Jacinto Caamaño, Teniente de Navío de la Real Armada y Comandante de la fragata *Aranzazu* desde el puerto de San Blas de donde salió el 20 de marzo del año 1792"
MAE mss. 10 y 11. See Caamaño; 1938, 1975
AGN Historia, vol. 71

Francisco Eliza:

"Resultas del viaje de las goletas *Activa* y *Mexicana* al mando del teniente de fragata D. Francisco Eliza en el reconocimiento de la costa de California desde la latitud de 41º a 47º" (1792)
MN ms. 273, fol. 250 y ss.
MN ms. 331, fol. 283
MN ms. 575 bis, doc. 8
"Extracto de lo acaecido en la navegación hecha en el Bergantín del Rey nombrado el *Acctibo*" (1793)
AHN Estado, leg. 4290, cp. 4
MN ms. 332, fol. 63. See Wagner; 1931

Francisco Eliza and Juan Martínez Zayas:

"Expedición de D. Francisco Eliza y el piloto D. Juan Martínez Zayas a la costa de San Francisco y al estrecho de Juan de Fuca"
AGN Historia, vol. 71, exp. 8

Chief of the Point of Lángara. José Cardero.
Museo Naval.

Bibliography

Abbad y Lasierra, Iñigo: 1981. *Descripción de las costas de California*. Ed. by Sylvia Lyn Hilton. Madrid.

Adam, L.: 1936. "North-West American Indian Art and its Early Chinese Parallels". *Man*. London. Vol. 36, no. 3.

Alcalá Galiano, Antonio: 1955. *Obras escogidas de don Antonio Alcalá Galiano*. Preface and edition by Jorge Campos. Madrid.

Alcalá Galiano, Dionisio: 1890. *Recuerdos de un anciano*. Madrid. Vol. 8.

Alcalá Galiano, Dionisio y Valdés, Cayetano: 1792. *Extracto del diario de la campaña ejecutada por las goletas "Sutil" y "Mexicana"*. See Wagner, H. R. California, 1933.

Alvarez López, Enrique: 1946. "Noticia acerca de las plantas ultramarinas estudiadas por Cavanilles y en particular de las recolectadas por Luis Neé". *Revista de Indias*. Madrid, no. 25, july-september, 1946, pp. 503-540.

—— 1951. "Noticias y papeles de la expedición científica mejicana dirigida por Sessé", *Anales del Jardín Botánico de Madrid*, 2, pp. 5-79.

—— 1952. "Las tres primeras campañas de la expedición científica dirigida por Sessé, y sus resultados botánicos", *Anales del Instituto Botánico A. J. Cavanilles de Madrid*, I, pp. 39-141.

Alvarez Terán, M.ª Concepción: 1980. *Catálogo XXIX. Mapas y dibujos (1503-1805) del Archivo General de Simancas*. Vol. 1. Valladolid.

Ames, Kenneth M.: 1981. "The evolution of social ranking on the Northwest Coast of North America". *American Antiquity*. Salt Lake City. Vol. 46, pp. 789-805.

Anderson, Bern: 1960. *The Life and Voyages of Captain George Vancouver*. Seattle.

Anónimo: 1778. *Voyage dans L'Hemisphére austral et autour du Monde fait sur les vaisseaux L'Avanture et la Resolution 1772-75*. París, 6 vols.

Anson, G.: 1749. *A voyage round the world in the years MDCCXL, I, II, III y IV*. London.

Arias Divito, Juan Carlos: 1968. *Las expediciones científicas españolas durante el siglo XVIII. Expedición Botánica a Nueva España*. Madrid.

Armillas Vicente, José Antonio: 1973. "Relaciones diplomáticas entre España y los Estados Unidos de Norteamérica a fines del siglo XVIII, 1789-1802". *Estudios del departamento de Historia Moderna*. Zaragoza, pp. 103-120.

Arteaga, Ignacio de: 1975. "Diario de la navegación que con el favor de Dios y de la Virgen de Regla espera hacer el Teniente de Navío...", in *Colección de Diarios y Relaciones para la Historia de los Viajes y Descubrimientos*. Madrid, t. VII, pp. 17-162.

Artiñano, Gervasio de: 1920. *La arquitectura naval española (en madera). Bosquejo de sus condiciones y rasgos de su evolución*. Barcelona.

Babio Walls, Manuel: 1981. *El Real Colegio Seminario de San Telmo, 1681-1981. Bosquejo de su fundación*. Sevilla.

Bancroft, Hubert Howe: 1884. *History of California*, volume XVIII of *The words of Huber Howe Bancroft*. San Francisco.

—— 1884. *History of the Northwest Coast*, volume XXVII. San Francisco.

—— 1886. *History of Alaska*. San Francisco.

Barbeau, Marius: 1950. "Totem Poles". *National Museum of Canadá: Anthropological Series*. Ottawa, no. 30. Bulletin no. 119, 2 vols.

Barcia: 1901. *Catálogo de los retratos de personajes españoles que se conservan en la Sección de Estampas y Bellas Artes de la Biblioteca Nacional*. Madrid.

Barras de Aragón, Francisco de las: 1935. *Estudios sobre la ciencia española del siglo XVII*. Madrid.

—— 1953. "D. Esteban José Martínez, alumno del Colegio de San Telmo de Sevilla". *Publicaciones de la Real Sociedad Geográfica*. Madrid, Series B, no. 312.

—— 1954. "Reconocimiento de las islas Hawaii Sandwich por el marino español Quimper". *Publicaciones de la Real Sociedad Geográfica*. Madrid, Series B, no. 318.

—— 1956. "Los Rusos en el Nororeste de América", *Anales de la Asociación Española para el progreso de las ciencias*. Madrid, no. 31, pp. 111-126.

—— "Un gran marino español del siglo XVIII: don Francisco Antonio Mourelle". *Las Ciencias*, year XVI, no. 1, pp. 161-210.

Barreiro-Meiro, Roberto: 1962. "El primer encuentro entre españoles y rusos en América". *Revista General de Marina*. Madrid, April 1962.

Barrington, Daines: 1781. *Miscellanies*. London.

Barrow, John: 1846. *Voyages of Discovery and Research within the Arctic Regions*. London.

Barry, John Neilson: 1926. "Broughton on the Columbia in 1792". *Oregon Historical Quarterly*, 27, pp. 397-411.

—— 1931. "Broughton, Up the Columbia River, 1792". *OHQ*, 32, pp. 301-12.

—— 1932. "Columbia River Exploration, 1792". *OHQ*, 33, pp. 31-42, 143-55.

—— 1938. "Who Discovered the Columbia River?". *OHQ*, 39, pp. 152-61.

Bayle, C.: 1933. *Historia de los descubrimientos y colonización de los P.P. de la Compañía de Jesús en la Baja California*. Madrid.

Beaglehole, John C.: 1955-1967. *The Journals of Captain James Cook on His Voyages of Discovery*. Vol. 3: *The Voyage of the Resolution and Discovery*. Cambridge.

—— 1974. *The Life of Captain James Cook*. Stanford, California.

Beals, Herbert, ed.: 1985. *For Honor and Country: the Diary of Bruno de Hezeta*. Portland.

Beerman, Eric: 1982. "Basque sailer at Bucareli Bay". *The Alaska Journal*. Austin.

Benedict, Ruth: 1971. *El hombre y la cultura*. Barcelona.

Berg, L.: 1926-28. *The Pacific-Russian scientific investigation*. Leningrado.

Berkh, Vasilii Nikolaevich: 1823. *Khronologicheskaia istoriia otkrytiia aleutakiks ostrovov*. St. Petersburg. (English edition, Seattle, 1938).

Bernard, E.: 1962. *The Viceregency of Antonio María Bucareli*. Austin.

Blanca Carlier, José M.: 1979. "El Cuerpo de pilotos de la Armada". *Revista General de Marina*, Agoust-September 1979.

Boas, Franz: 1897. *The social organization and the secret societies of the Kwakiutl indians*. Washington.

—— 1947. *El arte primitivo*. México.

Bodega y Cuadra, Francisco Antonio: 1865. (1775 y 1779) "Diarios de los viajes de Bodega y Cuadra de 1775 y 1779". *Anuario de la Dirección de Hidrografía*. Madrid, t. III.

—— 1943 (1775). "Navegación hecha por Juan Francisco de la Bodega y Quadra, Teniente de Fragata de la Real Armada y comandante de la goleta 'Sonora': A los descubrimientos de los mares y costa septentrional de California". *Colección de diarios y relaciones para la historia de los viajes y descubrimientos*, 2. Madrid, pp. 102-33.

—— 1959 (1779). "Navegaciones y descubrimientos hechos por oden de su magestad en la latitud en que se halla el Departamento y puerto de San Blas de 21 grados 30 minutos hasta los 61 grados, por el teniente de navío de la Real Armada, D. ... del orden de Santiago y Comandante de la fragata de S. M. 'Nuestra Señora de los Remedios' alias 'la Favorita', de 39 codos de quilla y 13 de manga, calada de popa en 14 pies y de proa en 13. Año de 1779". See *Noticias y Documentos*. Madrid, 1959.

Bolin, L. A.: 1959. "Nombres españoles en las Costas de Alaska". *Revista General de Marina*. May 1959.

Bona, Emma: 1931. "Sulla vita et viaggi di Alessandro Malaspina di Mulazzo, 1754-1810". *Bolletino della R. Società Geografica Italiana*. Roma, series VI, vol. VIII, Janvier 1931.

—— 1935. *Alessandro Malaspina sue navigazioni ed esplorazioni*. Roma.

Boone, Lalla Rookh: 1934. "Vancouver on the Northwest Coast". *Oregon Historical Quarterly*, 35, pp. 193-227.

Borden, Charles E.: 1975. "Origins and development of early Northwest Coast culture to about 3000 B.C.", *Archaeological Survey of Canada*. Paper no. 45. Ottawa.

Bougainville, L. A.: 1771. *Voyage autour du Monde, par la Frégate la "Boudeuse" et la Flate "l'Étoile", en 1766-7-8 et 9*. Paris.

—— 1921. *Viaje alrededor del Mundo, por la Fragata "La Boudese" y la fusta "La Estrella", en 1767, 1768 y 1769*. T. I y II. Translated from french by Josefina Gallego de Dantín. Madrid (reprinted in Madrid, 1936 and 1966).

Broughton, William Robert: 1804. *A Voyage of Discovery to the North Pacific Ocean...* London.

Brand, Donald Dilworth: 1956. "The Development of Pacific Coast Ports During the Spanish Colonial Period in Mexico". *Estudios antropológicos publicados en homenaje al Doctor Manuel Gamio*. México, pp. 577-91.

Buache, Philippe: 1753. *Considérations géographiques et physiques sur ce que la Carte des Nouvelles Découvertes au Nord de la Mer du Sur offre de plus particulier*. Paris.

—— 1781. *Considérations géographiques et physiques sur les nouvelles découvertes au Nord-Est de l'Asie et au Nord-Ouest de l'Amerique, avec les memoires relatifs presentées à l'Academie Royale des Sciences*. Paris.

Bustamante y Guerra, José: 1868. "Relación de las navegaciones que ejecutó separadamente la Corbeta de S. M. la 'Atrevida' en el viaje verificado unida a la 'Descubierta' en los años de 1789 a 1794". *Anuario de la Dirección de Hidrografía*. Madrid. Year VI.

Caamaño, Jacinto: 1939. "The Journal of Jacinto Caamaño". Translated by Harold Greenfell, introduction and notes by H. R. Wagner and W. A. Newcombe. *British Columbia Historia Quarterly*. VII.

—— 1975 (1792). "Extracto del diario de las navegaciones, exploraciones y descubrimientos hechos en la América septentrional por D... Año de 1792". *Colección de Diarios y Relaciones para la Historia de los Viajes y Descubrimientos*. Madrid, t. VII, pp. 173-238.

Cabello, Paz: 1983. "Coleccionismo americano y expediciones científicas del siglo XVIII en la museología española". *Archivio per l'Antropologia e la Etnologia*. Firenze. Vol. 113, pp. 115-135.

Calatayud Arinero, M.ª de los Angeles: 1984. *Catálogo de las expediciones y viajes científicos españoles a América y Filipinas (siglos XVIII y XIX), Fondos del Archivo del Museo Nacional de Ciencias Naturales*. Madrid.

Calderón Quijano, José Antonio: 1967. *Lo virreyes de Nueva España en el reinado de Carlos III*. Sevilla, 2 vols.

—— 1972. *Los virreyes de Nueva España en el reinado de Carlos IV*. Sevilla, 2 vols.

—— 1978. *Cartografía militar y marítima de Cádiz de 1513 a 1878*. Sevilla, 2 vols.

Candolle, Aphonse Louis de: 1862 (ed). *Mémoires et souvenirs de Agustin-Pyramus de Candolle*. Geneva, 1862.

—— 1874. *Calques des dessins de la flore de Mexique de Mociño et Sessé*. Geneva, 1874.

Cantillo, Alejandro: 1843-1869. *Tratados, convenios y declaraciones de paz y de comercio que han hecho con las potencias extranjeras los monarcas españoles de la Casa de Borbón. Desde el año 1700 hasta el día*. Madrid.

Capel, Horacio: 1982. *Geografía y Matemáticas en la España del siglo XVIII*. Barcelona.

Cárdenas de la Peña, Enrique: 1968. *San Blas de Navarit*. Méjico.

Cardero, José: 1802. *Relación del viaje hecho por las goletas "Sutil" y "Mexicana" en el año de 1792*. Madrid, 1 volume and atlas.

Carey, Charles H.: 1929. "Some Early Maps and Myths". *Oregon Historical Quarterly*, 30, pp. 14-32.

Carrasco y Guisasola, Francisco: 1882. *Documentos referentes al reconocimiento de la costa de las Californias desde el Cabo de San Lucas al de Mendocino, recopiladas en el Archivo de Indias*. Madrid.

Carreño, Alberto M. (ed): 1913. *Noticias de Nutka*. México.

Carril, Bonifacio del: 1961. *La expedición Malaspina en los mares americanos del sur: la colección Bauza, 1789-1794*. Buenos Aires.

Carteret, Philip. See Hawkesworth, J.

Caselli, Carlo: 1929. *Alessandro Malaspina e la sua spedizione scientifica intorno al mondo, con documenti inediti*. Milán.

Castillo Ledon, Luis: 1945. "El Puerto de San Blas. Su fundación y su historia". *Boletín de la Sociedad Mexicana de Geografía y Estadística*, 60, pp. 583-95.

Catálogos:

—— 1980. *Catálogo XXIX. Mapas y dibujos (1503-1805) del Archivo General de Simancas*. Vol. 1. See Alvarez Terán, M.ª Concepción.

—— 1982. *Catálogo de la Exposición "La Corona y las expediciones Científicas Españolas a América en el siglo XVIII"*. Instituto de Cooperación Americana. Cádiz.

—— 1984. *Catálogo de la exposición "La expedición Malaspina, 1789-1794"*, celebrated in the Centro Cultural de la Villa. Madrid.

—— *Catálogo XII. Secretaría de Guerra (siglo XVIII). Hojas de Servicios de América*. Archivo General de Simancas. Valladolid.

Ceballos, Ciriaco: 1798. *Disertaciones sobre la navegación a las Indias occidentales*. Isla de León.

Cervantes, Vicente: 1794. "Discurso pronunciado en el real jardín botánico de México el 2 de junio de 1794", *Suplemento a la Gaceta de Literatura de México*, 2 July 1794.

Colección: 1943-1975. *Colección de Diarios y Relaciones para la Historia de los Viajes y Descubrimientos*. Madrid, 7 vols. See Arteaga, Bodega, Caamaño y Martínez.

Convención: —1790 *Convención entre el Rey nuestro señor y el Rey de la Gran Bretaña, transigiendo varios puntos sobre pesca, navegación y comercio en el Océano Pacífico y los mares del sur, firmada en San Lorenzo el Real a 28 de octubre de 1790, cuyas ratificaciones se canjearon en el mismo sitio a 22 de noviembre siguiente*. Madrid.

Cook, James: 1784. *A voyage to the Pacific Ocean*. London, 3 vols. and atlas.

—— 1784. *A voyage Towards the South Pole and round the World performed in his Majesty's Siph Resolution and Aventure in the years 1772-75. 4th ed*. London, 2 vols.

—— 1785. *Voyage a L'Ocean Pacifique ordonné par le roi D'Agleterre. Executé sous la direction des capitaines Cook, Clarke y Gore sur les voisseaux la Resolution et la Découverte en 1776-80*. Paris, 8 vols.

—— 1832-33. *Viaje al Polo Austral o del Sur y alrededor del mundo hecho en los navíos... Resolución y Aventura en los años 1772 a 1775*. Translation and notes by Santiago Alvarado y Peña. Madrid, 8 vols.

—— 1853. *Historia de sus viajes por mar y tierra*. Translated by J. M. y P. y S. C. Madrid.

—— 1922. *Relación de su primer viaje alrededor del Mundo durante los años 1768, 1769, 1770 y 1771*. Translated from english by M. Ortega y Gasset. Madrid (reprinted in Madrid, 1936).

—— 1922. *Viaje hacia el Polo Sur, y alrededor del Mundo. Realizado a bordo de los navíos Reales "Resolution" y "Adventure", durante los años 1772, 1773, 1774 y 1775, y que comprende también las narraciones del Capitán Fourneaux, acerca de su actuación en el "Adventure" durante la separación de los dos navíos*. Translated from english by M. Ortega y Gasset. Madrid, 3 vols. Reprinted in Madrid 1938 and 1939.

Cook, J. y Forster, J. R.: 1777. *A voyage round the world in his Britannia Majesty's Sloop Resolution*. London.

Cook, J. y King: 1785. *A voyage to the Pacific Ocean, undertaken by the comand of his Majesty for making discovaries in the Northen Hemisphere*. London, 3 vols.

Cook, J., King y Bayle, P.: 1782. *The original astronomical observations made in the course of a voyage to the Northen Pacific Ocean in his Majesty Ships the Resolution and Discovory in the years 1776-77-78-79-80*. London.

Cook, Warren L.: 1973. *Flood Tide of Empire: Spain and the Pacific Northwest, 1543-1819*. New Haven.

Costansó, Miguel:

—— 1790. *An hist. Journal of the exped... to the North of California, in 1768, 1769 and 1770...* Translated by William Reveley. London.

—— 1950. (1770) *Diario histórico de los viajes de mar y tierra hechos al norte de California*. México.

Coxe, William: 1780. *Russians Discoveries between Asia and America*. London.

—— 1781. *Les nouvelles decouvertes des russes entre L'Asie et L'Amerique avec l'histoire de la conquiste de la Siberie et du comerce des russes et chiners*. Paris.

—— 1847. *España bajo el reinado de la Casa de Borbón, desde 1700 hasta 1788*. Translated by Jacinto de Salas Quiroga. Madrid, 4 vols.

Coyle, Jeannette, and Norman C. Roberts: 1975. *A Field Guide to the Common and Interesting Plants of Baja California*. La Jolla.

Cutter, Donald C.: 1960. *Malaspina in California*. San Francisco.

—— 1961. "California, training ground for spanish naval heroes", in *California Historical Society Quarterly*, xxx, June 1961, 40, 109-122.

—— 1963. "Early spanish artist, on the Northwest Coast". *Pacific Northwest Quarterly*, 59: 150-157.

—— 1963. "Spanish Scientific Exploration along the Pacific Coast". *The American West an Appraisal*. Santa Fe.

—— 1972. "Malaspina at Yakutat Bay... encounters between the Spaniards and the Indians in 1771", *Alaska Journal*, 2, pp. 42-49.

—— 1975. "Spain and the Oregon Coast". *The Western Shore: Oregon Country Essays honoring the American Revolution*. Portland, pp. 29-46.

—— 1978. "The Return of Malaspina: Spain's Great Scientific Expedition to the Pacific, 1789-1794". *American West*, 15, pp. 4-19.

Cutter, Donald C. y Mercedes Palau de Iglesias: 1977. "Malaspin's Artists". *The Malaspina Expedition*. Santa Fe.

Chapman, Charles Edward: 1915-16. "The Difficulties of Maintaining the Department of San Blas, 1775-1777". *Southwestern Historical Quarterly*, 19, pp. 261-270.

—— 1916. *The Founding of Spanish California; the Northwestward Expansion of New Spain, 1687-1773*. New York.

—— 1919. *Catalogue of materials in the Archivo General de Indias for the history of de Pacific Coast and the american Southwest*, volume VIII. "University of California publications in History". Berkeley (California).

—— 1921. *A History of California: the Spanish Period*. New York.

Chappe d'Auteroche: 1772. *Voyage en Californie, pour l'Observation du Passage de Vénus en 1769*. Paris.

Dalrymple, Alexander: 1767. *An Account of the Discoveries made in the South Pacific Ocean, previous to 1764*. London.

—— 1770-71. *An Historical Collection of the Several Voyages and Discoveries in the South Pacific Ocean*. London, 2 vols.

—— 1773. *Memorial original d'Arias sur les Découvertes à faire dans L'Hemisphère Austral*. Edimburgh.

—— 1775. *A Collection of Voyages chiefly in the Southern Atlantick Ocean, published from original Mss*. London.

—— 1790. *The Spanish Memorial of 4th June considered*. London.

—— *Nautical Memoirs and Journals*. London, 5 vols.

Davis, Robert T.: 1949. *Native arts of the Pacific Northwest*. Palo Alto. California.

Deslandes: 1736-1750. *Recueil de Traités de Physique et d'Histoire naturelle*. Paris, 2 vols.

Díaz-Trechuelo, María Lourdes: 1958. "Dos nuevos derroteros del galeón de Manila (1730-1773)". *Anuario de Estudios Americanos*, Sevilla, vol. XII.

Dixon, George: 1789. *A voyage Round the World but more particularly to the North-West Coast performed in 1785, 1786, 1787 and 1783 in the King George and the Queen Charlotte: Captains Portlock and Dixon*. London.

—— 1790. *Remarks on the voyages of John Meares*. London.

—— 1791. *Farther Remarks on the voyages of John Meares*. London.

Dmytryskyn, Basil, Crownhart-Vaughan, E. A. P. and Vaughan, Thomas: 1976. *Colonial Russian America: Kyrill Khlehnikov's Account*. Portland.

—— 1979. *The End of Russian America*. Portland.

—— 1982. *Civil and Savage Encounters: The Travel Letters of an Imperial Russian Naval Officer*. Portland.

—— 1986. *Russian penetration of the North Pacific, 1700-1799: A Documentary Record*, (volume II of the three-volume series, *To Siberia and Russian America: Three Centuries of Russian Eastward Expansion, 1554-1867*). Portland.

Dockstader, Frederick J.: 1961. *Indian Art in America*. Greenwich.

Domínguez Bordona: 1935. *Manuscritos de América* (Biblioteca del Palacio Real). Madrid.

Drucker, Philip: 1943. "Archaeological survey on the Northern Northwest Coast". *Anthropological Paper*, no. 20. Bulletin 133. Washington.

—— 1951. "Northern and Central Nootkan Tribes". *Smithsonian Institution*. Bulletin 144. Washington.

—— 1955. *Indians of Northwest Coast*. New York.

—— 1965. *Cultures of the North Pacific Coast*. San Francisco.

Duff, Wilson: 1956. "Prehistoric Stone Sculpture of the Fraser River and the Gulf of Georgia". *Anthropology in British Columbia*. Victoria, no. 5.

—— 1964. "Contributions of Marius Barbeau to West Coast Ethnology". *Anthropologica*. Vol. VI, no. 1.

Dumont D'Urville, Julio Sebastián César: 1841-1843. *Viaje pintoresco alrededor del mundo. Resumen general de los viajes y descubrimientos de Magallanes, Tosman, Dampier, Anson, Byron, Wallis...* Barcelona, 6 vols.

Eliza, Francisco de: 1791. *Extracto de navegación hecha en la goleta Santa Saturnina, del puerto de Sta. Cruz de Nutka a los reconocimientos de la costa sur de dicho puerto y llegada al Departamento de San Blas*. See Wagner. California, 1933.

—— 1793. *Extracto de lo acaecido en la navegación hecha en el Bergantín del Rey nombrado el Activo...* (4 November 1793). See Wagner. California, 1931.

Elliott, Thompson Coit: 1928. "Cook's Journal of His Approach to Oregon". *Oregon Historical Quarterly*, 29, pp. 265-277.

Emmons, G. T.: 1911. "Native Account of the meeting between La Perouse and the Tlingit". *American Anthropologist*. Vol. 13, April-June, 1911, pp. 294-298.

Engel, Le Bailli d': 1765. *Mémoires et Observations sur les Pays Septentrionaux entre l'Asie et l'Amérique*. Lausanne.

—— 1779. *Mémoirs sur la Navigation dans les Mers du Nord*. Berne.

—— 1791. *Remarques sur la partie de la Relation de Cook qui concerne le Détroit entre l'Asie et l'Amérique*. Berne.

Engstrand, Iris H. Wilson: 1969. "Spanish Scientist in the Pacific Northwest, 1790-1792", in *Reflections of Western Historians*. Tucson.

—— 1970. *Noticias de Nutka, an Account of Nootka Sound in 1792*. Seattle see Moziño Suárez de Figueroa, José Mariano.

—— 1974. "Scientists in New Spain: The Eighteenth Century Expeditions". *The Spanish Borderlands: A First Reader*. Los Angeles.

—— 1981. *Spanish Scientist in the New World. The Eighteenth century expeditions*. Seattle.

Espinosa y Tello, José: 1802 (1792). *Relación del viaje hecho por las goletas "Sutil" y "Mexicana" en el año 1792*. Madrid.

—— 1809. *Memorias sobre las observaciones astronómicas hechas por los navegantes españoles en distintos lugares del globo, las quales han servido de fundamento para la formación de las cartas de marear publicadas por la dirección de Trabajos Hidrográficos de Madrid, ordenadas por Don... gefe de esquadra de la real armada y primer director de dicho establecimiento*. Madrid, 2 vols.

Estrada Catoira, Rafael: 1930. *El viaje de las corbetas "Descubierta" y "Atrevida" y los artistas de la expedición, 1789-1794*. Madrid.

Feder, Norman: 1971a. *Two hundred years of North American Indian Art*. New York.

—— 1971b. *American Indian Art*. New York.

Feder, N. y E. Malin: 1962. *Indian Art of the Northwest Coast*. Denver.

Foest, Christian F.: 1980. *Native arts of North America*. London.

Fernández, Justino: 1939. *Tomás de Suria y su viaje con Malaspina*. México.

Fernández Almagro, Melchor: 1946. *Política naval de la España moderna y contemporánea*. Madrid.

Fernández Duro, Cesáreo: 1879. *Disquisiciones Náuticas*, 4, Madrid.

—— 1889. *Noticia Breve de las Cartas y planos existentes en la Biblioteca de S. M. el Rey*. Madrid.

—— 1895-1903. *La Aramada Española desde la unión de los reinos de Castilla y de Aragón*. Madrid, 9 vols.

—— 1901. "Tadeo Haenke, naturalista en el viaje alrededor del mundo de las corbetas 'Descubierta' y 'Atrevida', al mando de Alejandro Malaspina, desde 1789 a 1794". *Boletín Academia de la Historia*, 39.

Fernández Navarrete, Martín: 1802. *Noticias históricas de las expediciones hechas por los españoles en busca del paso del N.O.* Madrid.

—— 1825-1837. *Colección de los viajes y descubrimientos que hicieron los españoles desde fines del siglo XV*. Madrid, 5 vols.

—— 1846. *Disertación sobre la Historia de la Náutica y de las Ciencias Matemáticas que han contribuido a su progreso entre los españoles*. Madrid.

—— 1849. "Examen histórico-crítico de los viajes y descubrimientos apócrifos del capitán Lorenzo Ferrer Maldonado, de Juan de Fuca y del almirante Bartolomé de Fonte", in *Documentos inéditos para la Historia de España*, by D. Miguel Salvá N. O. Pedro Sáiz de Baranda. Madrid, t. xv, pp. 5-213.

—— 1851. *Biblioteca marítima española, obra póstuma*. Madrid, 2 vols.

—— 1919. *Viajes y descubrimientos españoles en el Pacífico. Magallanes, Elcano, Loaysa, Saavedra*. Madrid.

Ferrari Bono, Bruno P.: 1960. *El viaje de Malaspina y su vinculación en el movimiento revolucionario*. Buenos Aires.

Ferrer Maldonado, Lorenzo: 1885. "Relación del descubrimiento del Estrecho de Anian que hice yo... en el año de 1588...", in Alejandro Malaspina, *Viaje político-científico...* Madrid, pp. 137-44.

Fireman, Janet R. and M. Weber: 1977. "In Pursuit of Knowledge: The Malaspina Expedition". *Terra*, 15, pp. 18-24.

Fisher, Raymond H.: 1943. *The Russian fur trade, 1550-1700*. Berkeley.

Fladmark, Knut R.: 1975. "A paleoecological model for Northwest Coast prehistory". *Archaeological Survey of Canada*. Ottawa. Paper no. 43.

Fleurieu: 1773. *Voyage fait par ordre du Roi en 1768 y 1769 a differentes parties du monde pour éprouver en mer les horloges marines*. Paris, 2 vols.

—— 1798. *Voyage autour du monde, pendant les années 1790, 1791 y 1792*. Paris, 1798 (English edition, London, 1801).

Floridablanca, Conde de: 1982. *Escritos políticos, la instrucción y el memorial*. Edición y estudios de Ruiz Alemán. Murcia.

Fonte, Bartholomew de: 1708. "A letter from Admiral Bartholomew de Fonte the Admiral of New Spain and Perú and now Prince of Chile", in *Monthly Miscellany or Memoirs for the Curious*, London, April and June.

Forster, George: 1777. *A Voyage round the World, during the Years 1772-3-4 and 5*. London, 2 vols.

Forster, John Reinold: 1778. *Observations made during a Voyage round the World, on physical Geography, natural History, and ethic Philosophy*. London.

—— 1786. *History of the Voyages and Discoveries made in the North* (translated from the German). London.

Fraser, Douglas: 1962. *Primitive Art*. New York.

Galbraith, Edith C.: 1924. "Malaspina's Voyage around the World". *California Historical Society Quarterly*, 3, pp. 215-37.

Ganiushkina, T., R. Razumovskaya, and I. Shavrina: 1973. *Museum of Anthropology and Ethnography*. Leningrad.

García Franco, Salvador: 1947. *Historia del arte y ciencia de navegar*, Madrid. 2 vols.

—— *Instrumentos náuticos en el Museo Naval*. Madrid.

Garrigues, Emilio: 1965. *Los españoles en la otra América*. Madrid.

Gayangos, Pascual: 1977. *Catalogue of the Manuscripts in the Spanish Lenguague, in the British Museum*. London.

Gibson, James R.: 1975. "Bostonians and Muscovites on the Northwest Coast, 1788-1841". *The Western Shore: Oregon Country Essays honoring the American Revolution*. Thomas Vaughan, ed. Portland, pp. 81-120.

Gilbert, Thomas: 1789. *Voyages from New South-Walles to Canton, in the Year 1788*. London.

Godoy, Manuel: 1965. *Memorias*. Edición y estudio preliminar de Carlos Seco Serrano. Madrid.

Golder, F. A.: 1922-25. *Bering's Voyages*. Washington. 2 vols.

Gómez Campillo: 1944. *Relaciones diplomáticas entre España y los Estados Unidos según documentos del Archivo Histórico Nacional*. Madrid, 2 vols.

Gough, Barry M.: 1975. "The Northwest Coast in Late 18th Century British Expansion". *The Western Shore*. Portland, pp. 47-80.

Grepi, E.: 1883. "Un italiano alla corte di Spagna nel Secolo XVIII. Alezando Malaspina". *Nuova Antologia*. March 1883.

Guillén y Tato, Julio: 1930. *Pabellón de la Marina de Guerra. Exposición Ibero-Americana. Correspondencia relativa al viaje de Malaspina*.

—— 1932. *Repertorio de los manuscritos, cartas, planos y dibujos relativos a las Californias existentes en este Museo*. Madrid.

—— 1961. "Biografías desconocidas: el teniente de navío don Juan Manuel Quimper del Pino". *Revista General de Marina*. january 1961.

—— 1961. *Historia Marítima Española*. Madrid, 2 vols.

Gunther, Erna: 1962. *Northwest Coast Indian Art*. Seattle.

—— 1966. *Art in the Life of the Northwest Coast Indians*. Portland.

—— 1972. *Indian Life on the Northwest Coast of North America*. Chicago.

Guitiérrez Camarena, Marcial: 1956. *San Blas y las Californias. Estudio histórico del Puerto*. México.

Harnoncourt, René d': 1941. *Indian Art of the United States*. New York.

Harris, Marvin: 1978. *El desarrollo de la teoría antropológica. Una historia de las teorías de la cultura*. Madrid.

Harris, Nancy: 1983. "Reflections on Northwest Coast silver", in Holm, B.: *The box of daylight*. Seattle, pp. 132-136.

Hawthorn, Audrey: 1967. *Art of the Kwakiutl Indians and other Northwest Coast tribes*. Seattle.

Haves, Edmund (ed.): 1941. *Voyages of the Columbia to the Northwest Coast.* Boston.

Hernández Sánchez-Barba, Mario: 1953. "Españoles, Rusos e Ingleses en el Pacífico Norte, durante el siglo XVIII". *Información jurídica.* Madrid, no. 121, pp. 549-66.

—— 1957. *La última expansión española en América.* Preface by Manuel Ballesteros-Gaibrois. Madrid.

—— 1962. *Juan Bautista de Anza. Un hombre de fronteras.* Madrid.

Hervey, Frederic: 1780. *The Naval History of Great Britain from the first Times to the Year 1779.* London, 5 vols.

Herrera y Tordesillas, Antonio de: 1925. *Por Castilla y por León. Historia del descubrimiento de América, por el Cronista de Indias.* Barcelona.

Heverdahl, Thor: 1952. *American Indians in the Pacific. The theory behind the Kon Tiki Expedition.* London.

Hidalgo Sereno, Jacinto: 1961. "Un viaje de descubrimiento por la costa del Pacífico norteamericano". *Revista de Indias.* Madrid, no. 84, April-June 1961, p. 293.

History: —1764 *History (The) of kamtschatka:* (Transl. from the Russian language). London.

Holm, Bill: 1965. *Northwest Coast Indian Art: an analysis of form.* Seattle.

—— 1933. *The box od daylight. Northwest Coast Indian Art.* Seattle.

Howay, Frederick William: 1911. "Early Navigation of the Straits of Fuca". *Oregon Historical Quarterly,* 12, pp. 1-32.

—— 1917. "The Spanish Settlement at Nootka", *Washington Historical Quarterly,* 8, pp. 163-171.

—— 1923. "The Spanish discovery of British Columbia in 1774". *Canadian Historical Assoc.,* pp. 49-55.

—— 1929. *The Dixon-Meares Controversy.* Toronto.

Huish, Robert: 1851. *The Northwest Passage: A History of the Most Remarkable Voyages.* London.

Humboldt, Alexander von: 1811. *Essai politique sur le royaume de la Nouvelle Espagne.* Paris, 4 vols and atlas.

—— 1941. *Ensayo político sobre el Reino de Nueva España.* Edición crítica con introducción bibliográfica, notas y arreglo de la versión española por Vito Alessio Robles. México.

—— 1966. *Ensayo político sobre el Reino de la Nueva España.* Edited by Juan A. Ortega y Medina. México.

Humphreys, Robin A.: 1938. "Richard Oswald's Plan for an English and Russian Attack on Spanish America, 1781-1782". *Hispanic American Historical Review,* 18, pp. 95-101.

Instrucciones:

—1873. *Instrucciones que... los Virreyes de Nueva España dejaron a sus sucesores:* México, 2 vols.

Inverarity, Robert B.: 1950. *Art of the Northwest Coast Indians.* Berkeley y Los Angeles.

Jonaitis, Aldona: 1983. "Style and menning in the shamanic art of the northern Northwest Coast". In Holm, B.: *The box of daylight.* Seattle, pp. 129.131.

Juan, Jorge: 1757. *Compendio de Navegación para el uso de los Cavalleros Guardias-Marinas.* Cádiz.

Kerguelen: 1771. *Voyage dans la Mer du Nord, en 1767 et 1768.* París.

King, J. C. H.: 1979. *Portrait Masks from the Northwest Coast of America.* London.

Kippis, Andrés: 1795. *Historia de la vida y viages del Capitán Jaime Cook.* Translated by Cesáreo de Nava Palacio. Madrid, 2 vols.

Kotzbue, Otto von: 1821. *A voyage of discovery in to the south seas and Beering's Straits in the years 1815-1818.* London.

Krasheninnikov, Stepan Petrovich: 1755. *Opizanie Zmli kamchatki.* St. Petersburg.

—— 1972. *Explorations of Kamchatka: North Pacific Scimitar* (English edition). E. A. P. Crownhart-Vaughan. Translator and editor. Portland.

Krause, Aurel: 1956. *The Tlingit Indians.* Translated by Ema Gunther. Seattle.

—— 1972. "Under Mount Saint Elias. The History and culture of the Yakutat Tlight", *Smithsonian Contribution Anthropology.* Washington, vol. 7. 2 vols.

Krickeberg, Walter: 1946. *Etnología de América.* México.

Kroeber, Alfred Louis: 1925. "Handbook of the Indias of California". *Smithsonian Institution.* Washington. Bulletin 78.

Kruzenstern, Adam J. von: 1813. *A voyage round the world.* London, 2 vols.

La Bastide, Martín de: 1790. *Mémoires sur un nouveau passage de la Mer du Nord à la Mer du Sud.* Paris.

La Montan: 1702. *Voyage dans l'Amérique Septentrionale, le Canada.* Le Haye, 2 vols.

La Pérouse, Jean François Galaup: 1799. *A Voyage around the World in the Years 1785, 1787 and 1788.* London, 3 vols.

Lafuente, Antonio: 1982. *la enseñanza de las ciencias durante la primera mitad del siglo XVIII* (Estudios dedicados a Juan Peset Aleixandre). Valencia, 3 vols.

Lafuente, Antonio y Selles, Manuel: 1985. "La formación de los pilotos en la España del siglo XVIII". In *La Ciencia Moderna y el nuevo Mundo.* Madrid.

Laguna, Federica de: 1972. "Under Mount Saint Elias. The History and culture of the Yakutat Tligt". *Smithsonian Contribution Anthropology.* Washington, vol 7, 2 vols.

Lamb, Ursula: 1981. "The London years of Felipe Bauzá, Spanish Hidrographer in exile, 1823-1834". Separate of *Journal of navigation,* vol 34, no. 3, september 1981.

Landin Carrasco, Amancio: 1967. *Mourelle de la Rúa y sus viajes por el Pacífico.* Conference in the "Cátedra de Alta Cultura naval Arzobispo Gelmírez", Universidad de Santiago. Marín.

—— 1968. "Los últimos descubridores (España, Rusia e Inglaterra en el NE. del Pacífico)". In *Estudios de Derecho Internacional marítimo* (Homenaje al Profesor José Luis de Arcárraga). Madrid, pp. 197 y ss.

—— 1969. "España, Rusia e Inglaterra en el Noroeste del Pacífico". *Revista General de Marina.* June 1969.

—— 1971. *Mourelle de la Rúa, explorador del Pacífico.* Madrid. Reprinted in Madrid, 1978.

Langsdorff, George Heinrich von: 1813-14. *Voyages and travels in various parts of the world.* London.

Lasso de la Vega, Jorge: 1856-1863. *La Marina Real de España a fines del siglo XXVIII y principios del XIX...* Madrid, 2 vols.

Ledyard, John: 1963. *Journal of Captain Cook's Last Voyage.* Corvallis.

Lefan, Luis: 1942. "Un Departamento maritimo español del siglo XVIII en el Pacífico". *Revista General de Marina,* july 1942.

León Tello, Francisco José: 1979. *Mapas, planos y dibujos de la Sección de Estado del Archivo Histórico Nacional.* 2ond ed. Madrid.

Lévi-Strauss, Claude: 1968. *Antropología estructural*. Buenos Aires.

—— 1981, *la vía de las máscaras*. México.

Lisiansky, Urey Fedorovich: 1814. *A voyage round the world in the years 1803-4-5 and 6*. London.

L'Isle, Joseph-Nicolás de: 1752. *L'Astronome. Explication de la Carte des Nouv. Découvertes au Nord de la grande Mer du Sud*. París.

Little, C. H.: 1967. "Early voyages to Alaska", in *Explorers Journal*. New York, march 1967.

Lomgenbamgh, Dee: 1984: "From Anian to Alaschka. The mapping of Alska to 1778". *Map. Collector*, no. 29.

López Piñero, José M.ª: 1979. *El arte de navegar en la España del renacimiento*. Barcelona.

Lowery, Woodbury: 1912. *A descriptive lis of maps of the spanish possessions within the present limits of the United States, 1505-1820*, notes by Philip Lee Phillips. Washington.

Llabrés Bernal: 1934. *Breve noticia de la labor científica del Capitán de Navío Don Felipe Bauzá y de sus papeles sobre América (1764-1834)*. Palma de Mallorca.

Macintyre, Donald, R. N.: 1962. *Admiral Rod ney*. New York.

Majo Framis, Ricardo: 1956. *Vida y hechos de Fray Junípero Serra*. Madrid.

Malaspina, Alejandro: 1885. *Viaje político científico alrededor del mundo por las corbetas "Descubierta" y "Atrevida"*. Introduction by Pedro Novo y Colson. Madrid.

—— 1984. *Viaje científico y político a la América Meridional a las Costas del Mar Pacífico y a las islas Marianas y Filipinas*. Edition, introduction and notes by Mercedes Palau. Madrid.

Malo de Luque: 1784-90. *Historia política de los establecimientos ultramarinos de las naciones europeas*. Madrid, 5 vols.

Manfredi, Darío: 1984. *Alessandro Malaspina dei marchesi di Mulazzo. Le inclinazioni scientifiche e riformatrici*. I. I. S. L.

Manjarres, Ramón de: 1915-1918. "En el Mar del Sur. Expediciones españolas del siglo XVIII". *Boletín del Centro de Estudios Americanistas*. 1915, III, no. 16, pp. 1-16; 1916, IV, no. 17, pp. 44-47; 1918, V, no. 18, pp. 1-26 and no. 21, pp. 1.17.

Manning, William R.: 1905. "The Nootka Sound Controversy". *American Historical Association Annual Report of 1904*. Washington, pp. 279-478.

Manrique García, José: "El Oeste Español". *Revista Ejército*, 3/82, pp. 57-63.

Mariñas Otero, Luis: 1967. "El incidente de Nutka". *Revista General de Indias*. Madrid, nos. 109-110, july-december, 1967.

Marti Alanais: 1980. *Canadá en la correspondencia diplomática de los embajadores de España en Londres*. Madrid.

Martín-Meras, M.ª Luisa: 1984. "Vocabularios indígenas recogidos en las expediciones de Malaspina y de las goletas "Sutil" y "Mexicana". *Revista de Historia Naval*. Madrid, a. II, no. 6, pp. 57-73.

Martínez, Esteban José: 1964 (1789). "Diario de la Navegación que Yo el Alf(ére)z de navío de la R(ea)l, Arm(a)da, D(o). Estevan Josef Martínez boy a executar al P(uer)to, de S(a)n. Carlos... 1789". Edited by Roberto Barreiro-Meiro. *Colección de diarios y relaciones para la historia de los viajes y descubrimientos*, 6. Madrid, pp. 19-148.

Martínez Zayas, Juan: 1931 (1793). "Voyage a la Costa comprehendiendo entre la Boca Sur de Fuca y el Puerto de San Francisco...". *Quarterly California History Society*. December.

McVaugh, Rogers: 1977. "Botanicat Results of the Sessé & Mociño Expedition (1787-1803)". *Contributions from the University of Michigan Herbarium*, vol. 2, no. 3, pp. 97-195.

Meares, John: 1790. *Voyages made in the years 1788 and 1789 from China to the New York coast of America with an introductory narrative of a voyage performed in 1786, from Bengal in the ship Nootka, to which are annexed observations an the probable existence of a North Passage*. London.

—— 1791. *An answer to Mr. George Dixon... in which the remarks of Mr. Dixon on the voyages to the North West Coast of America and lately published*. London.

Mochon, Marion J.: 1966. "Masks of the Northwest Coast". *Publications in Primitive Art*. Milwaukee, no. 2.

Morales Padrón, Francisco: 1955. "Descubrimiento y toma de posesión". *Anuario de Estudios Americanos*. Sevilla, vol. XII.

—— 1963. *Historia del descubrimiento y conquista de América*. Madrid.

Moreno de Guerra y Alonso, Juan: 1917. *Relación de los Caballeros Cadetes de las Compañías de Guardias Marinas en los departamentos de Cádiz, Ferrol y Cartagena desde la creación de este cuerpo en 1717*. Madrid.

Morse, William I., editor: 1944. *Letters of Alejandro Malaspina (1790-1791)*. Boston.

Mortimer, George: 1791. *Observations and Remarks made during a Voyage to the Islands of Tenerife, Amsterdam [l'ile Saint-Paul des Hollandais], Maria, near van Diemen-Land, and others in the Pacific Ocean, and on the N, W. Coast of America, and fron thence to Canton, in the Brig Mercury, Cap. John Henry Cox*. London.

Mourelle, Francisco Antonio: 1781 (1775). «Journal of a Voyage in 1775. To Explore the Coast of America Northward & California» in *Miscellanies* of Daines Barrington. London.

—— 1971 (1779): "Navegación hecha por el Alférez de Fragata (...) a los descubrimientos de la Costa septentrional de California, 1779". In Landin Carrasco, A.: *Mourelle de la Rúa, explorador del Pacífico*. Madrid, pp. 217-269.

Mourelle, José María: 1856 y 1877. *Biografía del Excmo. Sr. D. Francisco Antonio Mourelle, Jefe de escuadra de la Armada. Publicada en la Crónica Naval de España*, dos ediciones, la última de ellas dice estar aumentada con notas y copias de documentos oficiales por su hijo don... Madrid.

Mourelle-Lema, M.: 1967. "Un navegante ilustre: el jefe de escuadra F. A. Mourelle". *Revista General de Marina*. Juny, 1967.

Moziño Suárez de Figueroa, José Mariano: 1913. *Noticias de Nutka. Diccionario de la lengua de los Nutkeses y descripción del volcán de Tuxtla*. México.

—— 1970. *Noticias de Nutka, and Account of Nootka Sound in 1792*. Translated from english by I. H. W. Engstrand. Seattle.

Muller, G. P.: 1766. *Voyages et Découvertes faites par les Russes, le long des Cotes de la Mer Glaciale et sur l'Ocean Oriental, tant vers le Japon que vers l'Amerique, avec l'Hist. du Fleuve Amur*. Amsterdam, 2 vols.

Murdock, George Peter: 1960. *Ethnographic Bibliography of North America*. 3rd ed. New Haven.

Museum of New Mexico, Ed. Santa Fe (USA): 1976. "The Malaspina Expedition. In the Pursuit of Knowledge". *El Palacio*. Vol. 82, no. 4.

Narborough, John: 1738. *Voyage à la Mer du Sud; se trouve à la suite du Voyage de Coreal*, Amsterdam. 3 vols.

Navarro García, Luis de: 1960. "El norte de Nueva España como problema politico en el siglo XVIII". *Revista estudios americanos*. Sevilla, no. 101, pp. 15-31.

Newcombe, C. F. (ed.): 1914. *The first circumnavigation of Vancouver Island*. Victoria, B. C.

—— 1923. *Menzies' Journal of Vancouver's Voyage, April to October, 1792*. Victoria, B.C.

Noticias:

—— 1757. *Noticias de California*. See Venegas, Miguel.

—— 1959 (1764-1795). *Noticias y Documentos acerca de las Californias, 1764-1795*. Madrid.

Novo y Colson, Pedro: 1880. *Historia de las exploraciones árticas hechas en busca del paso del nordeste*. Preface by Cesáreo Fernández Duro. Madrid.

—— 1881. *Sobre los viajes apócrifos de Juan de Fuca y de Lorenzo Ferrer Maldonado*. Recopilación y estudio. Madrid.

—— 1885. *Viaje político-científico alrededor del mundo por las corbetas "Descubierta" y "Atrevida", al mando de los capitanes de navío Don Alejandro Malaspina y don José de Bustamante y Guerra desde 1789 a 1794*. See Malaspina, Alejandro.

Official papers:

—— 1790. *Official papers relative to the dispute between the courts of Great Britain and Spain on the subject of the ships captured in Nootka Sound, and the negotiation that followed thereon*. London.

Ordenanzas:

—— 1748 *Ordenanzas Generales de la Armada*.

—— 1786. *Ordenanzas para el Real Colegio de San Telmo de Sevilla*. Madrid.

—— 1787. *Ordenanzas para el Real Colegio de San Telmo de Málaga*. Madrid.

Orozco y Berra, Manuel: 1881. *Apuntes para la Historia de la Geografía en México*. México.

—— 1938. *Historia de la dominación española en México*. México.

Ortega y Medina, Juan A.: 1966. *Ensayo político sobre el reino de la Nueva España*. See Humboldt, Alexander von.

Páez Ríos: 1948. *Iconografía Britana. Catálogo de personajes ingleses de la Biblioteca Nacional*. Madrid.

—— 1966. *Iconografía Hispana. Catálogo de los retratos de personajes españoles de la Biblioteca Nacional*. 2ond. ed. Madrid.

Pagés: 1782. *Voyages autour du Monde et vers les deux Poles, par terre en par mer, de 1767 à 1776*. Paris, 2 vols.

Palacio Atard, Vicente: 1945. *El Tercer pacto de Familia*. Preface by V. Rodríguez Casado. Madrid.

—— 1949. "El equilibrio de América en la diplomacia del siglo XVIII". *Estudios Americanos*, I. Sevilla, no. 3, pp. 461-479.

Palau, Mercedes.

—— 1980. *Catálogo de los dibujos, aguadas y acuarelas de la Expedición Malaspina*. Madrid.

—— 1984. *Viaje científico y político a la América Meridional a las Costas del Mar Pacífico y a las islas marianas y Filipinas*. See Malaspina, Alessandro.

Palou, Fr. Francisco: 1944. *Relación histórica de la vida y apostólicas tareas del venerable padre fray Junípero Serra y de las Misiones que fundó en la California septentrional y nuevos establecimientos de Monterrey*. Madrid.

Parkinson, J.: 1784. *A journal of a voyage to the South Seas in his Majesty's ship the Endeavour*. London.

Parry, William E.: 1945. *Tercer viaje para el descubrimiento de un paso por el Noroeste*. Buenos Aires.

Pérez Embid, Florentino: "Una sistematización de la historia de los descubrimientos geográficos", *Reviste Arbor*, no. 15, pp. 377-400.

—— "La expansión geográfica de Nueva España en el siglo XVII". *Revista de Indias*. Madrid, year XI, no. 45, pp. 501-531.

Pericot, Luis: 1962. *América Indígena*. In *Historia de América y de los Pueblos Americanos*. Barcelona, tomo I, 2ond. ed.

Phipps, John Constantine: 1774. *A Voyage towards the North Pole, in the year 1773*. London.

Piette, J. G. M.: 1946. "The *Diarios* of Early California, 1769-84", *The Americas*. Washington, no. 4, pp. 409.22.

Pino Díaz, Fermín del: 1982. "Los estudios etnográficos y etnológicos en la Expedición Malaspina". *Revista de Indias*. Madrid, nos. 169-70, pp. 393-465.

Porrúa Turanzas, José: 1958. *Relación del viaje hecho por las goletas "Sutil" y "Mexicana" en el año 1792*. Madrid, 1958.

Portillo, Alvaro del: 1977. *Descubrimientos y exploraciones en las costas de California*. Madrid.

Portlock, Nathaniel: 1789. *A Voyage round the World, but more particuliarly to the N. W. Coast of America, in 1785-6-7 and 8*. London.

Portillo y Díez de Sollano, Alvaro del: 1947. *Descubrimientos y exploraciones en las costas de California*. Madrid.

Presi, C. B.: 1825-1835. *Reliquia Haenkeana*. Praga, 2 vols.

Prévost: 1746 y ss. Histoire générale des Voyages par mer et par terre. Paris, 19 vols.

—— 1763. *Historia general de los viajes por mar y por tierra*. Madrid, 28 vols.

Priestly, Herbert Ingram. 1916. *José de Gálvez. Visitor General of New Spain 1765-1771*. Berkeley.

—— 1920. "The Log of the Princesa by Estevan Martínez: What does it Contribute to Our Knowledge of the Nootka Sound Controversy?". *Oregon Historical Quarterly*, 21, pp. 21-31.

Princeton University Art Museum: 1969. *Art of the Nortwest Coast*. Seattle.

Pulido Rubio, José: 1950. *El Piloto Mayor de la casa de Contratación de Sevilla. Pilotos Mayores, Catedráticos de Cosmografía y Cosmógrafos*. Sevilla.

Purchas, Samuel: 1225. *Hackluytus posthumus, or Purchas his Pilgrims, containing a History of the World in Sea Voyages and Land Travels by Englishmen, and others*. London, 5 vols.

Quesada, Vicente G.: 1917. *la vida intelectual en la América Española durante los siglos XVI, XVII y XVIII*. Buenos Aires.

Quimper, Manuel: 1792. *Drama de Quimper en su expedición al estrecho de Fuca*. See Wagner, H. R. California, 1933.

Ramos Catalina y de Bardazi, María Luisa: 1956. "Expediciones científicas a California en el siglo XVIII". *Anuario de estudios americanos*. Sevilla, vol. 13, pp. 217-230.

Rasmussen, Louise: 1941. "Artists with Explorations on the Northwest Coast". *Oregon Historical Quarterly*. 42, pp. 311-316.

Raynal, Guillaume Thomas: 1780. *Histoire philosophique et politique des Etablissement et du Commerce des Europeens dans les deux Indes*. Gènova, 5 vols.

Relación: 1802. *Relación del viage hecho por las goletas Sutil y Mexicana en el año 1792 para reconocer el Estrecho de Fuca, con una introducción en que se da noticia de las expediciones executadas anteriormente por lo españoles en busca del paso del noroeste de la América. De orden del Rey.* Madrid. See Wagner. California, 1933.

Richman, Irving Berdine: 1911. *California under Spain and Mexico, 1535-1847.* New York.

Rodríguez, Santiago: 1974. *Los manuscritos del Archivo General y Biblioteca del Ministerio de Asuntos Exteriores.* Madrid.

Rodríguez Casado, Vicente: 1950. "El Pacifico en la política internacional española hasta la emancipación de América". *Revista Estudios Americanos,* t. II, no. 5, january 1950, pp. 1-30.

—— 1962. *La política y los políticos en el reinado de Carlos III.* Madrid.

—— 1968. "La política de reformismo de los primeros Borbones en la Marina de guerra española", *Anuario de Estudios Americanos,* t. XXV, pp. 601-618.

Rohner, Ronald P. y Evelyn C.: 1970. *The Kwakiutl. Indians of British Columbia.* New York.

Salvatierra, Juan María, S. J.: 1946. *Misión de la Baja California.* Introduction and notes of R. P. C. Bayle, S. J. Madrid.

Sánchez Diana, José María: 1952. "Relaciones diplomáticas entre Rusia y España en el siglo XVIII, 1780-1783". *Rev. Hispania,* no. 12, pp. 590-605.

Sanfeliú Ortiz, Lorenzo: 1944. *62 meses a bordo. La expedición Malaspina según el diario del teniente de navío don Antonio de Tova Arredondo, segundo comandante de la 'Atrevida', 1789-94.* Madrid.

Santos, Angel S. J.: 1943. *Jesuitas en el Polo Norte.* Madrid.

Sapir, Edward: 1911. "Some aspects of Nootka language and Culture". *American Antropologist,* 13, pp. 15-28.

Schmieder, Oscar: 1947. *Geografía de América.* México.

Schurz, W. L.: 1922. "The Spanish lake". *Hispanic American Historical Review.*

Servicio Geográfico e Histórico del Ejército: 1949. *Cartografía de Ultramar.* Madrid.

Servin, Manuel P.: 1961. "Instructions of Viceroy Bucareli to Ensign Juan Pérez". *California Historical Society Quarterly,* 40, pp. 237-48.

Sherwood, M.: 1967. *Alaska and his history.* Seattle and London.

Shop Soler, Ana María: 1971. *Las relaciones entre España y Rusia en la época de Carlos IV.* Barcelona.

Shor Account:

—— 1976. "Short Account of Some Voyages Made by Order of the King of Spain, to Discover the State of the West American Coast from California Upward. Dated Madrid, 24 March, 1776". *Summary observations and facts collected from late and authentic accounts of Russian and other navigators, to show the practicability and good prospect of success in enterprises to discover a northern passage for vessels by sea, between the Atlantic and Pacific Oceans.* London.

Siebert, Erna y Werner Forman: 1967. *El arte de los indios norteamericanos de la costa del Noroeste.* México.

Sierra, Benito de la: 1930. "The Ezeta Expedition to the Northwest Coast in 1775". *California Historical Society Quarterly,* t. IX, pp. 201-42.

Simpson, Lesley Byrd (ed. and trans.): 1961. *Journal of José Longinos Martínez. Notes and observations of the Naturalist of the Botanical Expedition in Old and new California and the South Coast.* San Francisco.

Solórzano y Peyrera, Juan: 1776. *Politica Indiana,* I. Madrid, 2 vols.

Sota, José de la: 1985. *Bodega y Quadra y la Expedición de Límites.* Memoria de Licenciatura ms. Universidad Complutense. Madrid.

Sotos Serrano, Carmen: 1982. *Los pintores de la Expedición de Alejandro Malaspina.* Madrid, 2 tomos.

—— 1984. "Relación de documentos del Archivo General de la Nación de Méjico, para el estudio de las expediciones marítimas españolas del siglo XVIII a la costa del noroeste americano". *Revista de Historia Naval.* Madrid, year II, no. 4, p. 101.

Stewart, Hilary: 1973. *Indian artifacts of the Northwest Coast.* Seattle.

Swanton, John R.: 1952. "The Indian Tribes of North America". *Bureau of American Ethnology.* Bulletin 145. Smithsonian Institution. Washington.

Sykes, JOHN. *A Log of... His Majesty's sloop Discovery.* London.

Taylor, George P.: 1958. "Spanish-Russian Rivalry in the Pacific, 1769-1820". *The Americas,* 25, pp. 109-27.

Testart, Alain: 1982. "The significance of food storage among hunter-gatherers residence patterns, population densities and social inequalities". *Current Anthropology.* Chicago, vol. 23, pp. 523-37.

Thurman, Michael E.: 1963. "The Establishment of the Department of San Blas and Its Initial Naval Fleet: 1767-1770". *HAHR,* 43, pp. 65-67.

—— 1967. *The Naval Department of San Blas, New Spain's Bastion for Alta California and Nootka, 1767 to 1798.* Glendale, California.

Torquemada, Juan de: 1723. *Monarquía Indiana.* Madrid, 3 vols.

Torre Revello, José: 1944. *Los artistas pintores de la expedición Malaspina.* Buenos Aires.

Tudela de la Orden, José: 1954. *Los manuscritos de América en las Bibliotecas de España.* Madrid.

Vaillant, George C.: 1939. *Indian Arts in North America.* New York.

Valgoma y Díaz Varela, Dalmiro: 1944. *Real Compañía de Guardias Marinas y Colegio Naval. Catálogo de pruebas de Caballeros aspirantes.* Madrid.

Vallve, Manuel: 1933. *El Capitán Cook. Viajes y exploraciones de este célebre navegante.* Barcelona.

Vancouver, George: 1798. *A Voyage of Discovery to the North Pacific Ocean and round the World; in which the Coast of North-West America has been carefully examined and accuraiely surveyed, in the Years 1890-1-2-3-4 and 5, in the "Discovery" stoop of war and armed tender "chatau".* London, 3 vols and atlas.

Vaughan, T. H., E. A. P. Crowhart-Vaughan y Mercedes Palau: 1977. *Voyages of Enlightenment. Malaspina on the Northwest Coast, 1791-92.* Portland.

Veitia y Linaje: 1672. *Norte de la Contratación de las Indias.* Sevilla.

Vela, V. Vicente: 1951. "Expedición de Malaspina: Epistolario referente a su organización". *Revista de Indias,* Madrid, 11, pp. 193-218.

Venegas, Miguel: 1757. *Noticia de California.* Madrid.

—— 1759. *A natural and civil History of California* (Transl. from the Spanish Tongue). London, 2 vols.

Verdún, Pingré and Borda: 1778. *Voyage en différentes Parties de l'Europe, de l'Afrique et de l'Amérique, pour éprouver diverses Horloges et Montres marines.* Paris, 2 vols.

Viana, Francisco Xavier de: 1849. *Diario del teniente de navío don... trabajado en el viaje de las corbetas de S. M. C. Descubierta y Atrevida en los años 1789-90 a 1793*. Madrid.

—— 1958. *Diario del teniente de navío don... trabajado en el viaje de las corbetas de S. M. C. Descubierta y Atrevida en los años 1789-90 a 1793*. Colecc. Clásicos Uruguayos, vols. 27 y 28. Montevideo.

Vigón, Ana M.ª: 1986. *Guía Documental del Archivo General de Marina. Alvaro de Bazán*. Madrid (in press).

Vila Vilar, Enriqueta: 1966. *Los rusos en América*. Sevilla.

Wagner, Henry Raup: 1924. *The Spanish Southwest, 1542-1794*. Berkeley.

—— 1926. "Some imaginary California geography". *Proceedings Am. Antig. Soc.* no. XXXVI. April.

—— 1930. "Fray Benito de la Sierra's acount of the Hezeta experidition in 1775". *Quarterly Cal. Hist. Soc.* September.

—— 1931. "The Last Spanish Exploration of the Northwest Coast and the Attempt to Colonize Bodega Nay". *CHSQ*, 9, pp. 313-45.

—— 1933. *Spanish Explorations in the Strait of Juan de Fuca*. Santa Ana, California.

—— 1935. "An exploration of the coast of Southern Californian in 1782". *Quarterly Hist. Soc. of Calif*. December.

—— 1936. "Four Early Sketches of Monterey Scenes", *California Historical Society Quarterly*, 15, pp. 213-16.

—— 1936. "Journal of Tomás de Suria of His Voyage with Malaspina to the Northwest Coast of America in 1791". *Pacific Historical Review*, 5, pp. 234-76.

—— 1937. *The Cartography of the Northwest Coast of America to the Year 1800*. Berkeley and Amsterdam, 1968.

—— 1937. "The Spanish Soutwest, 1542-1794 an annotated bibliography". *The Quivira Society*.

—— 1966. *Spanish voyages to the nortwest coast of America in the sixteenth century*. Amsterdam.

Wardweel, Allen: 1978. *Objects of Bright pride. Northwest Coast Indian Art from the American Museum of Natural History*. New York.

Wardwell, A. y León Lebou: 1980. *Annotated Bibliography of Northwest Coast Indian Art*. New York.

The bird «Tetra Regio-montanus». José Cardero. Museo Naval.

231

Index of Names References

234

Chief of the Mouths of Wentusen. José Cardero.
Museo Naval.

Index of Geographical References

Produced under the Direction of Santiago Saavedra by
Gabriela Bernar, Rufino Díaz, M.ª Victoria Lasso de la Vega y
Juan Pérez de Ayala.

Documentation	Aranzazu Zabala (Museo Nacional de Ciencia y Tecnología)
	Blanca Saiz (Historian), Madrid
Translations	Dragoman Traducciones, Madrid:
	Colin Barry Anderton
	John E. Kennedy
	Bruce McCann
	Tradux, Madrid
	Roberta Quance, Madrid
Photographs	Jaume Blassi, and
	Archivo General de Indias, Sevilla
	Archivo Histórico Nacional, Madrid
	Archivos Oronoz, Madrid
	Toby Molenaar, Paris
	Beinecke Library, Yale University, Connecticut
	Hunt Institute for Botanical Documentation, Pittsburgh
	Museo de América, Madrid
	Servicio Geográfico del Ejército, Madrid
Maps	Santiago de la Sota, Madrid
Typesetting	Pérez-Díaz, S. A. Madrid
Photolithography	Cromoarte, Barcelona
Printing	Julio Soto
	Av. de la Constitución, 202, Torrejón de Ardoz, Madrid
Binding	Hermanos Ramos, Madrid
ISBN:	84-86022-20-7
Dep. Legal.:	M-9825-1986
Design	Jaume and Jordi Blassi

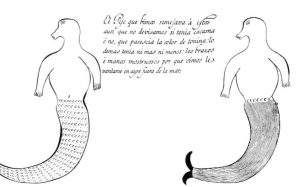

Copy of drawings from Hernando de Grijalva's
first voyage. Atlas de las goletas *Sutil* y *Mexicana*, 1802.
Museo Naval.